FRITZ BAUER

GERMAN JEWISH CULTURES

Matthew Handelman, Iris Idelson-Shein, Samuel Spinner,
Joshua Teplitsky, and Kerry Wallach, *editors*

FRITZ BAUER

*The Jewish Prosecutor
Who Brought Eichmann and
Auschwitz to Trial*

RONEN STEINKE

Translated by Sinéad Crowe
With a foreword by Andreas Vosskuhle

INDIANA UNIVERSITY PRESS

This book is a publication of

Indiana University Press
Office of Scholarly Publishing
Herman B Wells Library 350
1320 East 10th Street
Bloomington, Indiana 47405 USA

iupress.indiana.edu
Published in German as *Fritz Bauer oder Auschwitz vor Gericht*
© 2013 by Piper Verlag GmbH, Munich and Berlin
© 2020 by Indiana University Press

All rights reserved

No part of this book may be reproduced or utilized in any form or by any means, electronic or mechanical, including photocopying and recording, or by any information storage and retrieval system, without permission in writing from the publisher. The paper used in this publication meets the minimum requirements of the American National Standard for Information Sciences—Permanence of Paper for Printed Library Materials, ANSI Z39.48-1992.

Manufactured in the United States of America

Library of Congress Cataloging-in-Publication Data

Names: Steinke, Ronen, author. | Crowe, Sinead, [date], translator. | Vosskuhle, Andreas, writer of foreword.
Title: Fritz Bauer : the Jewish prosecutor who brought Eichmann and Auschwitz to trial / Ronen Steinke ; translated by Sinead Crowe ; with a foreword by Andreas Vosskuhle.
Other titles: Fritz Bauer, oder, Auschwitz vor Gericht. English
Description: Bloomington, Indiana : Indiana University Press, 2019. | Series: GJC/German Jewish Cultures | Includes bibliographical references and index.
Identifiers: LCCN 2019020825 (print) | LCCN 2019021900 (ebook) | ISBN 9780253046895 (ebook) | ISBN 9780253046857 (hardback : alk. paper) | ISBN 9780253046864 (pbk. : alk. paper)
Subjects: LCSH: Bauer, Fritz, 1903-1968. | Lawyers—Germany—Biography. | Public prosecutors—Germany—Biography. | Anti-Nazi movement—Germany—Biography. | Auschwitz Trial, Frankfurt am Main, Germany, 1963-1965. | Auschwitz (Concentration camp) | Eichmann, Adolf, 1906-1962.
Classification: LCC KK185.B38 (ebook) | LCC KK185.B38 S7415 2019 (print) | DDC 340.092 [B] —dc23
LC record available at https://lccn.loc.gov/2019020825

1 2 3 4 5   25 24 23 22 21 20

Supported by the Axel Springer Stiftung

CONTENTS

Foreword by Andreas Vosskuhle vii

Acknowledgments ix

1 The German Who Brought Eichmann to Justice: His Secret   *1*

2 The Secret Jewish Life of Postwar Germany's Most Controversial Jurist   *12*

3 The University Years (1921–1925): A Gifted Student   *32*

4 A Judge in the Weimar Republic: Bauer's Attempts to Avert Catastrophe   *50*

5 Concentration Camp and Exile (1933–1949)   *64*

6 Rehabilitating the Plotters of July 20, 1944   *86*

7 "Murderers Among Us": The Psychology of a Prosecutor   *106*

8 Bauer's Greatest Achievement: The Auschwitz Trial (1963–1965)   *125*

9 The Fight for Gay Rights: Bauer's Dilemma   *156*

10 Bauer's Path to Isolation   *171*

11 1968: The Body in the Bathtub   *188*

Bibliography   *195*

Index of Names   *203*

FOREWORD

WITH FEARLESSNESS AND TENACITY, WITH COMBATIVENESS AND UNFLAGGING stamina, Fritz Bauer devoted his life to humanity. His passionate advocacy of an enlightened society—in the best sense of the word "enlightened"—is one of the recurring motifs of his biography. This motif emerges in his championing of rational penal practice during his time as a young judge in Stuttgart. It is also present in his spirited defense of the Weimar Republic as the first democracy on German soil. But nowhere is it more evident than in the fight he began in the early years of the West German republic and continued until his premature death in the watershed year 1968. As attorney general of the state of Brunswick and later of Hesse, Bauer dragged Nazi tyranny into the spotlight. He forced German society—a society whose self-definition largely refused to acknowledge its past, despite the fact that this past clearly continued to be very present—to examine its history. Bauer confronted the young republic with a disturbing and shameful panorama of injustice. His fight for a legal reckoning with Nazi society and its crimes culminated in the first Frankfurt Auschwitz trial, which took place between 1963 and 1965.

Bauer met with opposition and hostility throughout his life. He was ostracized, persecuted, and forced into exile. Though he counted prominent figures such as Willy Brandt, Kurt Schumacher, and Theodor W. Adorno among his acquaintances, his position was always that of an outsider. One can only imagine the mental and physical toll exacted by his restless life.

While Bauer devoted great efforts to generating public interest in prosecutions of Nazi criminals, he was first and foremost a practical jurist, and his biography serves as a reminder to jurists of their potential to act courageously. All law is man-made. Human beings are responsible for creating it, enforcing it, and interpreting it. The law does not exist of its own accord; it is reliant on people who dedicate their lives to actualizing it. At a time when legal investigations into Nazism were carried out sporadically at best, Bauer showed just what could be achieved by means of the law.

Bauer's commitment to the law is even more remarkable when one considers the attitude pervading the West German judiciary at the time. Many of Bauer's colleagues had served as jurists under the Nazi regime, and they cultivated the convenient self-exculpatory myth that they had been victims of their own judicial probity. Their obedience to the law had put them at the mercy of forces beyond their control and implicated them in Nazi rule, they said, insisting that their moral integrity had nonetheless remained intact.

The restrictions imposed by the law continue to be an everyday experience for jurists. However, Fritz Bauer's life provides examples of how moral freedom can be exercised within the framework of the law. He demonstrated what the law can achieve in the hands of a jurist with courage, argumentative brilliance, and an unflagging work ethic. Bauer's biography therefore serves as a source of inspiration and a yardstick by which to evaluate the work of today's jurists.

Fritz Bauer was a democrat and a patriot who shaped German history and helped change it for the better. It is vital that we remember his life and honor his achievements. This book will make an important contribution to that end.

Prof. Andreas Vosskuhle
President of the Federal Constitutional Court of Germany
Karlsruhe, May 2013

ACKNOWLEDGMENTS

I WISH TO THANK THE FRITZ BAUER INSTITUTE in Frankfurt, which in affording me the status of visiting researcher provided me with access to invaluable expertise, resources, and technical support. I am particularly grateful to Werner Renz, who generously shared his extensive knowledge with me, as well as to Dorothee Becker, Dmitrij Belkin, Raphael Gross, Werner Lott, and Katharina Rauschenberger. I shared material with Monika Boll, curator of the Frankfurt Jewish Museum's 2014 exhibition on Bauer's life and work, and together we discovered new information on Bauer's time as a young judge, on his problems with the Danish authorities while in exile, and on his run-ins with the law because of alleged homosexual activities. This information is discussed in Chapters 4, 5, and 9 of this book and formed part of the exhibition.

Marcel Böhles, Michael Buchholz, and Patrick Schwentke assisted me with my research and helped uncover material relating to Bauer's student fraternity and membership of the Reichsbanner. Rolf Tiefenthal, Bauer's nephew, gave me access to private photos from the family archive, for which I am very grateful. Irmtrud Wojak was kind enough to provide me with scans of these photos. I discussed Bauer's numerous publications with Lena Foljanty, whose annotated collection of Bauer's articles and essays was published in 2018. I would also like to thank Elena Lefevre Georgescu, whose many translations from Danish into German enabled me to examine in more detail the books Bauer wrote while in exile.

I am deeply appreciative of the support provided by the staff of Indiana University Press, in particular Dee Mortensen and Paige Rasmussen, and of the excellent work done by my translator, Sinéad Crowe. My thanks also go to my agent, Barbara Wenner, and to Joachim Käppner for his consistently sound advice.

Finally, this book would not have been possible without Ulrike. She reminds me every day that even the greatest humanism is ultimately expressed in our love for a single human being. This book is dedicated to her in appreciation of her patience and tremendous support.

FRITZ BAUER

1

THE GERMAN WHO BROUGHT EICHMANN TO JUSTICE

His Secret

The heavy oak door on Gerichtsstrasse in downtown Frankfurt opened with barely a sound, and nobody noticed as twenty-seven-year-old Michael Maor slipped into the darkened building beyond. Maor knew exactly where to go, as they had meticulously mapped out his route for him beforehand. He made his way up the stone steps on the right until he reached the third floor, which stretched out ahead of him like a grand courtyard made of green linoleum. Moonlight streamed in through the windows. Maor's attention was immediately drawn to a prominent white door flanked by marble columns, which, in the dark, looked pitch-black rather than their usual reddish-brown color. The door led to the office of Fritz Bauer, attorney general of the state of Hesse; you can't miss it, they had told him.

The former Israeli paratrooper's mission: to photograph the file he would find on the left-hand side of Bauer's desk. The smell of cigars hung in the air, the long drapes were drawn, the walls were decorated with modern art, and, sure enough, on the left-hand side of the desk, Maor found a neat stack of papers. "The documents were emblazoned with SS insignia," Maor later recalled, "and a photo of a man in uniform was stuck to the first page."[1]

The file was that of Adolf Eichmann, the fiercely ambitious chief organizer of the Holocaust, the man who had planned the murder of millions of Jews down to the tiniest bureaucratic detail. On the evening of May 11, 1960—just a few weeks after Maor's nocturnal operation—the Israeli secret service, Mossad, kidnapped Eichmann from his hideout in Buenos Aires. Mossad then sedated him, dressed him in an El Al airline uniform, and flew him first class on a passenger plane to Israel. The capture resulted in one of the most important trials of the twentieth century, a trial that would shape the development of the still nascent Israeli society. But the vital clue that triggered the chain of events leading to Eichmann's capture had first appeared in a letter delivered in Frankfurt in 1957.[2]

The letter was from a German-born Jew named Lothar Hermann, who had been living in Argentina since fleeing the Nazis. Hermann wrote that Eichmann was living under an assumed name in a suburb of Buenos Aires. Hermann had discovered this by chance when it emerged that his own daughter had fallen in love with the mass murderer's son. At the time, there was hardly anyone to whom the horrified father could turn. The Israeli government was tied up with its own urgent national security issues, the Americans had long since handed responsibility for prosecuting Nazi crimes over to the Germans, and the German judiciary was riddled with judges and prosecutors who had themselves been involved with the Nazi regime. The attorney general of Hesse was the only figure who appeared willing to take action—unilaterally, if necessary—in the hunt for Eichmann.

One reason why Bauer's renown had spread as far as Argentina and Israel was that he was markedly different from most other high-profile German jurists. A Social Democrat of Jewish descent, he had managed to flee Germany in 1936, returning after the war to work in the judiciary, the branch of the German civil service where the old Nazi networks of power were most pervasive. Bauer's work focused on bringing Nazi criminals to justice, and so it was to Bauer's office that Lothar Hermann sent his revelation about Eichmann's whereabouts.

The Israeli agent had just finished setting up his camera in Bauer's office when he jolted to attention: "Suddenly I heard footsteps, and light came shining in under the door." Hearing someone slowly shuffling across the green linoleum toward the office, Maor dived for cover behind Bauer's desk. It sounded as if whoever was outside was dragging something across the floor.

Maor remained frozen in position until he realized it must be the cleaner. "She was obviously a bit lazy," he said later, pointing out that she didn't bother to clean the attorney general's smoky sixty-square-meter office. The woman shuffled on past the office—"luckily for her," Maor said ominously; failure was simply not an option for him that night. The light went out again.

It was no accident that the Eichmann file—the contents of which were passed straight on to Mossad—had been left open. Bauer himself had invited the nocturnal visitor, and so the operation was more of a clandestine handover of information than a break-in. Indeed, the operation was so covert that nobody—not even Bauer's most trusted legal colleagues—knew anything about it.

Over the preceding years, Bauer had repeatedly seen his work thwarted by civil servants leaking sensitive information and warning Nazi suspects about their impending arrests. The police force had proven to be full of such leaks. Bauer's small team of investigators avoided using police telex lines, as this would give several employees access to their messages. According to Joachim Kügler, a member of Bauer's team, "Whenever I needed to send a telegram while I was working on the Auschwitz trial, I would go down to the market and ask a vegetable seller to send it."[3]

Discretion was of paramount importance, as, in the 1950s and 1960s, warnings were being systematically leaked to Nazi criminals who had gone to ground. There was even a newsletter called *Warndienst West* (Western Warning Service) specifically devoted to issuing such alerts. *Warndienst West* was distributed by the Hamburg branch of the German Red Cross—itself run by a former SS *Obersturmbannführer*—to Wehrmacht and SS veterans' associations in various countries. The source of the warnings was to be found right in the center of Bonn's government district. Established in 1950 and led by a former prosecutor at a Nazi "special court" in Breslau, the Central Office for the Legal Protection of Nazi Suspects was based in the ministry of justice until 1953, after which it relocated to the foreign ministry.[4] Once, when pursuing Reinhold Vorberg, the most active contributor to the Nazi regime's policy of euthanizing people with disabilities, Bauer's team filed a request with a court in Bonn for permission to launch secret investigations. The judge personally passed this confidential information on to a local lawyer, and Vorberg promptly fled to Spain.[5]

Former Nazi officials had regrouped to form more than just a few disparate networks; by the 1950s, they comprised a broad front running across state institutions. Thanks to the amnesty laws of 1949 and 1954, most Nazi criminals sentenced by German courts had already been pardoned. Moreover, both their sentences and the verdicts of the denazification courts had been stricken from their records. In the early days of the West German republic, the Allies and German democrats had hoped for a clean break, or at the very least a cleanup of state institutions. Since then, however, civil servant unions had successfully fought for the rights of almost all former Nazi officials to be reemployed. As a result, former Nazis were working in government ministries, holding positions up to the level of undersecretary. During the 1950s, virtually all former Nazi Party members were able to reassume positions within the West German judicial and administrative systems.

In July 1957, Paul Dickopf, a former SS *Untersturmführer* who now headed up the international division of the Bundeskriminalamt (the Federal Criminal Police Office), informed Bauer that the German police force would not be able to assist in the search for Eichmann. Dickopf claimed that as Eichmann's offences had been political in nature, the Interpol charter prohibited the police from launching a manhunt.[6] In 1958, thirty-three of the Bundeskriminalamt's forty-seven senior officials were former members of the SS. When Bauer invited them to a meeting in 1960 to discuss investigations into suspected Auschwitz criminals, they sent a head of division who, as a former SS *Sturmbannführer* in Russia, had overseen the deportation of civilians to concentration camps.[7] Erwin Schüle, the head of the newly established Central Office for the Investigation of National Socialist Crimes, commented in 1960 that West German police officials—many of whom were back in top positions—had been complicit "to an alarming degree" in Nazi crimes.[8] The irony was not lost on anyone when it later emerged that Schüle had himself been a member of both the Nazi Party and the SA (Hitler's storm troopers).

Even those Nazis hiding in far-off places like Buenos Aires were protected by vigilant, well-connected friends. This made the hunt for Eichmann exceptionally difficult. The German ambassador to Argentina, Werner Junker—who had once served as a diplomat under the Nazi regime—kept in close contact with right-wing exiles and personal acquaintances of Eichmann's.[9] Bauer was unaware that the Bundesnachrichtendienst, West Germany's intelligence agency, had known about Eichmann's address and assumed name in Argentina since 1952 but had chosen to keep this information to itself. "Carefully gather everything you can on Eichmann," the agents had noted in a file that was only opened decades later.[10] But while Bauer didn't know that the Bundesnachrichtendienst had been suppressing information about Eichmann's whereabouts, he nonetheless knew not to expect help from the intelligence service. The appointment of Reinhard Gehlen as its head made Bauer even more aware of the need to play his cards close to his chest. Gehlen had been responsible for Eastern espionage during the German war of extermination against the Soviet Union, and in his new position in postwar Germany, he continued to surround himself with his old cronies.

The story of how Bauer contributed to the arrest and prosecution of the world's most famous living Nazi is thus the story of how he managed to beat all these odds. It is also the story of a series of lonely decisions Bauer was forced to make. In early November 1957, he met for the first time with the State of Israel's representative in Germany, Felix Schinnar, to pass on his Eichmann tip-off. At the meeting, which took place at a secret location, Bauer told Schinnar that the only other person who knew about the clue pointing to Buenos Aires was the state premier of Hesse, Georg August Zinn, who was a friend of Bauer's and a fellow member of the Social Democratic Party. Bauer stressed that no one else could be allowed to find out. Too much was at stake. Bauer intended to quietly circumvent the German institutions that had repeatedly perverted the course of justice.[11]

Shortly afterward, in January 1958, a Mossad agent working on Bauer's information made an initial attempt to track down Eichmann in Buenos Aires. However,

Eichmann's alleged house at Calle Chacabuco 4261 turned out to be small and dilapidated. It didn't remotely resemble the hideout of a powerful Nazi, and so the disappointed agent returned to Israel without investigating any further.[12]

Bauer wasn't prepared to give up so easily, however. On January 21, 1958, he met for a second time with an Israeli contact, this time in Frankfurt, where he secured a promise that Mossad would track down Bauer's informant, Lothar Hermann. Bauer even issued a fake ID document to enable the Israeli agent to pose as one of the attorney general's officials.

But the second Mossad mission also ended in disappointment when it emerged that Hermann was almost blind and lived several hours away from Buenos Aires in the city of Coronel Suarez. It turned out that Hermann hadn't lived in Buenos Aires for years. No longer willing to take Hermann at his word, Mossad was reluctant to make a third expedition to South America. The trail to Buenos Aires was about to go cold when Bauer noticed that some of his political adversaries seemed more agitated than usual.

On June 24, 1958, the German ambassador in Buenos Aires informed Bauer that all the embassy's efforts to determine Eichmann's whereabouts had reached a dead end. Paradoxically, however, he also insisted that Eichmann was unlikely to be hiding in Argentina and that in all probability he was in the Middle East. Shortly afterward, this odd message was echoed by another former Nazi, Paul Dickopf, the head of the Bundeskriminalamt's international division. For the first time in his career, Bauer received a visit from Dickopf, who advised against searching for Eichmann in Argentina. There was no way that Eichmann was there, Dickopf insisted.[13] This intervention only strengthened Bauer's hunch that he was on the right track.[14] When in August 1959 a third former Nazi—senior state's attorney Erwin Schüle, head of the Office for the Investigation of National Socialist Crimes—contacted Bauer to say that he, too, had been informed that Eichmann was far more likely to be in the Middle East than in South America, Bauer became extremely suspicious.[15]

His response was two-pronged. First, he tried to assuage the fears of his nervous adversaries. From fall 1959 onward, he issued a series of press releases announcing that the search for Eichmann was now confined to the Middle East. In the first of these—a press release that, according to the Eichmann expert Bettina Stangneth, was "obviously completely made up"—Bauer said he had reason to believe that Eichmann was now working for a sheikh as a "representative of West German companies" but that out of courtesy to these companies, he would refrain from naming them.[16] Even the member of Bauer's team in Frankfurt officially responsible for the Eichmann file, a senior prosecutor, was kept in the dark, informing Hesse's minister of justice in 1959 that Eichmann had most likely been hiding in Egypt until recently.[17]

Bauer gave a highly publicized press conference just before Christmas 1959. Afterward, the news agencies wired a sensational report: "In early 1960, the relevant ministries in Bonn, acting on behalf of the state's attorney general, Fritz Bauer, will call on the emirate of Kuwait to extradite Eichmann."[18] None of this was true—the press conference was all an act that had been arranged in advance with Mossad—but it had the desired effect. Even Argentine newspapers carried reports on Bauer's supposed new line of enquiry, and these reports served to give Eichmann and his supporters the all-clear.

The second prong of Bauer's response was to urge the Israelis to step up their covert hunt for Eichmann. The government in Jerusalem was hesitant, however. It had political misgivings. Capturing Eichmann in Argentina without first following official diplomatic protocol would be considered an international affront and an attack on Argentine sovereignty, and so it was likely to cause difficulties for the young Jewish state, which sought respect from the international community. Yet following diplomatic protocol would ruin any chance of capturing Eichmann. Bauer traveled to meetings in Israel in summer 1959 and at the beginning of December 1959 in an attempt to change the Israelis' minds. Eventually, he issued an ultimatum, saying that if they dithered any longer, he would drop his "Kuwait" charade and request an extradition order from Argentina, which would result in Eichmann receiving due warning.

On December 6, 1959, the Israeli prime minister, David Ben-Gurion, noted in his diary, "My proposal was that [Fritz Bauer] say nothing and rather than requesting extradition, give us [Eichmann's] address. If it turns out [Eichmann is] there, we'll capture him and bring him here."[19] With that, the decision was made. "Isser will take care of it," added Ben-Gurion. Isser Harel, director of Mossad, personally headed up the operation.

Bauer continued to provide the Israelis with evidence on Eichmann; this was why he invited Michael Maor to break into his office that night in 1960. But after Maor's visit, Bauer received no further updates on Mossad's progress. Eventually, on May 22, after weeks of radio silence, an Israeli contact phoned Bauer in Frankfurt to request a meeting the next day, indicating that he "might" have some good news to share.[20] The two men arranged to meet in a restaurant in Frankfurt, but the Israeli didn't show up at the agreed time. Bauer waited, becoming increasingly agitated with each minute that went by—partly out of a growing sense of foreboding about Eichmann, partly because he was worried something had happened to the contact. Half an hour had passed when the Israeli finally appeared at the door. His hands still covered in oil from repairing his tire, he immediately blurted out the news.

Isser Harel later wrote in his memoirs that Bauer had tears in his eyes as the two men embraced.[21] Two-and-a-half hours later in Jerusalem, at 4:00 p.m.

local time, Ben-Gurion made a statement in the Knesset, and the news spread to the rest of the world that Eichmann had been arrested and flown to Israel.

What the rest of the world didn't know was that a lone German state's attorney general had been the driving force behind Eichmann's capture—and Bauer wanted to keep it that way. He fiercely guarded the secret, because if his flagrant violation of the rules were to become public knowledge, it would instantly cost him his job.

Haim Cohn, the Israeli attorney general, wrote to Bauer, "I hardly need tell you—and in any case I can't write it down in a letter—how indebted I am to you, not just in terms of gratitude, but also bearing in mind our shared goal and success."[22]

We can only imagine the twinge of envy Bauer must have felt when in 1960, the whole world's attention turned to the massive theater auditorium in Jerusalem where Eichmann was brought to trial. The Israeli judiciary staged the trial as a media event, presenting it as a confrontation with the Holocaust that would shatter the silence that had prevailed up to that point. Bauer also dreamed of such a reckoning with the past, as he once confided to his staff in Frankfurt, though he regretted the fact that the Israeli court wished to apply the death penalty, partly because this meant Eichmann would not be available to serve as a witness at future trials.[23]

Bauer tried to persuade the Adenauer government to send an extradition request to Israel. He wanted to let the world know that, with many Germans still unconvinced of the Nazi regime's wrongdoings, Germany was desperately in need of the kind of moral clarification that might be achieved by putting Eichmann on trial. But Bonn refused. Bauer's attempt didn't even impress those of his contemporaries who were usually well disposed toward him. In general, the Germans were reluctant to confront their past, the political philosopher Hannah Arendt wrote at the time to her friend Karl Jaspers, dismissing Bauer's lone voice as an inconsequential exception: Fritz Bauer was "a Jew, so it doesn't count."[24]

"I heard it was you who caught Eichmann," a young friend in Frankfurt once said to Bauer.

Evidently unable to keep his Eichmann secret entirely to himself, Bauer had shared it with another friend, who in turn couldn't resist sharing it with others. "Who told you that?" Bauer asked in surprise, but the young man refused to reveal his source. Noting that Bauer didn't deny playing a role in the capture of Eichmann, the friend persisted. "What about Simon Wiesenthal?" he asked. "Everyone says he tracked Eichmann down." Laughing quietly, Bauer replied, "Yes, he calls himself 'the Eichmann Hunter.' He can call himself that if he likes; he may have hunted Eichmann, but he didn't catch him."[25]

The world didn't discover the true extent of Bauer's role in the hunt for Eichmann until August 1968, when the Israeli newspaper *Ma'ariv* divulged the secret. The story was then corroborated by a confidant of Ben-Gurion, the novelist Michael Bar-Zohar. It is striking that the Israelis waited until Bauer was dead and the truth could no longer harm him.[26]

It took several decades for the full drama that had unfolded behind the scenes to come out into the open. This silence is baffling, particularly given the dearth of positive role models in postwar German history and the lack of examples of civil courage within the German legal profession in particular.

Bauer had a profound understanding of how a small courtroom could spark major political debates. Nowhere did this understanding come more into play than in the Auschwitz trial, which took place in Frankfurt from 1963 to 1965. Initiated by Bauer himself, this trial served "in many respects as a supplement to the Jerusalem trial," Hannah Arendt noted at the time.[27] Today, Bauer is most famous for the Eichmann and Auschwitz trials, neither of which would have taken place without him. But his own story, the life story of a man who confronted the Germans with their history, is also a fascinating one. Two scholarly works have been published on Bauer to date: Matthias Meusch's 2001 monograph, *Von der Diktatur zur Demokratie. Fritz Bauer und die Aufarbeitung der NS-Verbrechen in Hessen (1956–1968)* (From Dictatorship to Democracy: Fritz Bauer and the Investigation Of National Socialist Crimes in Hesse, 1956–1968), and Irmtrud Wojak's 2009 biography, *Fritz Bauer 1903–1968: Eine Biographie*. Though they are excellent, these works haven't brought Bauer's story to the wider audience it deserves, and they neglect several important aspects of Bauer's life.

When filling out forms in the postwar period, Bauer described himself as having "no religion." He stubbornly refused to talk about his youth and kept a remarkable distance from other Jews. For these reasons, it has hitherto been assumed that Bauer, who came from an assimilated Jewish family, never felt any close ties to his Jewish heritage. But new sources reveal a different story. The teenage Bauer enjoyed a vibrant relationship with Judaism and played an active role in Württemberg's small Jewish world. In 1945, he was still proudly describing himself as Jewish. It was only in 1949, when he returned to Germany after years in exile, that he began to keep this aspect of his biography out of the public eye. Bauer's awkward efforts to play down his Jewish heritage reveal a great deal about the German political climate of the time. His fraught dealings with anti-Semites as a young local court judge have also remained unexplored, the details lying dormant in court records.

As a young man in exile in Denmark, Bauer was questioned by police about alleged homosexual activities. Tied together with a piece of red-and-white string, these police reports have been gathering dust deep in the Danish national archives in Copenhagen for decades. Had they surfaced while Bauer was attorney general of Hesse, they could have ended his career, as homosexuality was still a crime in 1960s Germany. The only reason the reports are significant today is that they raise the possibility that Bauer had yet another secret to guard. They may also help us develop a better understanding of his antiauthoritarian streak.

Equal parts politician and bohemian, Bauer greeted inmates with the words "My comrades!" when he visited a prison in Hesse in 1958.[28] This would have been considered an outrageous way for an attorney general to address prisoners during the Adenauer era. On another occasion, he was asked during a panel discussion, "What can be done to reduce the general aggressiveness that is the root of so much harm in society?" Bauer called back into the auditorium, "More sexuality! In literature too! I disagree with the ban on the Marquis de Sade."[29] On yet another occasion in the late 1950s, Georg August Zinn, Hesse's state premier, invited a group of publishers, ministry officials, and journalists to sit down together to discuss a draft of a new, modernized press law for Hesse. Over the course of the meeting, the most radical proposals for absolute freedom of the press were made by the quick-witted chain-smoking attorney with the unkempt hair, until eventually an unwitting journalist asked, "Excuse me, what newspaper do you work for?"[30]

The role Fritz Bauer played throughout his life was that of a prosecutor driven not by ruthlessness or a desire for retribution but by profound liberalism. He shone some light on his country at a time when it was still very dark, and he changed it forever, both as a prosecutor and as a criminal justice reformer. To understand Bauer's achievements, this book examines numerous documents, including previously unseen ones. It also draws on the insights provided by the people who knew him best. Some of these people loved Bauer, some suffered as a result of his vulnerability and fear of intimacy, and some turned against him toward the end of his life.

Bauer's home telephone would often ring in the middle of the night. When he picked up, he would hear an unknown caller screaming "Die, you Jewish pig!" through the earpiece. From spring 1964 onward, the rooms in which the Auschwitz trial took place had to be searched for explosives at the start of each day. Bauer's office itself received a bomb threat.[31] He had the piles of letters he received filed away into folders, some labeled "Letters of Support," others labeled "Crank Letters."[32] Yet in the late 1960s, when the author Ingrid Zwerenz asked him to send her some abusive letters for a book project she was working on, Bauer demonstrated an ability to find humor in the vitriol. Whereas novelists such as Heinrich Böll, Günter Grass, and Martin Walser waved Zwerenz's request aside or claimed they never held on to hate mail, Bauer sent a friendly reply accompanied by a particularly odd specimen, a postcard covered on both sides by a densely typewritten message. The sender, identified only as "Kölner Kreis" (The Cologne Circle), had addressed the card to "Attorney General Fritz Bauer, Bigwig 1a, Frankfurt" but provided no further details about the location of Bauer's office.

Perhaps Bauer was amused by the fact that the postman knew where to deliver the postcard despite the paucity of information. Or perhaps it was the crude text that made him smile: "Our idea of a prosecutor is someone who stands up for order, morals, and cleanliness!" According to this anonymous author, Fritz Bauer was the complete opposite.[33]

Notes

1. *Der Spiegel*, "Feindliches Ausland," July 31, 1995.
2. Bettina Stangneth highlights the possibility that Hermann initially contacted Arnold Buchthal, a Jewish senior prosecutor; see Stangneth, *Eichmann vor Jerusalem. Das unbehelligte Leben eines Massenmörders* (Zürich and Hamburg: Rowohlt, 2011), 406. However, Buchthal, who worked as a state prosecutor in Frankfurt until 1957, was Bauer's direct subordinate. Investigations into violent Nazi crimes—or "old political cases," as they were termed in the bureaucratese of the time—had to be reported to and authorized by state attorney generals.
3. Joachim Kügler, interview by Werner Renz, May 5, 1998.
4. For further details on the Central Office for the Legal Protection of Nazi Suspects—which performed the opposite function of, and was established before, the Central Office for the Investigation of National Socialist Crimes—see Annette Weinke, *Eine Gesellschaft ermittelt gegen sich selbst. Die Geschichte der Zentralen Stelle Ludwigsburg 1958-2008*, 2nd ed. (Darmstadt: Wissenschaftliche Buchgesellschaft, 2009), 126-135.
5. Johannes Warlo, interview with the author, October 9, 2012.
6. Cf. Stangneth, *Eichmann vor Jerusalem*, 407.
7. On Bernhard Niggemeyer's participation in this meeting, see the note made on March 8, 1960, by the prosecutor Georg Friedrich Vogel in file number 4 Js 444/59, Landgericht Frankfurt am Main. On Niggemeyer's past, see Dieter Schenk, *Auf dem rechten Auge blind. Die braunen Wurzeln des BKA* (Cologne: Kiepenheuer & Witsch, 2001), 187-190.
8. Quoted in Andreas Eichmüller, *Keine Generalamnestie. Die Strafverfolgung von NS-Verbrechen in der frühen Bundesrepublik* (Munich: Oldenbourg Verlag, 2012), 375.
9. See Stangneth, *Eichmann vor Jerusalem*, 413.
10. Quoted in ibid., 533.
11. See ibid., 407.
12. See ibid.
13. See Irmtrud Wojak, *Fritz Bauer (1903-1968). Eine Biographie* (Munich: C. H. Beck, 2009), 296.
14. See Stangneth, *Eichmann vor Jerusalem*, 430.
15. See Wojak, *Fritz Bauer*, 298.
16. Stangneth, *Eichmann vor Jerusalem*, 438.

17. Wojak, *Fritz Bauer*, 298.
18. Quoted in Stangneth, *Eichmann vor Jerusalem*, 435.
19. Quoted in Michael Bar-Zohar, *Ben-Gurion*, vol. 3 (Tel Aviv: Am Oved, 1978), 1,374.
20. See Isser Harel, *Das Haus in der Garibaldistraße* (Frankfurt am Main: Ullstein, 1976), 279.
21. See ibid., 280.
22. Haim Cohn to Bauer, May 22, 1960, Fritz Bauer papers, Archiv der sozialen Demokratie, Bonn.
23. Warlo, interview.
24. Hannah Arendt to Karl Jaspers, August 6, 1961, published in *Hannah Arendt/Karl Jaspers Briefwechsel 1926–1969*, ed. Lotte Köhler and Hans Saner, 2nd ed. (Munich: Piper, 1987), 483.
25. Manfred Amend, interview with the author, November 14–15, 2012.
26. See *Süddeutsche Zeitung*, "Israelischer Autor: Fritz Bauer verriet uns Eichmann," February 19, 1969.
27. Hannah Arendt, "Der Auschwitz- Prozeß," in *Nach Auschwitz, Essays & Kommentare 1*, ed. Eike Geisel and Klaus Bittermann (Berlin: Edition Tiamat, 1989), 117.
28. Quoted in *Der Spiegel*, "Personalien," March 20, 1957.
29. Quoted in Robert Neumann, *Vielleicht das Heitere. Tagebuch aus einem andern Jahr* (Munich: Heyne, 1968), 386.
30. Ernst Müller-Meiningen Jr., "Wenn einer nicht im Dutzend mitläuft. Erinnerungen an den hessischen Generalstaatsanwalt Bauer, der am 16. Juli 65 Jahre alt geworden wäre," *Süddeutsche Zeitung*, July 16, 1968.
31. See Wojak, *Fritz Bauer*, 307.
32. See Irmtrud Wojak, "'Die Mauer des Schweigens durchbrochen.' Der erste Frankfurter Auschwitz-Prozess 1963–1965," in *"Gerichtstag halten über uns selbst..." Geschichte und Wirkung des ersten Frankfurter Auschwitz-Prozesses*, ed. Fritz-Bauer-Institut (Frankfurt: Campus, 2001), 23.
33. See Ingrid Zwerenz, ed., *Anonym. Schmäh- und Drohbriefe an Prominente* (Munich: Rütten & Loening, 1968), 89.

2

THE SECRET JEWISH LIFE OF POSTWAR GERMANY'S MOST CONTROVERSIAL JURIST

The Reticent Hothead

"Did you experience any anti-Semitism when you were younger?"[1] Bauer let the interviewer's question hang in the air for a moment before replying in his deep, Swabian-inflected voice. The question was an innocent one, but for Bauer, the lawyer who confronted the Germans with Auschwitz, it was fraught with danger.

It was August 1967. Illuminated by lights that had been arranged around the corduroy armchairs in his Frankfurt office, Bauer was seated beside a dark, wild painting by the Frankfurt expressionist Siegfried Reich an der Stolpe. Wearing his trademark horn-rimmed glasses, his hair disheveled as usual, Bauer slouched in his armchair, his pant leg riding up to reveal a light-colored sock and a glimpse of his leg. He was smoking a small cigar, his favorite accompaniment to reflective discussions like this one. By now, Fritz Bauer no longer needed any introduction to the many German TV viewers watching at home. A large number of these viewers found Bauer's approach to confronting the past too extreme. At the time of the interview, he was the most famous—and, if the number of threatening letters he received is anything to go by, the most hated—prosecutor in the country. A plot to kill him had recently been uncovered. The year before, two right-wing extremists had hatched a plan to assassinate Bauer, whom they regarded as "the main culprit behind the trials against war criminals." The would-be assassins' targets also included Willy Brandt and the writer Günter Grass. Their plot was complicated by several factors, not least the fact that Bauer carried a pistol in his pocket.[2]

Bauer's detractors accused him of being vengeful. "Anyone who watches you on TV, Dr. B., can immediately see that you are filled with boundless hatred," wrote the author of one typical piece of hate mail.³ Another letter writer asked, "Has your rage blinded you to the fact that the vast majority of Germans are sick to the teeth of these so-called Nazi criminal trials? Go back to where you belong!!!"⁴ Such cranks were not the only ones wondering whether Bauer was driven by personal motives. Many other Germans had been questioning whether Bauer's concern with the Nazi past was rooted in his own encounters with anti-Semitism, and so he had to choose his words carefully.

He could have told viewers about his student days, when he was prohibited from joining sports clubs and fraternities because he was Jewish; about how he was attacked by the National Socialist press, which referred to him as "the Jew Bauer," when he was a twenty-eight-year-old local court judge; about how he was barred from the legal profession from 1933 onward; about how his family had been dispossessed and forced to flee twice; or about how his return to German public service after the war was obstructed by those who saw it as "inopportune." But instead, Bauer chose to recount a single, relatively innocent, anecdote about his schooldays. The story went like this: As a bespectacled first-grader, Bauer was beaten up by a couple of other pupils, who were jealous because the teacher had praised him. During the row, one of the children told Bauer, "Your family killed Jesus."

And that was it. In their religion class, Bauer's Christian classmates had learned that "the Jews" were the killers of Jesus Christ, an idea that neither emerged nor disappeared with National Socialism.⁵ Compared to the experiences Bauer might have described, this childhood incident seems fairly harmless.

Bauer was loath to talk about his personal experiences as a Jew. On October 24, 1943, the Swedish police had recorded "persecution of Jews" as his reason for fleeing his first country of exile, Denmark.⁶ Yet after 1949, whenever he was asked whether he had been subjected to "political, racist, or religious persecution," Bauer always claimed that he had been persecuted for purely political reasons, and not because he was Jewish.⁷ In 1960, when the mayor of his home city, Stuttgart, invited him to share some personal memories to be included in an exhibition on the persecution of "fellow Jewish citizens" in Stuttgart, Bauer refused point-blank.⁸ "I doubt anyone else in my family would want to share their experiences either," he added.⁹

Bauer and his TV interviewer, Renate Harpprecht, had agreed in advance on the questions that would be asked during the TV interview on the corduroy armchairs.¹⁰ Like Bauer, Harpprecht was a Jewish survivor of the Nazi regime. By the age of twenty-one, she had been incarcerated in the concentration camps at Auschwitz and Bergen-Belsen. Years later, she described her memories of being freed by the British, saying that she would never forget the oppressive heat and the sickly sweet stench of thousands of rotting corpses.[11] We know, then, that Bauer had plenty of time to prepare his answers to Harpprecht's questions and that he knew he was talking to somebody who would understand what he had been through. Yet neither Harpprecht nor Bauer brought up the experiences that would expose the massive biographical chasm separating them from most of their German TV audience.

Instead, Bauer used the interview as an opportunity to emphasize the exact opposite, claiming that his personal background gave him a special understanding of German anxieties. As he came to the end of his anecdote about being teased as a Jewish schoolchild, he said, "It was then, at the age of six, that I began to suffer from what's now known as collective guilt." "Collective guilt" was a politically charged concept at the time. It was frequently invoked by those Germans who believed that Allied attempts to prosecute Nazi crimes resulted in all Germans being unfairly tarred with the same brush. In claiming that even as a boy he had rejected the concept of collective guilt, Bauer sought to assuage his German audience's fears. The parallel he drew was absurd, but it nonetheless helped drive home his point that he wasn't seeking to blame all Germans for the crimes of the past.

Bauer's Jewish heritage was a matter of great interest at the time, not just for the anonymous letter writers and night-time callers who accused him of being out for revenge but also for politicians and journalists. Indeed, even Bauer's friends seemed to think of him as first and foremost a Jew. "Fritz Bauer was a wonderful hothead," recalled one of his political colleagues, Jürgen Baumann, a member of the Freie Demokratische Partei (Free Democratic Party) who had once served as minister of justice in West Berlin. "A great man. He was three-quarters Jewish, I believe. So he was a Jew. But he was a socialist really."[12] This emphasis on Bauer's Jewishness stands in stark contrast to the way in which Bauer sought to present himself in postwar Germany; when filling out forms from 1949 onward, Bauer always described himself as having "no religion."[13]

In the mid-1960s, a young friend of Bauer's innocently asked, "Is it true that you're Jewish?" Bauer gave a chilly response: "According to the Nuremberg Laws, yes."[14] Bauer was certainly not the first well-known German to claim it was Hitler who had turned him into a Jew, but his young friend would later wonder whether Bauer had ever felt a connection to Judaism that went beyond the identity forced upon him by anti-Semitism.

"According to the Nuremberg Laws, yes." How strange these words would have sounded to Bauer's grandfather, a man who had been a leading figure in Tübingen's Jewish community during the Wilhelmine era, a man who had sung prayers and knelt while recounting tales from the Torah and Talmud to a rapt audience of one: his grandson, Fritz. The reason for Fritz Bauer's reluctance to talk about his Jewish background after 1945 was certainly not that he had nothing to say.

A Family Determined to Fit In: Bauer's Childhood in Wilhelmine Germany

When Bauer was a small child, his grandparents lived in a corner house at the end of a cobbled lane in Tübingen, a small town in the south of Germany, in what was then known as the Kingdom of Württemberg. This house seemed like a magical world to the young Bauer. "Everything, absolutely everything, was a source of fascination," he remembered later. "Number 6 Kronenstrasse was full of secrets."[15] It was here, and not in his own parents' home, that Fritz Max Bauer, born in Stuttgart on July 16, 1903, learned about his family's heritage. "Everything seemed shrouded in a mysterious dusky light, though these were in fact the most ordinary things in the world, often things that were just one or two generations old," he explained.

This house revealed "the deeper, personal significance of 'religion,'" Bauer wrote in a 1938 letter to his mother. "The pictures of past generations looking down at me, the old furniture, and Grandfather himself, who himself seemed like an Old Testament figure, especially after the death of my beloved grandmother, made the Old Testament come alive in a way it never did at school." The shelves were full of books, photo albums, and mysterious illustrated volumes, one of which was entitled *Flowers of Jerusalem*. The Promised Land was perceptible in the scents that wafted through the house, too: "Olive blossoms, orange blossoms, and other flowers from the Orient had been gathered together in bunches and stored. It was like a herbarium," Bauer later reminisced. Beneath the bouquets were written the names of places in what was then Palestine: "A Souvenir of Samaria," "Blossoms from the Mount of Olives," "Violets from Nazareth and Tiberias."[16] As a grown man in 1938, Bauer could still recall these biblical place-names, which indicates that he was aware of their significance even as a boy.

As soon as he was tall enough to stick his head up over his grandparents' windowsill, Bauer loved to gaze out at the brightly colored little houses huddled along the banks of the Neckar river. As an adult, he waxed lyrical about "rooftops nestling into one another, windows filled with flowers, sheets hanging out to dry, and the proud, defiant Gothic church towering over it all."[17] The young Bauer, who wore small metal-framed glasses from an early age, would scamper around the upstairs apartment where his grandparents lived, skirting past their heavy, bourgeois furniture. The dark wood and expensive leather objects filling the home evoked the opulence of bygone days, while the faded chrysanthemum wallpaper in the guestroom had a quainter, more whimsical flavor. As he

Figure 2.1. The family: Ella, Margot, Ludwig, and Fritz Bauer, around 1910.
Credit/Source: *Tiefenthal family*.

Figure 2.2. In Bauer's childhood memories, his sister Margot features prominently. Credit/Source: *Tiefenthal family*.

clambered over the sagging sofa, "which concealed its innards within a heavy fabric covered in a bright floral pattern," his sister Margot, who was almost three years younger, was never far behind.[18] As his mother had five siblings, Bauer had several cousins, but most of these had emigrated to the United States when they were very young. In later life, the only person Bauer could remember playing with as a child was Margot. And nothing gave the two children a greater thrill than the wonders contained on the floor below the apartment, where their grandparents ran a clothing store.

Every now and then, Fritz and Margot would be left alone in the store. They loved pretending that the sumptuous clothes belonged to them, but they also secretly hoped they wouldn't have to deal with any actual customers, as "neither of us had the slightest idea what to say if someone came in looking for something."[19] The children preferred to devote their attention to exploring the store's treasures. One of the most memorable of these appeared one day in the form of a large sealed box labeled "Workwear." The label stirred the children's imagination. Having observed the comings and goings of the store's many customers, Fritz and Margot surmised that the box must contain at least one officer's uniform, like the one their father used to wear when he was a soldier, with gold buttons, shiny epaulets, and opulent fabric. Or perhaps they would find a uniform for a policeman with "a spiked helmet, cavalry saber, and military mustache." Bauer later admitted that he thought policemen were "the greatest thing on earth" when he was a child.[20] Fritz and his sister opened the mysterious box and began to empty it. As the contents piled up in front of them, their disappointment grew: all they found were plain overalls and aprons.[21]

Fritz and Margot had already internalized their family's worldview. The family did not maintain a skeptical distance from the cavalry sabers and military mustaches of the authoritarian Wilhelmine monarchy. Quite the opposite; the family's attitude was characterized by loyalty and admiration, even though Jews faced discrimination under this regime. Bauer's Tübingen-born grandfather, Gustav Hirsch, a man with gray hair, gentle eyes, and a bushy mustache, was a respected businessman. As Fritz's mother explained to her amazed son, Hirsch was also a politician of sorts in Tübingen, a university town dominated by national conservatives.[22] Hirsch served as secretary and treasurer of the board of the citizens' association, where he toasted the king of Württemberg, helped organize the town's commercial activities, behaved like a model citizen, and cultivated a close, respectful relationship with the men with the spiked helmets and shiny epaulets.[23] As head of the synagogue, Hirsch also served as leader of the Jewish community in Tübingen. He took over this role from his father, Leopold, in 1900 and would pass it on to his own oldest son, who was also called Leopold, in 1925.[24] Hirsch was therefore the main point of contact in Tübingen for the state-run Israelite Senior Church Authority at a time when rabbis and Jewish religion teachers were employees of the German state. Bauer described his grandfather as someone who was always "ready to lend a helping hand to anyone who needed it" and who impressed everyone with his ability to provide "detailed explanations of everything under the sun."[25] The young Fritz Bauer deeply admired his grandfather. In later years, too, Bauer liked to believe he resembled Hirsch: "Scientists now believe that grandfathers are reflected in their grandchildren," he wrote to his mother in 1938.[26]

Jews in the state of Württemberg had been able to apply for full civil and political rights since the 1860s, but each application had to be individually filed with the local council. Hirsch didn't gain his rights until 1875, when he was twenty-seven years old. Jews accounted for less than 1 percent of the total German population at the time. As they had long been prohibited from farming, most Jews lived in larger German cities such as Hamburg and Berlin, where they accounted for a somewhat larger percentage of the population. Tübingen, however, was a small town surrounded by vineyards, and its university had only admitted Jewish students since 1819. Thus, when Bauer was a child, the town's entire Jewish population consisted of a few families. In the year 1910, just 139 of the town's estimated 19,000 inhabitants were Jewish.[27]

Jews were still unwelcome in several of the Kingdom of Württemberg's state institutions. This placed limits on any political ambitions Gustav Hirsch may have harbored. His brother Robert had been repeatedly passed over for positions as a judge, despite having passed his bar exam in Tübingen in 1884. In fact, Robert received so many rejections that in February 1886, the Württemberg minister of justice personally advised him not to submit any more applications, as he was "damaging his religion's reputation."[28] Jews were not yet fully emancipated, which made many of them keen to prove they were in no way different from their Christian neighbors. Gustav Hirsch instilled in his six children a belief in the importance of education and hard work, just as his own father had done. Every morning, Hirsch's father had sent him and his seven brothers off on the long journey to school in the next village. He had also insisted that they were to revere their German fatherland at least as much as their non-Jewish neighbors did.[29] Gustav Hirsch's daughter Ella and her husband raised their own children, Fritz and Margot, in much the same spirit.

The golden rule at the family dinner table, Bauer remembered, was "Sit down and keep quiet. Don't dare open your mouth if your father is speaking." Decades later, he was still plagued by "nightmares recalling the moment at one Sunday lunch when I had the cheek to move my left arm instead of keeping it motionless by the table."[30] Bauer's parents were not well matched. His mother, a kind and gentle woman, showered her children with affection and attention; "She completely understood Fritz," Margot recalled.[31] Later, after his mother developed cancer, Fritz Bauer wrote to her every day up to her death in 1955.[32] "If he opened up to anyone," Margot said, "then it was our mother."[33] Fritz and Margot's father, Ludwig, was usually away on business during the week, but when he returned on the weekends, the family home would become a stricter, more severe place.[34]

Fritz Bauer was sent to Eberhard-Ludwigs-Gymnasium, an academic high school for boys. The school's façade resembled a fortress, and its front garden was laid out in a rigid geometric pattern. An institution steeped in tradition, Eberhard-Ludwigs-Gymnasium specialized in Greek and Latin and was largely attended by the sons of pastors, businessmen, civil servants, industrialists, and aristocrats. One of its pupils, a scion of the Württemberg baron Freiherr Konstantin von Neurath, would later become Hitler's foreign minister. Neurath was "such a brilliant student," Bauer later noted sarcastically, "that he even needed extra tuition in geography."[35] Graf von Stauffenberg, then lord chamberlain to the king of Württemberg, also sent his sons to the school, where Bauer encountered them in a theater group.[36]

Around this time, the piano became the ultimate trapping of the German middle class. The Bauers' decision to send Fritz and Margot to piano lessons therefore had more to do with convention than any real talent or interest. At the age of nine or ten, the children would knock on Fräulein Heimberger's door, sit down on her little revolving stool, and play pieces from Czerny's *School of Velocity*, a collection of difficult finger-training exercises. These were to be performed quickly and efficiently without the pedal, which usually serves to soften individual notes by adding a warm, forgiving reverberation.[37] As a result, even the tiniest mistakes were clearly audible. "Within a few moments, a few hours, I was furious," Fritz Bauer recalled. Fräulein Heimberger "had the nerve to beat me, a boy. She hit me on the arm with the metronome, a punishment I didn't feel I deserved. After a while I'd had my fill of Czerny and his ilk."[38]

While rummaging around at home one day, the young Fritz Bauer found something much more interesting: a book of sheet music belonging to his father. "Stretching my little hands as far as I could across the piano, I reached the deep, dark tones at the lower end. They expressed the murmur of the Rhine, all the beauty of the *Rheingold*. I reveled in these tones; they enthralled me. I felt as if I had plumbed the most profound depths of German music."[39] The music in question was the overture to Richard Wagner's *Rheingold*. Wagner's anti-Semitic essay *Das Judenthum in der Musik* (Jewishness in Music)—first published in 1850 and republished in an expanded edition in 1869—had caused a stir some years previously, yet during his lifetime, Wagner's work was admired by many Jews.[40] One of these admirers was evidently Ludwig Bauer.

Born in 1870 into a Jewish family in the rural town of Ellwangen, Ludwig Bauer was the second of five children. By virtue of sheer self-discipline, he managed to work his way up through society. Just one generation earlier, Jews in many parts of Germany had been prohibited from selling new clothes, and so they had had to rely on the second-hand trade.[41] Nevertheless, Ludwig and his brother Julius grew up to run a successful textile business together. The business, which sold fabric by the meter, employed five people, and, as a partner, Ludwig Bauer was bringing home an annual salary of 40,000 Reichsmarks by the 1930s.[42] This was a handsome sum at a time when deputy state ministers earned 26,500 Reichsmarks a year and the average doctor earned about 12,500 Reichsmarks.[43] Ludwig Bauer had become a wealthy man. While the family's day-to-day existence was by no means extravagant, Ludwig's wife, Ella, who was eleven years his junior, kept a fourteen-carat gold ladies' wristwatch and a diamond ring in her jewelry box.[44] When the outbreak of World War I was announced in 1914, the family was on holiday in the genteel Belgian seaside resort of Blankenberge. As an adult, Fritz Bauer recalled that the family had taken "four or five huge trunks" with them on this holiday. Fritz's mother spent her days dancing tango in a shimmering dress while the children gathered starfish on the beach.[45]

The Bauers reacted to the war's outbreak with the same odd equanimity demonstrated by millions of other Germans. For the eleven-year-old Fritz, the war was an inconvenience, as it forced the family to end their holiday prematurely, leaving their trunks behind them in Belgium. As an adult, Bauer recalled that "the Bauer family had no doubt that the German armed forces would quickly conquer Belgium. For us, the conquest of Belgium was tied up with the endeavor to recapture our trunks. . . . The Bauers' firm belief in the Germans' ability to conquer major cities like Antwerp was confirmed, as was our belief that our trunks would eventually be retrieved. I believe that in October or November a message arrived from the national railway saying 'Your trunks have made it to Stuttgart!'"[46]

Ludwig Bauer, a reader of the liberal *Frankfurter Zeitung* newspaper, was possibly too intelligent to muster up genuine enthusiasm for the war. "There'll be no wars in the twentieth century. It's impossible. We're an advanced people; war is out of the question," he used to say.[47] But whatever his personal views on the war may have been, Ludwig Bauer showed his children that demonstrative patriotism played just as important a role in the life of a prominent citizen as virtues such as hard work and competence. In 1894, when Jews were still prohibited from becoming army officers, the twenty-two-year-old Ludwig Bauer had volunteered for the military. After serving for a year in the eleventh company of Württemberg's "Queen Olga" grenadier regiment, he returned to Stuttgart to go into business.[48] When World War I broke out, he registered with the military again and was posted with the same regiment.[49] At the time, many Jews hoped that the war would help break down social barriers between Jewish and non-Jewish Germans. This hope seemed to materialize in 1916, when Württemberg's war ministry granted Jews the long-awaited right to be sworn in to the military in the presence of a Jewish chaplain. On July 16, 1916, an officer swore in Jewish recruits during a ceremony presided over by a rabbi at Ludwigsburg Synagogue.[50] Many Jews mistakenly believed that this development would mark an end to their discrimination.

A total of 520 Jews from Stuttgart and the nearby town of Cannstatt were sent to the front. Among them were Ludwig Bauer and his brother-in-law Leopold Hirsch, the son of the head of Tübingen's synagogue. The names of the ninety-eight Jewish soldiers killed in action would later be engraved in a special memorial garden in the Israelite Cemetery in Stuttgart.[51] The garden was created partly as a means of debunking the myth that Jews had shirked their military duties. The very emergence of this myth indicated that the trenches had not fostered the sense of community that so many Jews had hoped for. Instead, with defeat looming, many Germans were looking for scapegoats, and anti-Jewish discrimination intensified. In October 1916, German Jews were subjected to further humiliation when the Prussian war minister ominously announced that the military was planning to conduct a meticulous *Judenzählung* (Jewish census). The results of this census were never disclosed.

Fritz Bauer's Jewish heritage was no secret to anyone at his high school, as at the beginning of each school year, the teacher would ask each pupil in the class to state his name and religion.[52] Jewish pupils were aware that their behavior was monitored more closely. For example, when the war began to affect the supply situation in Stuttgart, a few pupils took to illicitly trading sugar and old gold. One of Bauer's classmates, Fred Uhlman, later recalled that "only a small group of boys took part in these activities, and not one of them was Jewish. Can you imagine the uproar if Jewish boys had been involved?!"[53]

During the war, Bauer happily joined his classmates in marking the advancing front lines on the huge maps of Europe hanging up in their classroom. When at one point he was confined to bed with scarlet fever, what upset him most was that he would miss out on the fun of moving forward the little black, white, and red flags on these maps. "First," Bauer said, "it was scarlet fever that prevented me from moving the flags. Later, it was the defeat at the Battle of the Marne." Bauer's description of the nationalism of his childhood is revealing; as a schoolchild, he said, he demonstrated nationalism to the extent that "my school demanded it."[54]

Bauer may have suffered under his father's severity when he was growing up, but he could well understand its reasons.

Hanukkah and Bar Mitzvah: Bauer's Upbringing and Sense of Identity

When he was six or seven years old, Bauer asked his mother, Ella, to explain what God is. Rather than attempting to provide a definition, Ella Bauer told her son that he need only remember one rule: "What is hateful to you, to your fellow don't do."[55]

This simple answer is not necessarily a sign that the Bauer family was unversed in Jewish doctrine. Instead, it probably indicates that Bauer's mother—a "smart" woman, according to her son—knew how to explain the essence of her faith in a child-friendly way.[56] Her response to her son's question recalls the famous anecdote about the eminent Jewish sage Rabbi Hillel. The story goes that a few decades before the birth of Jesus, a Gentile approached the rabbi with the following challenge: "I will become a Jew if you can recite the entire Torah while standing on one leg." In response, Hillel stood on one leg and said, "What is hateful to you, to your fellow don't do. That is the entirety of the Torah; everything else is elaboration. So go, study." It seems likely that Ella Bauer—the daughter of a synagogue head—invoked the Golden Rule not because she was stumped by her son's question but because she was deeply familiar with Jewish teachings, including those of Rabbi Hillel.

Looking back on their childhood, Fritz's sister, Margot, described the family home as a "liberally Jewish" one in which "we celebrated the festivals."[57] During the spring festival of Passover, Ludwig, Ella, Fritz, and Margot Bauer would all gather around the dining table to eat several courses, sing, and remember the Exodus from Egypt. To mark the beginning of the new year in the fall, they would dip the traditional slices of apple into honey. On Hanukkah, the winter festival of lights, they would light candles for eight days, lighting one more candle each day so that by the end, all eight candles were burning. But despite all these festivities, there was one thing the children missed: Christmas, the Christian festival of their neighbors.[58]

Perhaps Fritz and Margot felt that in the strict Bauer household, Jewish festivities did not generate quite enough warmth to compensate for the lack of Christmas. Margot later commented that the family had observed the Jewish festivals "because one of our grandmothers was still alive," which suggests that the Bauers were to some degree just going through the motions.[59] What is noteworthy, though, is the parents' firm refusal to let their children have a Christmas tree. Their refusal is all the more remarkable because it was common at the time for assimilated Jews to celebrate Christmas for the sake of their children, treating the festival more as a German than a Christian tradition; there was even a decorated tree in the Viennese home of the Zionist leader Theodor Herzl.[60]

But the Bauers refused to celebrate Christmas, insisting that only Jewish religious festivals were marked in their home. They had no intention of squeezing Christmas in between Hanukkah and Passover. Ludwig Bauer was adamant that German patriotism and a sense of Jewish identity weren't mutually exclusive, and he wasn't prepared to compromise either.

Stuttgart's synagogue—a large, cube-shaped building decorated with stained glass and Moorish mosaics—was located on Hospitalstrasse, just five hundred meters away from the town hall. The surrounding streets were named after great Swabian writers and thinkers like Hölderlin, Schiller, Mörike, Hegel, and Hesse.[61] Inside the synagogue, all the pews faced in the same direction: toward the lectern at the front. This church-like layout was unusual, given that lecterns are usually located in the center of synagogues. Within the synagogue, Württemberg Jews could feel that they had at last achieved their dream of leading a bourgeois German existence, a dream they had been permitted to pursue for only a few decades now. The Old Testament stories about Adam and Eve in paradise, about the trials and tribulations of Jacob's twelve sons, and about Moses leading the Jews out of slavery in Egypt came to life not in Hebrew but in the earthy Swabian dialect of the region.[62] This demonstrates the huge degree to which Stuttgart's Jews identified with their German environment. "It never occurred to us that the prophets spoke anything other than Swabian," commented a Jewish contemporary of Fritz Bauer's who had attended the synagogue.[63]

There had been a Zionist association in Stuttgart since 1918, but it had so few members that its meetings took place in a single room in an inn. The association sought donations to fund land purchases in Palestine, but its little blue collection cans marked with Hebrew script hung in only a handful of homes in Stuttgart.[64] For most Jews, the idea of seeking a home anywhere but Stuttgart was absurd; they felt it made more sense to emphasize their patriotic allegiance to Germany.[65] When frightened, destitute Jewish refugees arrived in the city after fleeing bloody Russian pogroms, many native Stuttgart Jews feared being tainted by association.[66] With their beards, side curls, and fur hats, the new arrivals didn't fit in at all; they came from the alien world of the shtetl, as immortalized in the work of Marc Chagall. "People who don't speak proper German, never mind Swabian, have no right to a voice within the German community," complained one born-and-bred Stuttgart Jew in 1919, the sharpness of his criticism betraying a deep sense of uneasiness.[67]

One of the leading figures in Stuttgart's Jewish community was Otto Hirsch, who in 1930 became president of the council of Württemberg's Israelite Religious Community and in 1933 took over as chairman of the Reich Deputation of German Jews. Hirsch, a former student of the same elite high school Fritz Bauer had attended, also worked for the state of Württemberg as a jurist. The Hirsch family in Stuttgart, though large and diffuse, was not related by blood to Fritz Bauer's maternal Hirsch relatives in Tübingen. The Stuttgart Hirsch family originally came from the town of Künzelsau and had moved to Stuttgart back in 1857, whereas the Tübingen Hirsch family originally came from the village of Wankheim. However, the two families had been connected by marriage for some time, as a cousin of Fritz Bauer's mother—a woman named Minna, daughter of the jurist Robert Hirsch—was married to Otto Hirsch's brother.[68]

Any documents relating to the synagogue membership of Fritz Bauer's parents went up in flames when the synagogue was burned down in 1938.[69] Nevertheless, there can be little doubt that the Bauers were indeed members, as right up to the Weimar period, the same law applied to Jews that continues to apply to members of the two main Christian churches in Germany today. Jews were automatically registered as members of their local Jewish community, to which they were required to pay a church tax.[70] This means that Ludwig and Ella Bauer would have been members of Stuttgart's Israelite Religious Community by default, unless they at some point underwent a formal procedure to leave it.[71] The latter seems unlikely given that, as the historian Michael Brenner writes in his classic *The Renaissance of Jewish Culture in Weimar Germany*, "anybody who left [the community] left Judaism at the same time."[72] In other words, he or she would no longer have been registered as "Israelite" in the local authority's list of residents. But when Fritz Bauer moved to Munich to study in 1922, he registered as "Israelite" with the local authorities.[73] This wouldn't have been possible unless his parents were still official members of the Jewish community.

Seeing as Bauer's family observed Jewish festivals, it is highly probable that Ella and Ludwig Bauer sent their son to the synagogue in Stuttgart at least once: for his bar mitzvah on his thirteenth birthday. At the time, bar mitzvah ceremonies—during which boys who have come of age are called to the synagogue's lectern to read from the Torah for the first time—were just as common in the Jewish community as communion and confirmation ceremonies were among Bauer's Christian classmates. Moreover, as we have seen, Bauer's maternal relatives formed the backbone of the Jewish community in Tübingen and as such needed to maintain their reputation as devout Jews. The Hirsch family would therefore presumably have viewed any refusal to follow the bar mitzvah convention as a grave affront.

While Bauer's Christian classmates attended religion class, he and his few Jewish classmates received instruction from a rabbi.[74] However, Bauer dropped religion before sitting his final exams; when asked to choose between learning Hebrew, the key to understanding the old biblical texts, and English, the language of international commerce, he opted for English.[75] It is apparent, then, that Bauer did not inherit the religiosity of his mother's side of the family. Indeed, at the age of eighteen, Bauer delivered a speech at his university in praise of Nietzsche's individualism and atheism.[76] Years later, at the age of thirty-three, he made his critical views on religion even more explicit when he wrote a newspaper article commending *Inside the Walls*, a play by the Jewish Danish writer Henri Nathansen about the relationship between a Jewish girl and a Christian boy. Bauer was struck by one particular line, an answer to the question of whether children should be brought up to be good Christians or good Jews: "They should be brought up to be human beings."[77] However, the critical attitude toward religious dogma evident in Bauer's response to this play should not be interpreted as a sign that he was already seeking at this point to distance himself from the Jewish milieu he had grown up in.

Several of Bauer's young socialist contemporaries left the Jewish community for political reasons. One prominent example is Rudolf Katz, a jurist from Kiel who would later pursue a successful legal career in postwar Germany, ultimately becoming vice-president of the Federal Constitutional Court. But whereas Katz left the Jewish community in 1930, Bauer was still describing himself as "Israelite" when he registered with the judicial authorities in 1928.[78] Furthermore,

Bauer accepted a remarkable number of invitations to speak at Jewish events. As his reputation as a gifted orator grew, Bauer became known as "the only Jew" to make public appearances in Stuttgart. His friend Helmut Mielke later recalled that those who attended such events were "hugely impressed by his erudition."[79] Bauer, the brilliant young jurist who was appointed to the position of local court judge at the age of just twenty-seven, thereby realizing the dream denied his great-uncle Robert Hirsch, was "very well known" among "Jews," in particular, Mielke pointed out. However, Bauer's speeches were likely to disappoint any listeners expecting him to address specifically Jewish issues; the only themes the young Bauer wished to speak about were democracy and socialism.[80]

When he wanted to, though, Bauer could call upon an extensive knowledge of religious vocabulary. This knowledge came to the fore when he was invited to speak to the Association of Jewish Craftsmen, an organization which, under the leadership of its chairman, Julius Landauer, helped young unemployed people in Stuttgart find apprenticeships. Landauer wanted Bauer to convince his protégés that the one thing they all had in common—namely, their Jewish background—could be a source of proletarian solidarity. In her account of Bauer's speech, the historian Maria Zelzer noted that "the speaker emphasized the importance of socialist ideas in the Torah. Dr. Bauer did not go so far as to suggest that the Jewish prophets were the original leaders of the proletariat, but he did describe them as the source and bastion of socialist thought. True Judaism provides a bridge to socialism, he argued."[81]

Bauer maintained ties with the Jewish community after he went into exile in 1936. In that same year, he wrote his article about the Danish dramatist Henri Nathansen's plea for tolerance, praising Nathansen's call for children to be brought up as human beings rather than good Christians or good Jews. Notably, this article appeared in the Jewish *CentralVereins-Zeitung*. Formerly known as the *Allgemeine Zeitung des Judentums*, this newspaper was published by the Central Association of German Citizens of Jewish Faith, the precursor to today's Central Council of Jews in Germany. As the newspaper's Scandinavia correspondent, Bauer learned a great deal about the history of Danish Jews.[82] He introduced his readers to the Jewish Norwegian poet Henrik Wergeland, for example, celebrating Wergeland as a writer as talented as Heinrich Heine, with whom he shared not just a first name but also a similar degree of political commitment. Bauer saw Wergeland's beautiful grave in Our Saviour's Cemetery in Oslo as a testament to his achievements. "Grateful Jews on the other side of the Norwegian border erected this monument," Bauer informed his readers.[83]

Statements like these suggest that Bauer's attitude toward his Jewish heritage was anything but cold and distant. He may not have been religious in any traditional sense, but as a young man in exile in Scandinavia, Bauer was familiar with the debates raging between Zionists and proponents of assimilation, such as the chief rabbi of Copenhagen, Dr. Friediger, and Professor Lund, a Jewish academic at Lund University in Sweden.[84] In 1947, shortly before he returned to Germany, Bauer wrote an article reminiscent of the speech he had made to the Association of Jewish Craftsmen back in 1930. This article insisted that the Old Testament prophets were "the first socialists" because they had dreamed of a "socialist kingdom of peace."[85] A couple of years previously, in August 1945, Bauer had voluntarily addressed the issue of his Jewish identity in an article for the *Sozialistische Tribüne*, a newspaper targeted at a non-Jewish readership. In the article, Bauer described his encounter with a fifteen-year-old member of Hitler Youth in a Danish refugee camp. "Hey, Fritz, what exactly are you, anyway? German, Jewish, or stateless?" the boy asked. "Well, Günther, you may laugh, but I'm German, Jewish, and stateless," Bauer replied.[86]

These words indicate that, at this point, Bauer still proudly identified as Jewish. Many years after Fritz's death, in the tranquil surroundings of a Swiss hotel, Margot Bauer commented on the wealth of vibrant quotations her brother had woven in and out of his essays and books. She was convinced that this stylistic technique could be traced back to Orthodox Judaism: "Fritz borrowed [the technique]," she said.[87] Of course, Margot may have been mistaken. The strikingly vivid style of Bauer's many written contributions to the central legal and political debates of the young West Germany may have had another source of inspiration. We cannot be sure that its roots go back to the world of the rabbis that Bauer had got to know as he was growing up in Stuttgart. Nevertheless, the fact that Margot *believed* her brother's writing to be so fundamentally influenced by his Jewish heritage reveals a great deal about the Fritz Bauer she knew in private. As far as she was concerned, Bauer never made a completely clean break with their shared Jewish roots. But in public, Bauer became more tight-lipped about his heritage after 1945. It was only after he returned to Germany alone, leaving his parents and sister behind in Sweden, that he began to cultivate his image as a figure with "no religion."

Notes

1. *Als sie noch jung waren. Gespräch mit Fritz Bauer*, television interview with Bauer, first broadcast on August 11, 1967, by WDR.
2. See Gerhard Mauz, "Schuhgröße neun reicht im allgemeinen," *Der Spiegel*, November 14, 1966.
3. Irmtrud Wojak discovered this undated letter, which was sent from Nuremberg, in the national archives in Wiesbaden. See Wojak, *Fritz Bauer*, 307.

4. Ibid., 307.

5. Another Jewish boy who went to school in Stuttgart at this time, Fred Uhlman, encountered an elementary school religion teacher who taught his students that "the Jews" had scourged Jesus. See Fred Uhlman, *The Making of an Englishman. Erinnerungen eines deutschen Juden* (Zürich: Diogenes, 1998), 37.

6. See Wojak, *Fritz Bauer*, 161.

7. Questionnaire issued by the higher regional court of Frankfurt am Main in 1956, judiciary personnel file, call number NL—08/03, Fritz Bauer Institute Archives, Frankfurt am Main.

8. See Alfred Tischendorf (on behalf of the mayor's office) to Fritz Bauer, March 23, 1960, inventory 8600, number 172 (filed under "Bauer, Fritz"), Stadtarchiv Stuttgart.

9. Bauer to Tischendorf, March 28, 1960, ibid.

10. Renate Lasker-Harpprecht, interview by author, January 5, 2013.

11. Renate Harpprecht, "Es war der Tag, an dem das Leben noch einmal begann. Renate Harpprecht erinnert sich an die Befreiung aus dem KZ Bergen-Belsen am 15. April 1945," *Frankfurter Rundschau*, April 13, 2002.

12. Quoted in Thomas Horstmann and Heike Litzinger, *An den Grenzen des Rechts. Gespräche mit Juristen* (Frankfurt am Main: Campus, 2006), 136. It's not clear why Baumann believed Bauer to be "three-quarters" Jewish, given that all of Bauer's grandparents were Jewish; Paul Arnsberg, a Jewish community leader in Frankfurt, wrote in 1968 that "from a Halachic perspective," Bauer was Jewish and that he was "of purely Jewish descent." Paul Arnsberg, "Nachrufe: Generalstaatsanwalt Dr. Fritz Bauer," *Frankfurter Jüdisches Gemeindeblatt*, July/August 1968, 15.

13. Questionnaire issued by the higher regional court of Frankfurt am Main in 1956.

14. Amend, interview by author.

15. Fritz Bauer to Ella Bauer, summer 1938, Rolf Tiefenthal's personal archive. The letter was never finished or sent. Bauer's friend Heinz Meyer-Velde found it within a book in Bauer's apartment and later passed it on to Bauer's nephew, Rolf Tiefenthal.

16. Ibid.

17. Ibid.

18. Ibid.

19. Ibid.

20. Fritz Bauer, "Im Kampf um des Menschen Rechte" (1955), republished in *Die Humanität der Rechtsordnung. Ausgewählte Schriften Fritz Bauers*, ed. Joachim Perels and Irmtrud Wojak, (Frankfurt am Main: Campus, 1998), 37.

21. Bauer once shared this story with his friends Heinz and Gisela Meyer-Velde. Heinz and Gisela Meyer-Velde, interview with the author, November 22, 2012.

22. See Bauer, "Im Kampf um des Menschen Rechte," 38.

23. Geschichtswerkstatt Tübingen, ed., *Zerstörte Hoffnungen. Wege der Tübinger Juden* (Tübingen: Theiss, 1995), 35.

24. Ibid., 27, 35.

25. Bauer, "Im Kampf um des Menschen Rechte," 38.

26. Fritz Bauer to Ella Bauer, summer 1938.

27. See Lilli Zapf, *Die Tübinger Juden. Eine Dokumentation* (Tübingen: Katzmann-Verlag, 1981), 38f.

28. Quoted in Stadtarchiv Ulm, ed., *Zeugnisse zur Geschichte der Juden in Ulm. Erinnerungen und Dokumente* (Ulm: Stadtarchiv Ulm, 1991), 14f.

29. See Geschichtswerkstatt Tübingen, ed., *Zerstörte Hoffnungen*, 30f.
30. *Heute abend Kellerklub. Die Jugend im Gespräch mit Fritz Bauer*, television interview with Bauer, first broadcast on December 8, 1964, by HR.
31. Margot Tiefenthal, interview by Walter Fabian, 1973. The transcript is available in file number EB 87/112 (papers of Walter Fabian), Deutsches Exilarchiv, Frankfurt am Main.
32. Ibid.
33. Ibid.
34. Ibid.
35. Bauer, *Als sie noch jung waren*.
36. See Eberhard Zeller, *Oberst Claus Graf Stauffenberg. Ein Lebensbild*, 2nd ed. (Paderborn: F. Schöningh, 2008), 6.
37. Bauer, *Als sie noch jung waren*.
38. Ibid.
39. Ibid.
40. See Amos Elon, *The Pity of It All: A Portrait of Jews in Germany, 1743–1933* (London: Picador, 2004), 261f.
41. See Geschichtswerkstatt Tübingen, ed., *Zerstörte Hoffnungen*, 30.
42. See letter from Ella Bauer's attorney, Ostertag, to the Landesbezirksstelle für die Wiedergutmachung (State District Office for Compensation), Stuttgart, April 22, 1950, file number EL 350 I Bü 23925, Staatsarchiv Ludwigsburg.
43. See Hans-Ulrich Wehler, *Deutsche Gesellschaftsgeschichte. Vierter Band: Von Beginn des Ersten Weltkriegs bis zur Gründung der beiden deutschen Staaten 1914–1949* (Munich: C. H. Beck, 2003), 725, 727.
44. Tiefenthal, interview by Walter Fabian. See also the letter from Ella Bauer's attorney, Ostertag, to the Landesbezirksstelle für die Wiedergutmachung (State District Office for Compensation), Stuttgart.
45. Bauer, *Als sie noch jung waren*.
46. Ibid.
47. Ibid.
48. See Wojak, *Fritz Bauer*, 58. Wojak viewed Ludwig Bauer's police clearance certificate in the personal archive of Fritz Bauer's nephew, Rolf Tiefenthal, in Denmark.
49. See Paul Sauer and Sonja Hosseinzadeh, *Jüdisches Leben im Wandel der Zeit. 170 Jahre Israelitische Religionsgemeinschaft, 50 Jahre neue Synagoge in Stuttgart* (Gerlingen: Bleicher Verlag, 2002), 81.
50. See Leo Adler, *Wandlungen bei dem Oberrat der Israelitischen Religionsgemeinschaft Württembergs, Feiertagsschrift der Israelitischen Kultusvereinigung Württemberg und Hohenzollern*, September 1962, Archiv Stadtbibliothek Stuttgart.
51. See Sauer and Hosseinzadeh, *Jüdisches Leben im Wandel der Zeit*, 86.
52. See Uhlman, *The Making of an Englishman*, 41.
53. See ibid., 52f.
54. Bauer, *Als sie noch jung waren*.
55. Ibid.
56. Quoted in Gerhard Zwerenz, "Gespräche mit Fritz Bauer," *Streit-Zeit-Schrift* 2 (September 1968): 89.
57. Tiefenthal, interview by Fabian.
58. See Wojak, *Fritz Bauer*, 69. Bauer shared this childhood memory with a friend of his in Frankfurt, Professor Ilse Staff, who mentioned it in a eulogy she delivered at a memorial

service attended by close friends of Bauer's in July 1968. Staff subsequently passed on the manuscript of her eulogy to Irmtrud Wojak.

59. Tiefenthal, interview by Fabian. Tiefenthal must have been referring here to her paternal grandmother, as her maternal grandmother, Emma—wife of the devout Gustav Hirsch—died in 1918. See Geschichtswerkstatt Tübingen, ed., *Zerstörte Hoffnungen*, 35.

60. See Elon, *The Pity of It All*, 285.

61. See Fred Uhlman, *Der wiedergefundene Freund* (Zürich: Diogenes, 1998), 56.

62. See Sauer and Hosseinzadeh, *Jüdisches Leben im Wandel der Zeit*, 95.

63. Dr. Ch. Lehrmann, "Ansprache," in *Festschrift zur Einweihung der Synagoge in Stuttgart*, ed. Israelitische Kultusvereinigung Württemberg und Hohenzollern (Stuttgart: Israelitische Kultusvereinigung Württemberg und Hohenzollern, 1952), 17.

64. Sauer and Hosseinzadeh, *Jüdisches Leben im Wandel der Zeit*, 92f.

65. Ibid., 95.

66. See ibid., 102.

67. Quoted in ibid., 99.

68. Hans George Hirsch, interview with author, March 16, 2013. (Born in 1916, Hans George Hirsch is Otto Hirsch's son. He now lives in Bethesda, Maryland, USA.)

69. Only post-1945 documents relating to Stuttgart's Jewish community are preserved in the city's archives.

70. See Michael Brenner, *Jüdische Kultur in der Weimarer Republik* (Munich: C. H. Beck, 2000), 62.

71. Extracts of the 1912 Israelite "constitution" were republished in Leo Adler, *Wandlungen bei dem Oberrat der Israelitischen Religionsgemeinschaft Württembergs*, 36. According to this constitution, "every member of the Israelite Religious Community is automatically a member of the religious community of his place of residence" (Paragraph 2), and "the responsible rabbi must be notified of the intention to withdraw from the religious community. Withdrawal comes into effect four weeks after notification and must be certified by the rabbi" (Paragraph 3). Prior to 1912, there were no official regulations governing withdrawal from the community.

72. Michael Brenner, *Jüdische Kultur in der Weimarer Republik*, 62.

73. See Wojak, *Fritz Bauer*, 529, footnote 71. The registration form of May 18, 1922, is preserved in Munich's city archives.

74. See Uhlman, *The Making of an Englishman*, 42.

75. See Wojak, *Fritz Bauer*, 82.

76. See *Monatsberichte des Bundes Freier Wissenschaftlicher Vereinigungen*, July 1922, call number MF B78, Leo Baeck Institute Archives, New York, 5.

77. Fritz Bauer, "Glückliche Insel Dänemark," *CentralVereins-Zeitung—Allgemeine Zeitung des Judentums* (C.V.-Zeitung), December 24, 1936.

78. See Fritz Bauer's judiciary personnel file, call number NL—08/03, Fritz Bauer Institute Archives, Frankfurt am Main.

79. Quoted in Wojak, *Fritz Bauer*, 109.

80. Ibid.

81. Maria Zelzer, *Weg und Schicksal der Stuttgarter Juden* (Stuttgart: Klett, 1964), 127.

82. See, for example, Fritz Bauer, "Panorama in Helsingör," *C.V.-Zeitung*, July 29, 1937.

83. Fritz Bauer, "Von unserem F.-B.-Berichterstatter/Kopenhagen, 'Der 'andere Heinrich,'" *C.V.-Zeitung*, April 14, 1937.

84. Fritz Bauer, "Juden in Europas Norden," *C.V.-Zeitung*, September 22, 1938, 5. Bauer's other articles include "Einwanderer in Skandinavien. Offiziöse Zahlen und Daten von unserem fb.-Berichterstatter, Kopenhagen," *C.V.-Zeitung*, April 29, 1937, and "Von unserem F.-B.-Berichterstatter/Kopenhagen, 'Das Nansen-Amt,'" *C.V.-Zeitung*, June 23, 1938. In the latter, Bauer recommends Norway as a country of exile.
85. Fritz Bauer, "Sozialismus und Sozialisierung," *Deutsche Nachrichten*, May 12, 1947.
86. See Fritz Bauer, "Brief aus Dänemark," *Sozialistische Tribüne*, September 1945, 25.
87. Tiefenthal, interview by Fabian.

3

THE UNIVERSITY YEARS (1921–1925)
A Gifted Student

Twenty-Three Friends

They had everything set up. It was November 1922, and Bauer, now a law student, had arranged to meet twenty-two friends, almost all of them Jewish, in Burg Raueck, an inn just off Munich's main square. As usual, the students' beer-stained books of drinking songs were open on the tables in front of them. But for once, Bauer and his friends weren't in the mood for singing. "Much as we had been looking forward to a night of carousing, each of us was acutely aware of the gravity of recent events, and we all felt the burden of responsibility weighing on our shoulders. We knew no amount of forced joviality would allow us to forget how serious the situation was," wrote one student present that evening. "What depressed us most of all was the fact that the university was dominated by groups engaged in political activities that ran counter to all our ideals," he added.[1]

The political climate in Munich had been fraught for several months. Walther Rathenau, the German foreign minister, had been assassinated in Berlin a few months previously, just as he had begun to garner support for the country's unpopular young democracy. Decades later, Sebastian Haffner, a journalist four years Bauer's junior, wrote of Rathenau: "Never in the history of the German republic had a politician so captured the imagination of both the masses and the younger generation. . . . It seemed as if, had he not been the German foreign minister in 1922, he could have been a German philosopher in 1800, an international financial mogul in 1850, a great rabbi, or an anchorite."[2]

Rathenau came from a well-respected assimilated Jewish family. His father, Emil, was known as the "Bismarck of the electrical industry," as he had introduced electric light and trams to most cities in Germany. Bauer, one of Walther Rathenau's many admirers, would later begin his doctoral thesis with a quote from the politician.

Figure 3.1. In the Jewish fraternity FWV, Bauer (on the right) makes friends.
Credit/Source: *Tiefenthal family.*

Bauer and his friends were deeply shocked when Rathenau was shot dead in his limousine in the leafy Berlin suburb of Grunewald on June 24, 1922. This brutal crime was just the most notorious in a series of 354 political assassinations that had been carried out since Germany became a democracy; Emil Julius Gumbel, a statistics professor at Heidelberg University, was keeping a running tally.[3] Investigators suspected that the assassins, who had sped away from the scene after opening fire on Rathenau from another car, were members of right-wing student fraternities.[4] The University of Berlin called off its memorial service for Rathenau because the chancellor feared the fraternities' celebrations would spin out of control.[5] "We were profoundly shaken," Bauer later recalled, "and we sensed that democracy was in grave danger. This was a matter very close to our hearts, because fundamental human rights were at stake."[6]

The "political activities" engaged in by groups of students at the University of Munich tended to be violent in nature. A student by the name of Rudolf Heß, who in 1922 was still attending lectures, submitting essays, and giving presentations in seminars, had mobilized a band of fraternity brothers.[7] Spurred on by the success of Mussolini's March on Rome in late October 1922, Heß's disciples carried out numerous vicious attacks. Hermann Göring was also enrolled at the University of Munich, where his subjects included political science. Munich provided the Nazis with exceptionally fertile ground, as the writer Ernst Jünger later explained. Jünger, then an up-and-coming star of the right-wing conservative scene, described Munich as "more fertile than Berlin. The people there are more impulsive; they have experienced the Bavarian Soviet Republic. I saw workers, demobilized soldiers wearing gray field tunics, young guys with faces that looked like they had been painted by Leibl. People came down from the mountains and into the city, where they were mesmerized [by Hitler] and hung on his every word."[8]

Heß's storm troopers, known as the SA, had not yet adopted their distinctive brown shirts, but with their puttees and swastika armbands, they were nonetheless a conspicuous presence in Munich's university district. "I witnessed the unrest in Munich and the initial emergence of Hitler's Nazi Party," Bauer said in a television interview years later. Looking back on his student days in Munich, he remembered seeing "'No access for Jews' emblazoned across huge bright red signs. These words were clearly written for all to see; no one should dispute their existence today."[9] The SA's eleventh *Hundertschaft*—the squad commanded by Heß until early 1923—was composed entirely of students.[10] These campus thugs were feeling triumphant in fall 1922, as just a few weeks earlier, ethno-nationalist groups had gained a majority in the German Student Union.[11] Indeed, it had become clear at National Students' Day in Erlangen in 1921 that Bavarian students counted among the nationalists' strongest supporters.[12] In response, the new majority's few opponents, who included in their ranks Bauer and his fraternity brothers, founded the Cartel of Republican Students in Munich in August 1922.[13] Before long, members of the cartel found themselves at the receiving end of the brutality meted out by the young men in puttees.

Bauer was one of those gathered in Burg Raueck on that dark November evening in 1922 to voice his opinion on the latest disturbing turn of events. Having just recently moved from Heidelberg to Munich, he was still a relatively unfamiliar face. All the other students knew about him was that he was a fan of Greek theater and Goethe and that he lived in Schwabing, Munich's bohemian quarter, where the renowned playwright Bertolt Brecht had recently celebrated his wedding. They were taken aback when the strong-willed, polemical Bauer erupted in fury. He had little patience for their "depressed" mood. They had become "far, far too willing to put up with it all," he exploded, an accusation he would later reiterate in writing, adding that his fraternity brothers didn't seem capable of getting fired up about anything. What was truly regrettable, Bauer said, was that "most people seem to regard this as an ideal situation. They believe we have achieved the ultimate goal of establishing harmony. Having given up the fight, they are just sitting back, looking to the past, and worshiping the law of inertia. And they will keep on muddling along like this until one day they realize that the heavy, clumpy, inelastic sphere has remained motionless while everything else around it keeps moving and changing."

Neither "tedious slogans" nor the traditional gymnastics exercises practiced by his liberal fraternity brothers were going to "have any impact on the world in 1923," Bauer said. He concluded his rant by exhorting his fellow students to "take a stand" and wage a political struggle. "We can practice gymnastics elsewhere," he added sardonically.[14]

That evening, the twenty-two friends elected the nineteen-year-old Bauer as their new president.[15]

A Jewish Fraternity

Before moving to Munich, Bauer had studied at Heidelberg University, commencing his studies there in spring 1921, when he was just seventeen years of age. He arrived in Heidelberg shortly after nationalistic German fraternities known as *Burschenschaften* passed the "Eisenach Resolutions," which prohibited "Jews and people of Jewish descent" from becoming members.[16] Bauer would later describe the Eisenach Resolutions, which also forbade *Burschenschaft* members from marrying "Jewish or colored women," as the first "Aryan paragraph."[17] (Under the Nazi regime, Aryan paragraphs were adopted by schools, universities, the civil service, the professions, and private organizations to effectively drive Jews out of public life.) The adoption of the Eisenach Resolutions led even the less regimented student fraternities in Germany to consider whether they should follow suit.[18] One of these was Allemannia, a fraternity based in a palatial villa close to the spectacular ruins of Heidelberg Palace. Several articles arguing for and against equality for Jews were published in Allemannia's magazine around this time. The main reason the issue was so hotly debated among Allemannia members was that an unusually high number of Jews had been prominent members of the fraternity in the past.[19] In contrast, the shift to the right was barely discussed in most of Heidelberg's other fraternities, and life at Heidelberg University, which had hitherto been known as a liberal oasis on the banks of the river Neckar, became smaller and more restrictive for Jewish students like Bauer.[20]

Bauer didn't have to join a fraternity. Like four out of every ten students at the time, he could simply have rented a room in an anonymous boarding house and explored the town's inns on his own.[21] Students who didn't belong to fraternities were at the very bottom of campus hierarchies in 1920s Germany, however, and Bauer looked with longing at the bright flags and crests adorning the fraternity houses dotted around Heidelberg's university district. At the age of eighteen, he explained rather emotionally that his wish to join a fraternity was driven by the "urge to be part of a community, the desire to come together and work with friends toward a common goal." This desire for community, claimed Bauer, constituted "a form of socialism based on the conviction that naked individualism is both impossible and ridiculous," because "the individual can only achieve something truly positive if he works closely with like-minded people."[22]

Bauer's only option was to apply to one of the university's few Jewish fraternities, which had been established in response to growing anti-Semitism on campus.[23] One such Jewish fraternity was called Bavaria. Wearing bright orange caps and blue, white, and orange ribbons, members of Bavaria formed a small but self-assured minority who made no attempt to blend in on campus. Quick to reach for their heavy sabers whenever other fraternities expressed anti-Semitic sentiments, they were regularly involved in duels until 1923, when the university rector intervened.[24] The combative Bavaria fraternity didn't appeal to Bauer, however. Instead, he opted to join a smaller, more moderate group called the Freie Wissenchaftliche Vereinigung (FWV: Free Academic Union) in May 1921. There were branches of this decidedly liberal, nondenominational fraternity at nine German universities. Members of the FWV were proud of their blue, red, and silver crest, but they didn't wear the brightly colored uniforms, caps, and ribbons favored by most other fraternities. Instead, Bauer and his FWV brothers wore formal black suits and ties around campus, and when they invited women to their dances, they eschewed the military-inspired garb worn by other fraternities.[25] Members of the FWV treated the university's few freshman students with more respect than other fraternities, and they regarded members of sororities, with whom they occasionally organized events, as their equals.[26] Bauer made several friends in the fraternity, some of whom he even took back to Stuttgart to meet his parents.[27]

To celebrate the completion of his first semester at Heidelberg, Bauer and his fraternity brothers gathered in the candlelit back room of a brewery at 6 Leyergasse, where Bauer was toasted with a "splendid peach punch."[28] The fraternity's monthly report records that afterward, the revelers "made a great hullabaloo" as they moved on to the terrace of Heidelberg Palace, "where we had a stunning view of the moonlit palace. For some of us, though, the vista was a little blurry." The pacifist essayist Kurt Hiller, who was awarded a doctorate in law by Heidelberg University in 1907, recalled that the FWV was involved in "less brawling, to be sure, but just as much boozing" as other fraternities. When Hiller first attended an FWV meeting, he encountered a "young gynecologist with a carrot-colored goatee beard" who greeted Hiller with the words "Down the hatch!," thereby "commanding me to swill down an entire bottle of beer in one go." Hiller was appalled: "I hadn't done anything to deserve this punishment, not even by the beer-fueled moral standards of this petit-bourgeois academic boor."[29]

It is possible that Bauer himself refrained from his fraternity's bawdier activities. Years later, a young student friend of Bauer's named Heinz Meyer-Velde felt he was being pressured into joining a fraternity in Göttingen. "They make you drink so much beer!" he complained to Bauer, who responded, "There are ways of avoiding it."³⁰ One photo from his student days captures Bauer and his friends at a dance. The women are wearing party dresses adorned with the latest Charleston-style feather accessories, and the men are wearing black bow ties. One man has pinned a couple of heart-shaped cookies to his lapel.³¹ Bauer is the only one not looking at the camera, and he doesn't seem to be paying any attention to the women beside him, either. Yet he doesn't look like a peripheral figure. Bauer's contributions to the debates taking place in the heat of Heidelberg's student inns would soon ensure that he became the center of attention.

The articles Bauer wrote for the FWV's monthly reports testify to his love of philosophy and literature. He appears to have been particularly drawn to the writings of Arthur Schopenhauer; "side by side with the history of nations, the history of philosophy, science, and art takes its innocent and bloodless way" is one of the Schopenhauer aphorisms quoted by the eighteen-year-old Bauer.³² Bauer's fraternity brothers shared these progressive, humanist ideals. They kept their distance from Heidelberg's fencing halls, preferring instead to meet on Friday evenings to listen to each other deliver speeches on great writers, such as Dostoevsky, Lessing, and the Romantic poet Christian Dietrich Grabbe.³³ In his very first semester, Bauer made a speech too, and it caused quite a stir.

According to one student who witnessed this speech, Bauer presented "historico-philosophical observations" from "a determinist perspective": "He shared his insights into the value and meaning of history, into its origins and progress, into the relationships between various cultural epochs, and so on."³⁴ Many years later, Bauer would share this materialist understanding of history with a larger audience. In this later speech, which he delivered at a 1962 conference for social workers organized by the German Workers' Welfare Association, Bauer provided further evidence of his extensive knowledge of German literature from Weimar classicism to twentieth-century left-wing theater. Quoting one of Brecht's most famous lines—"First comes food, then morality"—Bauer argued that the eighteenth-century poet and playwright Friedrich Schiller had anticipated Brecht's insight when he wrote, "The dignity of man, no more of that, I pray you. Give him food to eat, a place to live; if you have covered his nakedness, dignity will follow by itself."³⁵ Even as a student, Bauer's self-assured argumentation had been so watertight it rendered his audience speechless. "His observations did not meet with any opposition, and so no discussion of this interesting theme developed," noted the student responsible for taking the minutes.³⁶

Before he had even begun his second semester, Bauer was serving as the fraternity's spokesman. In an article published in the fraternity's journal, Bauer articulated his brothers' uneasiness about the growing power of right-wing figures on university campuses as he criticized "charlatans" who were "driving experienced lecturers out of their positions because of their political views." A "politicized university," Bauer explained, is "senseless, just as senseless as politicized science, just as paradoxical as a concept like 'social-democratic nitrogen' or 'a German-nationalist trial.' Because if there is one thing that forms the essence of the sciences and the academy, then it is surely their independence from current events, their freedom, and their separation from politics and parties."[37] In contrast to what many figures in "today's German universities" believed, the role of scholarship was not to serve the state, the eighteen-year-old Bauer wrote, "The state is nothing more than a rough husk that surrounds the core of life. It is the wall around the garden of human fruits and flowers," he noted, adding that the state's "moral raison d'être" is to "nurture scholarship, ensuring it advances and creates cultural assets." By the time his second semester began, Bauer had been appointed secretary of his fraternity.[38]

Bauer's speeches were never boring. One evening, he gave a short talk entitled "Goethe's Practical Reason," in which he argued that the ethics of Goethe and Kant are diametrically opposed. Not everyone gathered in the inn was wholly convinced by this thesis, yet by the end of the night, even Bauer's critics were impressed by his oratory skills. "It is fair to say that, thanks to the spirited delivery, the introduction provided to very different worldviews, and the superbly structured argumentation, this was a truly exceptional lecture in the tradition of Goethe," wrote the fraternity journal's reporter.[39] Admittedly, such journal reports tended to be kind to speakers. Even so, extravagant praise like this was rare, as was the barely concealed irritation triggered by Bauer's second talk, which bore the simple title "Decadence." Here, Bauer, whose self-confidence was growing all the time, took listeners on a dizzying journey through the history of civilization as he critiqued the values associated with soldierly obedience. Virtues such as self-restraint and conformity would ultimately lead to cultural decay, Bauer argued. "Of course, arguments like this are always rooted in the purely personal views of the speaker, and so needless to say, Bauer's understanding of concepts such as religion, God, Christianity, and history were hotly contested," one fraternity brother observed.[40]

Shortly afterward, Walter Einstein, a law student, gave a speech responding to Bauer's arguments. The fraternity journal noted that Einstein "held the completely opposite view, arguing that extreme individualism and the uncompromising preservation of originality—if indeed such a thing even exists—are not goals one should aspire to. To discover one's true identity, one should sacrifice oneself for others, for one's better self, for one's leader—both in the wider world beyond the fraternity and within the small circle of the FWV. Subordinating oneself to a leader means serving an idea; respecting nothing but oneself means chaos. Community depends on subordination of oneself to a leader in the service of an idea."[41]

Like Bauer, Einstein would soon move to Munich, where he would study the same subject as Bauer and become co-chairman alongside Bauer of the Munich FWV. It would appear, then, that the two young men got on well and that participants of FWV debates maintained a sporting attitude, no matter how heated these debates became. This helps to explain why Bauer was well liked despite his polemical speeches against religion, the state, and Kant. It helped that the fraternity members were able to laugh at themselves. On one particularly drunken evening, one brother generated much mirth when he began to mimic some of the more prominent members of the Heidelberg FWV: "Richard Sternheimer, the melodramatic dictionary of quotations; Hans Schwarz's God-filled self; Walter Einstein's asthmatic jurisprudence; Fritz Bauer's vigorous shalvation."[42] (Bauer's Swabian accent meant that he occasionally pronounced "s" as "sh.")

"Embracing Germanness": Disagreements with Heidelberg's Zionists

The question of whether the FWV was a Jewish fraternity was a contentious one. A correspondent for a magazine called *Der Jüdische Student* (The Jewish Student) wrote with disdain, "The Freie Wissenschaftliche Vereinigung is composed entirely—or almost entirely—of Jews, and yet it is the most vociferous in its insistence that it is not a Jewish fraternity. It is as if it considers such a designation an affront."[43]

The FWV described itself to the outside world as a "parity" fraternity—in other words, as a nondenominational group that welcomed Protestants, Catholics, and Jews alike.[44] In reality, though, almost all its members were Jewish, and so, with anti-Semitism growing in the world around them, FWV members in their subdued black suits soon faced the same level of discrimination as the members of the Zionist fraternity Bavaria in their bright orange caps.

Large nationalistic German fraternities dominated Heidelberg's fraternity scene. They also wielded a great deal of power over the town as a whole. A single boycott threat from them was all it took to force innkeepers, student organizations, and other fraternities to adopt their own private Aryan paragraphs.[45] As a result of such paragraphs, Bauer was turned away from a student sports club because he was Jewish, and he was left with no option but to sell the canoe he had just bought and abandon his plan to row it down the Neckar with a non-Jewish friend.[46] Bauer was also prohibited from entering many of Heidelberg's inns, as just before he began his studies, nationalistic fraternities had successfully demanded that several inns in the student district become "Jew-free" zones.[47]

Such developments didn't dent FWV members' patriotism. They established a special memorial foundation to honor former members of the fraternity who had fallen in World War I, and they sang all three verses of the national anthem.[48] Indeed, their motto—"Unity, Justice, Freedom!"—was borrowed from the anthem.[49] Their political credo—which Bauer helped draft after he moved to Munich—demanded that fraternity brothers adopt a "tolerant way of life" while "embracing Germanness."[50]

When asked outright about their religion, neither Bauer nor his fraternity brothers tried to hide the fact that they were Jewish.[51] Nevertheless, they firmly believed that religion should be a private matter. One former FWV brother noted that the fraternity "could understand the human reasons why" other Jewish students might want to come together in defiance to form Zionist associations. However, he also warned that such associations were having "a disastrous impact on the solidarity we seek to foster among all German students."[52] At the end of a heated round-table discussion, most FWV members voted against joining forces with the Zionists in upcoming university elections because they felt their political differences were too extreme. Whereas FWV members believed progress could only be achieved if Jewish and Gentile Germans "worked together hand-in-hand," the Zionists believed in "secession." Bauer and his fraternity brothers also refused to be part of a "Jewish list" of candidates in the student union election.[53] The aim of the "list" was to enable Jewish associations to wrest one or two seats from the nationalist German majority, but FWV members refused to collaborate with other Jewish fraternities until 1924, when they came together with the Bavaria and Ivria fraternities to form the neutral-sounding National Freedom Group.[54]

Unfortunately, such initiatives did nothing to stop anti-Semitism from spreading across the campus, and the FWV was soon barred from the Heidelberg University Fraternities' Association.[55] To make matters worse, the FWV's insistence on religious neutrality only served to antagonize all the other Jewish groups that had been barred: "Anyone with a duty to defend Jewish honor should not trivialize this duty. We are appalled to see that some people even ridicule our sense of honor," wrote a contributor to *Der Jüdische Student*.[56] Members of the FWV were therefore caught between German nationalists, who told them they didn't belong, and Zionists, who advised them to celebrate their otherness. Alfred Apfel, an FWV brother who would later become one of the Weimar Republic's most prominent lawyers, noted of this time, "The Zionist students' criticisms troubled us. They reproached us . . . for making supposedly loathsome attempts to assimilate while they themselves sought to resist German anti-Semitism with their own extreme form of Jewish nationalism."[57] Another Jewish fraternity member in Heidelberg recalled how when we had a few hours to spare, we would gather with like-minded students and reflect on the fate of the Jews. We would thrash out the problems that seemed to be cropping up all around us. And those of us who were fighting hardest and suffering most would go for nighttime walks, either alone or in pairs, along the banks of the Neckar or through the town's charming narrow lanes. Together, we sought to gain clarity. We were disappointed, bitter, and lonely, caught between Christian fraternity members, whose attitudes had rapidly been twisted by propaganda in all too tangible ways, and those students who believed that the solution was to be found in Zionism.[58]

Tübingen: The Lion's Den

In later years, Bauer wrote to his mother that whenever he thought about Tübingen—the university town where he finished his studies in 1924—beautiful images would flood his mind: images of "the bustling market with all its smells and noises, the idyllic tranquility of the alleys."[59] Bauer loved his mother dearly, and given that she came from Tübingen, complimenting the town was a way of indirectly complimenting her. A little florid hyperbole is understandable, then. However, during his paean to Tübingen, Bauer also referred to the "humanism of the Aula," a statement that is rather more baffling.[60]

The Aula, one of Tübingen University's main buildings, was at the heart of university life. Bauer transferred to Tübingen University in the summer of 1923 because at the time, law students were required to sit their bar exams in their home state.[61] He spent two semesters studying in the Aula, a rigorously classical box-shaped building with sharp corners and a copper roof, before sitting the first bar exam, where he achieved one of the top grades in his cohort. A highly charged, militant atmosphere pervaded the university at the time. The professors boasted about how Tübingen had been more successful than any other German university in mobilizing students to join the war effort. Rumors about secret military training exercises and hidden caches of weapons on the campus were rife.[62] In the evenings, members of various fraternities would congregate on the street outside the Aula—a street known to students as "the racetrack"—to parade with their sashes and sabers.[63] The notorious anti-Semitism of Tübingen students was what had put Bauer off enrolling at the university on first graduating from high school.[64] Now he couldn't even lean on the support of FWV members, as no branch of the fraternity existed here. In the winter semester of 1923 to 1924, the total number of Jewish students at Tübingen amounted to just ten, four of whom were in the law faculty.[65]

Bauer's mother was undoubtedly familiar with the Aula. As Bauer didn't seem to be concerned that his talk of the "humanism of the Aula" would arouse his mother's skepticism, we can assume that he never complained about the political atmosphere during his time at what was then Germany's most reactionary university. Yet the writer Fred Uhlman, who had studied there a year previously, remembered most of the university's Jewish students anxiously seeking to avoid any kind of attention.[66] Not so Bauer. In the summer of 1923, just a few months after he had furiously called on his FWV brothers to "take a stand," Bauer, though still studying law, began attending Protestant theology lectures at Tübingen.[67] Bauer's Jewishness was surely even more conspicuous at these lectures, where he was likely the only non-Christian present, than anywhere else on campus. Such behavior suggests that Bauer was anything but afraid of attracting attention.

Bauer could have sought common ground with another Tübingen campus minority: the university's few Catholic students. Catholics, who had only been permitted to assume high-level civil service positions in Germany since 1918, maintained a relatively open-minded attitude toward the Weimar Republic, which is why Catholic fraternities tended to form political alliances with liberal and Jewish ones.[68] But Bauer didn't join the Catholics. Instead, he joined the Protestant lectures, continuing in his second semester at Tübingen to enroll in lectures such as "The History of Dogma" and "New Testament Theology."[69]

Bauer, who many years later would draw on his theological knowledge to advance his political arguments, no doubt had good reasons for attending such lectures; it's unlikely he simply wished to send a signal. But whether it was intentional or not, his message was loud and clear: "I'm not afraid, and I'm not going to hide."

Bauer's Doctoral Thesis Impresses Germany's Industrialists

There were plenty of attractive career opportunities open to Bauer after he passed his bar exams with flying colors in 1925. He could certainly have avoided the long, onerous route into the minefield that was German criminal justice and opted instead for an easier, more lucrative profession. The world of corporate headquarters and chambers of commerce, of starched collars and polished cufflinks beckoned. The story of Bauer's doctoral thesis indicates that he was not completely immune to the temptations of this world.

This story began in Heidelberg in the summer semester of 1923, when the average price of a student textbook shot up overnight from 55,000 to 70,000 marks.[70] The university was far emptier than usual, as fewer and fewer families could afford the study costs. Week after week in October 1923, the value of the mark plunged to a tenth of its former value, wiping out the savings of middle-class families. A contemporary issue of the satirical magazine *Simplicissimus* features on its cover a picture of an exhausted man in a tattered suit slumped on a bench. "You must have a very strenuous job," comment two women; "Yes, I'm an eviction marshal," the man responds.[71] As a well-off law student eager to learn about the causes of the crisis, Bauer listened carefully to the lectures of Karl Geiler, a professor of commercial law.[72] He bought Geiler's most recent book, *Social Forms of Organization in Contemporary Commercial Law*, and annotated it heavily, highlighting in particular the sections dealing with cartels and trusts, conglomerates that had become powerful players in the German economy.[73]

Such conglomerates had seemed like a good idea when they first emerged at the turn of the twentieth century. With many German companies complaining about the ruinous competition they faced, the view began to gain currency that it would be in these companies' shared interest to set prices together rather than continually trying to underprice each other. This led to the emergence of major consortia such as the Saxon Pulp Manufacturers' Association in the Ore Mountains and the Rhenish-Westphalian Coal Syndicate in the Ruhr region. Some of these consortia took the form of cartels, while others, taking the Standard Oil Trust as their inspiration, modeled themselves on the Anglo-American trust form. Cartel members entered into price-fixing agreements but were otherwise competitors and ran their businesses independently of each other. Members of trusts, which can be seen as forerunners of today's corporate groups, worked together more closely. Each trust member was responsible for running its own business, but all profits were channeled into a shared pool.[74]

The most famous trust in Germany was IG Farben, a "community of interests of dye-making companies." Established at the start of the twentieth century by the biggest players in the German chemical industry, IG Farben was the largest chemical company in the world. From 1928 onward, its colossal headquarters—a six-story neoclassical office block made of yellow limestone—loomed over the city of Frankfurt as a symbol of the conglomerate's power. The board of directors—nicknamed by employees as "the board of the gods"—had themselves immortalized in an oil portrait.

At first, the German authorities let these new chemical and coal conglomerates do as they liked.[75] It was only when the economy collapsed in 1922 that the shady side of such conglomerates became more apparent and the judiciary began to consider forcing industrialists to open themselves up to competition. Just as Bauer was becoming interested in cartels, observers were realizing that cartel members were colluding to hike up their prices.[76] Political mistrust of the cartels further intensified when, with the prospect of badly needed capital arriving in Germany from the United States, American investors expressed uneasiness at the entangled nature of relationships within German industry. Back in the United States, the introduction of antitrust legislation had led to the breakup of Standard Oil Trust in 1911.[77]

Many German jurists were therefore concerned with the question of whether the cartels should be dismantled or whether they should resist American pressure.[78] In 1927, Bauer contributed to this debate with a doctoral thesis entitled *The Legal Structure of Trusts: An Examination of the Organization of Commercial Conglomerates in Germany in Comparison to Trust Forms in the United States of America and Russia*—a long-winded title with a somewhat "medieval quality," as Bauer himself later admitted.[79] Bauer prefaced his thesis, which argued that trusts should resist pressure from external free-market forces, with a long quote from Walther Rathenau, who in his role as a business leader had successfully pushed for syndicates to play a key role in the German war economy in the latter years of World War I.

Bauer made the case that trusts offered a middle way between the "individualistic economic ideology prevailing in the USA, with its battle cry of '*laissez faire, morbleu, laissez faire*,'" and the authoritarian planned economy of the Soviet Union. According to Bauer, coming together to form trusts would enable companies to combine "the spontaneity and autonomy of liberalism with the rationality of socialism." In doing so, he argued, they could avoid "forcing private entrepreneurialism into the Procrustean bed of bureaucratic schematism and thereby killing the dynamism necessary to drive *homo economicus*'s pursuit of profit."[80]

Bauer adopted the position of a true Social Democrat in his advocacy of a "third way" between the free market and state paternalism, yet he did so without alienating Germany's industrialists, who were sure to welcome the approach promoted in Bauer's thesis. After all, the idealistic young doctoral student had put forward several persuasive legal arguments for allowing the coal and chemical barons to continue profiting from conglomerates. It's safe to assume that the position put forward in Bauer's thesis could have opened many career doors for him in industry.[81] Bauer's remarkable work ethic can only have increased his attractiveness as a potential employee: at more than two hundred pages, his thesis was more than twice as long as the average law thesis of the time. In it, Bauer demonstrated his mastery of juristic conventions, his ability to structure his ideas precisely, his talent for cautious argumentation, and his respect for other jurists, including those professors whose views he wished to refute. Impressively, Bauer managed to complete his thesis within a year, working on it at night after spending his days completing a traineeship at a court in Stuttgart.[82]

When Bauer was awarded his doctorate *magna cum laude* in 1927, a new kind of jurist was emerging in Germany.[83] Commercial lawyers were sophisticated, eloquent men who offered their services to company headquarters and chambers of commerce without sacrificing their independence. They weren't just out to make money; they also sought to bring order and intellectual orientation to an economy that was still largely unregulated. Such men were to be found in law reform commissions, at opera premieres, in liberal debating circles, and behind university lecterns. Max Hachenburg was one of the Weimar Republic's most prominent commercial law experts. Photos of the time show him smiling benevolently, wearing a shirt with a fashionable rounded collar, a gleaming tiepin, and polished cufflinks.[84] Hachenburg was filled with a sense of patriotic duty when he was appointed to the National Economic Council, a panel of experts that advised the Weimar government. In his memoirs, Hachenburg wrote about how impressed he was by the "intelligence and energy" of the luminaries he met on the council, one of whom was a member of IG Farben's "board of the gods."[85]

It's not difficult to imagine Bauer carving out a successful career for himself in this world. Commercial law was still a relatively new, undeveloped field where talented young people could avoid the glass ceiling still in place within the civil service. Many gifted Jewish jurists, including Hachenburg, found their niche here. The nephew of a rabbi in Mannheim, Hachenburg had once harbored ambitions of becoming a university professor but had been thwarted by the virulent anti-Semitism of university appointments committees.[86] Making a virtue of necessity, he enthusiastically described a career in commercial law as "the most direct means of influencing the economic life of the people."[87]

Bauer's doctoral supervisor, Karl Geiler, could have helped Bauer enter this world. Like Hachenburg, Geiler was a practitioner, and as such he was something of an outsider among his colleagues at Heidelberg University. He had been hired as an honorary professor to report on the fast-moving developments taking place within the field of commercial law. Geiler, who had collaborated with Hachenburg on writing an annotated version of the German Commercial Code, maintained good contacts with German industry and was particularly well connected with Carl Zeiss, the major Jena-based manufacturer of optical systems. Geiler also had many close contacts in the Jewish community. His wife was Jewish, as was the partner of the law firm he worked for. Geiler's writings (and indeed Bauer's thesis) were published by Bensheimer Verlag, a Jewish publishing house that was later "Aryanized"—in other words, transferred to non-Jewish owners—under the Nazi regime.[88] It would appear that Geiler and Bauer enjoyed a good relationship; Geiler wrote in one letter of recommendation that it gave him "particular pleasure" to support Bauer, for "alone the style" of Bauer's work and "the manner in which he formulates his thoughts are evidence of his brilliant intellect."[89]

It wasn't long before Bauer was offered a job by a mineral oil company. To his parents' dismay, however, he turned it down. He decided instead to take his political struggle to the murky depths of the criminal justice system, a decision informed by his conviction that it was important to "take a stand" and fight for what he believed in. Many years later, when recalling what he was like as a young man, Bauer described himself as "leaping onto Don Quixote's Rocinante in the belief that the horse was in fact Trojan, and riding into the tumultuous world of the judiciary with the aim of changing it for the better."[90]

Notes

1. *Monatsberichte des Bundes Freier Wissenschaftlicher Vereinigungen*, November/December 1922, call number MF B78, Leo Baeck Institute Archives, New York, 6.
2. Sebastian Haffner, *Geschichte eines Deutschen. Die Erinnerungen 1914–1933*, 6th edition (Stuttgart and Munich: dtv, 2001), 47–49.
3. See Amos Elon, *The Pity of It All*, 368, 370.
4. See Wolfgang Zorn, "Die politische Entwicklung des deutschen Studententums 1918–1931," in *Darstellungen und Quellen zur Geschichte der deutschen Einheitsbewegung im neunzehnten und zwanzigsten Jahrhundert*, ed. Kurt Stephensen, Alexander Scharf, and Wolfgang Klötzer (Heidelberg: Universitätsverlag Winter, 1965), 274f.
5. See Elon, *The Pity of It All*, 265.
6. *Heute abend Kellerclub. Die Jugend im Gespräch mit Fritz Bauer*.
7. Kurt Pätzold and Manfred Weißbecker, *Rudolf Heß. Der Mann an Hitlers Seite* (Leipzig: Militzke, 2003).
8. Ernst Jünger, *Jahre der Okkupation* (Stuttgart: Klett, 1958), 248.
9. Bauer, *Als sie noch jung waren*.
10. See Pätzold and Manfred, *Rudolf Heß*, and Anselm Faust, *Der Nationalsozialistische Deutsche Studentenbund. Studenten und Nationalsozialismus in der Weimarer Republik*, vol. 1 (Düsseldorf: Schwann, 1973), 26.
11. See Faust, *Der Nationalsozialistische Deutsche Studentenbund*, 12.
12. See Zorn, "Die politische Entwicklung des deutschen Studententums 1918–1931," 270.
13. See Jürgen Schwarz, *Studenten in der Weimarer Republik. Die deutsche Studentenschaft in der Zeit von 1918 bis 1923 und ihre Stellung zur Politik* (Berlin: Duncker & Humblot, 1971), 262f.
14. Fritz Bauer, in *Monatsberichte des Bundes Freier Wissenschaftlicher Vereinigungen*, May/June 1923, 5.
15. See *Monatsberichte des Bundes Freier Wissenschaftlicher Vereinigungen*, November/December 1922. 6. In Munich in summer 1922, Bauer had been elected vice-chairman to Walter Einstein's chairman. See *Monatsberichte des Bundes Freier Wissenschaftlicher Vereinigungen*, August 1922, 3.
16. See Arne Lankenau, *"Dunkel die Zukunft–Hell der Mut!" Die Heidelberger Studentenverbindungen in der Weimarer Republik 1918–1929* (Heidelberg: Universitätsverlag Winter, 2008), 123.
17. Bauer, *Als sie noch jung waren*.
18. Cf. See the discussion of growing debates in student associations in 1921 in Schwarz, *Studenten in der Weimarer Republik*, 244.

19. Lankenau, *"Dunkel die Zukunft–Hell der Mut!,"* 122.
20. See Matthias Stickler, "Zwischen Reich und Republik. Zur Geschichte der studentischen Verbindungen in der Weimarer Republik," in *"Der Burschen Herrlichkeit." Geschichte und Gegenwart des studentischen Korporationswesens*, ed. Harm-Hinrich Brandt and Matthias Stickler (Würzburg: Veröffentlichungen des Stadtarchivs Würzburg, 1998), 98; and Lankenau, *"Dunkel die Zukunft–Hell der Mut!,"* 116, 222, 238. On Heidelberg's reputation at the time, see the description of the academic landscape of the Weimar period in Horst Göppinger, *Juristen jüdischer Abstammung im "Dritten Reich." Entrechtung und Verfolgung*, 2nd edition (Munich: C. H. Beck, 1990), 188.
21. See Michael Weiss, *Bücher, Buden, Burschenschaften. Tausend Semester Tübinger Studentenleben* (Tübingen: Attempto Verlag, 1991), 116.
22. Fritz Bauer, "Sinn und Wert der studentischen Kooperation," *Monatsberichte des Bundes Freier Wissenschaftlicher Vereinigungen*, September 1921, 9.
23. See *Monatsberichte des Bundes Freier Wissenschaftlicher Vereinigungen*, special issue for *Pfingstkartelltag 1921*, June 1921, 10.
24. See Gerhard Taus, "Studentische Vereinigungen, Begriffe und Abkürzungen," in *Freie Wissenschaftliche Vereinigung. Eine Berliner anti-antisemitische Studentenorganisation stellt sich vor–1908 und 1931*, ed. Manfred Voigts (Potsdam: Universitätsverlag Potsdam, 2008), 13.
25. See ibid.
26. See the report on FWV's "close contact" with sororities by Thea Wasservogel in *Monatsberichte des Bundes Freier Wissenschaftlicher Vereinigungen*, December 1921/January 1922, 4.
27. Tiefenthal, interview by Fabian.
28. See *Monatsberichte des Bundes Freier Wissenschaftlicher Vereinigungen*, June 1921, 11.
29. Kurt Hiller, *Leben gegen die Zeit, Band 1: Logos* (Reinbek: Rowohlt, 1969), 61–63.
30. Quoted in Meyer-Velde, interview by author.
31. See photo in Irmtrud Wojak, *Fritz Bauer*, 83.
32. See Voigts, *Freie Wissenschaftliche Vereinigung*, and Bauer's own text, "Hochschule und Politik," *Monatsberichte des Bundes Freier Wissenschaftlicher Vereinigungen*, September 1921, 9f.
33. See Matthias Hambrock, *Die Etablierung der Außenseiter. Der Verband nationaldeutscher Juden 1921–1935* (Cologne: Böhlau, 2003), 138, and Michael Buchholz, "Zur Geschichte der Freien Wissenschaftlichen Vereinigung," in *Freie Wissenschaftliche Vereinigung*, ed. Voigts, 216. In position papers, FWV members also demanded that other fraternities stop "playing with weapons."
34. *Monatsberichte des Bundes Freier Wissenschaftlicher Vereinigungen*, August 1921, 12.
35. Fritz Bauer, "Forderungen der Gesellschaft an die Strafrechtsreform. Vortrag gehalten auf dem Arbeiterwohlfahrt-Sozialarbeitertreffen 30. Mai bis 3. Juni 1962 in Bad Godesberg," *Schriften der Arbeiterwohlfahrt* 14 (1962), 5.
36. *Monatsberichte des Bundes Freier Wissenschaftlicher Vereinigungen*, August 1921, 12.
37. Bauer, "Hochschule und Politik," 9f.
38. See *Monatsberichte des Bundes Freier Wissenschaftlicher Vereinigungen*, December 1921/January 1922, 7.
39. Ibid.
40. *Monatsberichte des Bundes Freier Wissenschaftlicher Vereinigungen*, July 1922, 5.
41. Ibid.
42. *Monatsberichte des Bundes Freier Wissenschaftlicher Vereinigungen*, August 1922, 2.

43. Quoted in Manfred Voigts, "Einleitung," in *Freie Wissenschaftliche Vereinigung*, ed. Voigts, 6.
44. See Lankenau, *"Dunkel die Zukunft–Hell der Mut!,"* 138.
45. Ibid.
46. Bauer told his wife, Anna Maria Petersen, about this episode, and Petersen related the story to Irmtrud Wojak in 1997. See Wojak, *Fritz Bauer*, 529, footnote 72.
47. See Lankenau, *"Dunkel die Zukunft–Hell der Mut!,"* 136.
48. See *Liederbuch zum Festkommers der Freien Wissenschaftlichen Vereinigung an der Universität Heidelberg anläßlich des 35. Stiftungsfests 1927*, 3, papers of the FWV member Rudolf Zielenziger, Leo Baeck Institute, New York. Accessible at: http://archive.org/details/rudolfzielenziger.
49. See Gerhard Taus, "Studentische Vereinigungen, Begriffe und Abkürzungen," 16.
50. See *Monatsberichte des Bundes Freier Wissenschaftlicher Vereinigungen*, November/December 1922, 6.
51. See Wojak, *Fritz Bauer*, 529, footnote 71. When Bauer was filling out a police registration form in order to enroll for a third semester at the University of Munich, under "Religion," he wrote "Israelite." The form, which dates to May 18, 1922, is preserved in Munich's city archives.
52. Arthur Rosenberger, "Was wir tun" (1908), republished in *Freie Wissenschaftliche Vereinigung*, ed. Voigts, 72.
53. See *Monatsberichte des Bundes Freier Wissenschaftlicher Vereinigungen*, August 1922, 2.
54. See Lankenau, *"Dunkel die Zukunft–Hell der Mut!,"* 138, 198.
55. Ibid., 48.
56. Quoted in Voigts, "Einleitung," in *Freie Wissenschaftliche Vereinigung*, ed. Voigts, 6.
57. Alfred Apfel, *Hinter den Kulissen der deutschen Justiz: Erinnerungen eines deutschen Rechtsanwalts 1882–1933*, trans. Jan and Ursula Gehlsen (Berlin: Berliner Wissenschaftsverlag, 2013), 18.
58. Quoted in Lankenau, *"Dunkel die Zukunft–Hell der Mut!,"* 139.
59. Fritz Bauer to Ella Bauer, summer 1938.
60. Ibid.
61. See Fred Uhlman, *The Making of an Englishman*, 73.
62. See Weiss, *Bücher, Buden, Burschenschaften*, 108–118; Göppinger, *Juristen jüdischer Abstammung im "Dritten Reich,"* 187, 189; and Uhlman, *The Making of an Englishman*, 104–112.
63. See Weiss, *Bücher, Buden, Burschenschaften*, 99.
64. See Bauer, *Als sie noch jung waren*.
65. See Zapf, *Die Tübinger Juden. Eine Dokumentation*, 266.
66. See Uhlman, *The Making of an Englishman*, 112f.
67. *Monatsberichte des Bundes Freier Wissenschaftlicher Vereinigungen*, May/June 1923, 5.
68. See Schwarz, *Studenten in der Weimarer Republik*, 265f., 273.
69. See Wojak, *Fritz Bauer*, 104.
70. See Weiss, *Bücher, Buden, Burschenschaften*, 116.
71. Cover of *Simplicissimus* no. 21 (1925), reprinted in *Spott und Respekt–die Justiz in der Kritik*, ed. Anja Eichler (Petersberg: Michael Imhof Verlag, 2010), 113.
72. This is evident from the registration list for summer semester 1923 in Heidelberg University's archives; see Wojak, *Fritz Bauer*, 530, footnote 80.

73. See ibid.
74. See Matthias Schmoeckel, *Rechtsgeschichte der Wirtschaft. Seit dem 19. Jahrhundert* (Tübingen: Mohr Siebeck, 2008), 247–253.
75. The courts' friendly stance toward cartels was cemented in a landmark ruling on February 4, 1897, in favor of the Saxon Pulp and Paper Cartel. See *Reichsgerichtsentscheidungen in Zivilsachen*, vol. 38 (Berlin: de Gruyter), 155f.
76. See Schmoeckel, *Rechtsgeschichte der Wirtschaft*, 255f.
77. See ibid., 253–255.
78. Schmoeckel writes that there was a "never-ending series of articles on the cartel problem"; ibid., 248.
79. Fritz Bauer to Horkheimer, September 21, 1937, call number I/2 230, Max-Horkheimer-Archiv, Stadt-und Universitätsbibliothek Frankfurt am Main.
80. Bauer, *Die rechtliche Struktur der Truste. Ein Beitrag zur Organisation der wirtschaftlichen Zusammenschlüsse in Deutschland unter vergleichender Heranziehung der Trustformen in den Vereinigten Staaten von Amerika und Rußland* (Mannheim: Bensheimer, 1927), 2, 3.
81. See Bauer's judiciary personnel file. In an application for a position as a judge at the higher regional court of Brunswick in 1948, Bauer enclosed extracts from two journal reviews praising his thesis.
82. Bauer sat the first bar exam on December 9, 1924, in Tübingen; see Bauer's judiciary personnel file. He submitted his doctoral thesis "at the end of 1925," according to the introduction to the published version. According to Bauer's personnel file, he began serving as a judge at the regional court of Stuttgart in March 1928. As the typical training period at the time was three years, this indicates that Bauer began his training in March 1925.
83. Bauer informed his fraternity brothers that his thesis had been awarded this distinction in *Monatsberichte des Bundes Freier Wissenschaftlicher Vereinigungen*, April 1926, 8.
84. See Max Hachenburg, *Lebenserinnerungen eines Rechtsanwalts und Briefe aus der Emigration* (Stuttgart: Verlag W. Kohlhammer, 1978), figure 41.
85. Ibid., 191.
86. See Göppinger, *Juristen jüdischer Abstammung im "Dritten Reich,"* 187.
87. Hachenburg, *Lebenserinnerungen*, 56.
88. See Stefanie Weis, *Leben und Werk des Juristen Karl Hermann Friederich Julius Geiler (1878–1953). Ein Rechtswissenschaftler in Zeiten des Umbruchs* (Hamburg: Verlag Dr. Kovač, 2013), 132.
89. Karl Geiler, "Foreword," to Bauer, *Die rechtliche Struktur der Truste*, VII, and reference from Professor Karl Geiler dated 1926, Heidelberg University archives, quoted in Wojak, *Fritz Bauer*, 104.
90. Bauer, "Scham bei der Lektüre. Richter zerstörten die Demokratie," (review of Heinrich and Elisabeth Hannover's *Politische Justiz 1918 bis 1933*), *Die Zeit*, September 29, 1967.

4

A JUDGE IN THE WEIMAR REPUBLIC

Bauer's Attempts to Avert Catastrophe

A Rap at the Door

The brisk footsteps of police officers were becoming an increasingly common sound in the corridors of the local courthouse. When the twenty-nine-year-old Bauer, one of the court's judges, heard the steps drawing closer to his office on March 23, 1933, he may well have assumed that yet another of his political comrades had been arrested. By now, Social Democrats were being dragged in front of the court on an almost daily basis. Behind its angular sandstone façade on Stuttgart's Archivstrasse, the local court had become one of the city's key sites of repression.[1] Located in the political heart of Württemberg, a state around half the size of today's Baden-Württemberg, the local court was responsible for handling misdemeanors and midlevel criminal cases. Right next door was the next-highest court, the regional court, which was housed in a palatial Wilhelmine building with a wooden guillotine on display in one of its atriums.[2] For months now, left-wing figures were being thrown into the court's jail regardless of whether they had been convicted of any crime.[3] "Protective custody" was the euphemism coined by Germany's new rulers to refer to the incarceration of untried, unconvicted prisoners. One week previously, the court's cells had become so overcrowded that prisoners had to be transferred to a makeshift concentration camp.[4]

The police officers, wearing Württemberg state police uniforms and brandishing handcuffs, stopped at Bauer's door. They were from the "Political Police" department, which reported directly to the state's minister of the interior.[5] After making significant gains in the federal election of March 5, 1933, the Nazi Party had finally managed to win a majority in the Reichstag by forming a coalition with the German National People's Party (Deutschnationale Volkspartei, or DNVP). As a result, Stuttgart's police force now had a new chief: former SA general Dietrich von Jagow, a man Bauer had encountered before.[6]

Between 1931 and 1933, when Jagow had commanded the local SA squad, Bauer had been his direct left-wing counterpart as chairman of the Stuttgart branch of the Reichsbanner Schwarz-Rot-Gold (Black, Red, and Gold Banner of the Reich), a militant organization affiliated with the Social Democrats that sought to defend democracy in the Weimar Republic.

The police rapped on Bauer's door and entered his office. Hearing a commotion, some of Bauer's colleagues left their desks to see what was going on. They stood by their doors, watching in silence as he was arrested. Though he had been working there for just three years, Bauer—the youngest judge in the courthouse—already had a reputation as a controversial political figure. No one said a word as the police led him away.[7]

The Lone Social Democrat in the Conservative Judiciary

Bauer's colleagues had been keeping a close eye on him in the years leading up to his arrest. They all knew he was Jewish, as he had to say so in every personnel form he filled out. But he was not the only Jew working at the court; a Jewish judge called Robert Bloch had been hired at the same time, to name just one other example. (An unmarried son of a Stuttgart store owner, Bloch was fifteen years older than Bauer and had previously worked in the local court of Waiblingen, a town near Stuttgart.[8]) What made Bauer really stand out, then, was not his religion but his politics: From the late 1920s onward, Bauer was the only judge in Stuttgart who was a card-carrying member of the Social Democratic Party of Germany (Sozialdemokratische Partei Deutschlands, or SPD).[9]

In the 1920s, Stuttgart was a progressive city with thriving artistic and socialist scenes. Describing the city's atmosphere in 1927, the Russian author and journalist Ilja Ehrenburg wrote, "Under the linden trees one hears not the sighs of Schumann but the cacophony of jazz." In a travelogue entitled *Visa of the Times*, Ehrenburg observed that "in the city park, there is a 'Summer Fashion Show.' The massive café is packed: the lower middle classes, salesclerks, office clerks, doctors, and salesmen hawking sample books from the top twenty stores all ply their trade here."[10] The year 1927 also saw the construction in Stuttgart of the Weissenhof Estate, a bold residential project designed by some of the world's most exciting architects, including Ludwig Mies van der Rohe and Walter Gropius. Bauer approvingly described the style of these thirty all-white architectural works of art as "gleaming, expansive, and welcoming."[11] The city's politics were modern, too. By the end of the 1920s, Stuttgart was a small liberal stronghold in the middle of a rural state otherwise dominated by nationalistic voters. The SPD, which Bauer had joined when he was still at school, was the strongest party in the city, whereas the Nazis were a small splinter group, winning just 1.1 percent of the vote in the 1928 municipal elections.[12]

Stuttgart's judges inhabited another world, however. "They came from highly elitist student fraternities and were members of the reserve officers' corps. Their entire outlook was conservative and authoritarian in spirit," recalled Bauer, who after a few months working in the state's attorney's office became an assistant judge. "The kaiser had gone, but the generals, public officials, and judges remained," he noted.[13] When the political battle waged by the Nazis on the streets of Stuttgart escalated from 1930 onward, the police and the courts responded with leniency. Whereas they aggressively pursued communists, they turned a blind eye to Nazi rallies and marches—largely because they sympathized with the Nazis, according to Bauer. Most of the judges he worked with hated the Weimar Republic, which they believed had been "created by 'godless' and 'unpatriotic' scoundrels," Bauer claimed. "The judges weren't at all fond of the republic," he said, "and they used the guise of judicial independence to sabotage the new state."[14]

Over these years, Bauer had only once been directly involved in a political trial. In fall 1928, just after he had completed his three years of training, two teenage boys received letters from the state's attorney accusing them of selling "at least ten" copies of a newspaper entitled *Der Rote Jungfront* (The Young Red Front) to passers-by in Stuttgart one Sunday afternoon. The prosecutor demanded prison sentences of one and two weeks, respectively.[15] When the communists refused to accept this, the matter ended up before a judge. The complacent prosecutor, deeming it unnecessary to present the case himself, sent a relatively new recruit into the courtroom in his place. The twenty-five-year-old recruit in question, Fritz Bauer, reduced the sentence demanded by his more experienced colleague and was never allowed anywhere near political trials again.[16]

Shortly afterward, a judge named Frauenknecht was made solely responsible for trying anyone charged with political offenses.[17] Frauenknecht's rulings included a one-week prison sentence imposed on a twenty-two-year-old bricklayer for distributing a newspaper called *Der Rote Schulkamerad* (The Red Classmate) in a vocational school and urging students to go on strike "against voracious German capitalists."[18] Frauenknecht also sent people to prison for being involved in the Alliance of Red Front Fighters, an organization that had been banned since May 1929, and even for uttering antifascist slogans. Ruling that "it is self-evident that a speech containing the words 'defeat the fascists wherever you encounter them' clearly constitutes an incitement to violence against others because of their political activities," Frauenknecht sentenced the defendants to a week in prison.[19]

The severity of such punishment stands in stark contrast to a negligible prison sentence handed down to a Stuttgart member of the SA Brownshirts who had murdered a young communist worker named Hermann Weisshaupt by stabbing him several times in the stomach on November 8, 1930. When the Nazis took power in 1933, this already lenient sentence was quashed entirely.[20] As Bauer later commented, "there was an almost methodical imbalance in how justice was administered to the right [e.g., the Kapp Putsch and Beer Hall Putsch, Hitler's 'Oath of Legality,' the Boxheimer documents] and the left [e.g., the Bavarian Soviet Republic]."[21]

Bauer argued that by emboldening right-wingers, the German judiciary's political bias provided the "judicial overture" to the Nazi regime.[22] Even at the time, this bias was no secret; the pacifist Carl von Ossietzky, the anarchist Erich Mühsam, and the satirist Kurt Tucholsky are just some of the more entertaining commentators who, now that they were no longer reined in by imperial censorship, poked fun at it in their writing. A cartoon printed in the satirical magazine *Simplicissimus* in 1931 depicts two judges as slow, ancient lizards with leathery skin. Wearing voluminous robes and black hats, the two imperious creatures carry dark leather-bound lawbooks. "I don't see what people are getting so worked up about," one says to the other. "For every person who has been wrongfully convicted, there are at least ten guilty people walking around scot-free!"[23]

In the same year this cartoon was published, the Jewish lawyer Alfred Apfel—a former member of Bauer's student fraternity, the FWV—defended the freedom of *Weltbühne* (World Stage), a political magazine published by Carl von Ossietzky, at the Reichsgericht, the highest court in the land.[24] The trial centered on an article entitled "Dubious Affairs in German Aviation," which had revealed that the German army was rearming in violation of the Treaty of Versailles. The author's "breezy certainty" that the charge of treason would "burst like a bubble" was soon confronted by the reality that the highest German court wasn't remotely interested in defending the press's newly won freedom.[25]

The sharpest criticism of the judiciary's reactionary spirit came from the SPD. Gustav Radbruch, the party's foremost legal expert, had made it his mission to exorcise this old, malevolent spirit after being appointed as German minister of justice in 1921. Radbruch called on young people to enter the judiciary, and his party openly threatened to invoke Article 104 of the Weimar Constitution and give the judiciary's top levels a major shake-up if their hostility toward the republic persisted. Fearing the Social Democrats would be granted the power to carry out their threat, the conservative, nationalistic German Association of Judges did everything it could to discredit the SPD's legal policies.[26]

Though Bauer generally kept quiet about his determination to heed Radbruch's call to transform the judiciary, he did take some overt steps to help instigate such transformation from the inside. In 1928, a few years after the SPD newspaper *Vorwärts* (Forward) had called for the formation of a pro-republican association to serve as an alternative to the all-powerful German Association of Judges, Bauer established a Württemberg branch of the "red" Republican Association of Judges.[27] However, a mere 3 percent of Württemberg's judges joined it.[28] Radbruch, one of the editors of the association's journal, *Die Justiz* (Justice), railed against the judiciary's inability to accept criticism, warning that its "reflexive defense mechanism" would lead to its downfall.[29]

Though Bauer actively supported the SPD and the Weimar Republic, he took pains to avoid stirring up trouble in his daily working life in the courthouse. Displaying traits that would contribute to the extraordinary tenacity he demonstrated later in life, Bauer was a master tactician. Even as a rebellious young judge, he always kept a level head and chose his battles wisely. He thereby managed to swim against the political current without running the risk of losing his robe and, with it, the possibility of instigating change. After working for just two years as an assistant juvenile court judge, Bauer was promoted to a permanent position as a local court judge. This rise through the ranks was exceptionally rapid for the time.[30] Years later, observers would claim that Bauer had been the youngest local court judge in the Weimar Republic, a claim he never disputed, though no evidence exists to support it.[31] Bauer's politics didn't impede his meteoric rise. At night, he worked as an on-call judge; during the day, he dealt with the city's poverty-related crime.[32] Having moved on from juvenile offenses, the twenty-seven-year-old Bauer dealt with the cases of defendants whose surnames began with the letters Brb-Bz, G, and Se-Sz. He imposed sentences that were standard for the court, making no attempt to ameliorate the severity of the laws of the time, and so his colleagues couldn't accuse him of allowing his left-wing politics to influence his judgments.

A good example of Bauer's strategy can be found in his handling of the case of an unemployed piano maker who had been arrested for begging. As Bauer explained, this was a legally complex case involving "covert" begging. The piano maker hadn't begged for money in any straightforward sense; initially, he had begged for work, only asking for "a donation" after a local businessman refused to offer him a job. As the case was by no means clear-cut, there was scope for clemency. Bauer could have given the piano maker the benefit of the doubt and acquitted him (though of course the next court up might later quash this verdict). Yet Bauer found the piano maker guilty as charged and briskly ruled that "a sentence of two days' imprisonment seemed appropriate."[33]

Bauer demonstrated similar intransigence in another case, this time involving a destitute construction worker. One fall day, the man had caught five goldfinches in the district of Vaihingen and then attempted to sell the birds to workers at Nordbahnhof, Stuttgart's northern train station. Despite mass unemployment, the law was uncompromising: it was illegal to catch and roast birds without a permit. "It was obvious that the defendant had acted out of desperation," Bauer acknowledged, yet he insisted that "a sentence of fourteen days seemed appropriate."[34]

"Has the Ministry of Justice Been Covering Up the Actions of the Jew Bauer?"

"It's not the use of the word 'Jew' that prompted me to press charges," Bauer explained. "That's not what offends me."[35] On September 25, 1931, the courtroom gallery was a sea of brown and green. In their brown shirts were members of the SA, and in green were members of the pro-republican Reichsbanner Schwarz-Rot-Gold. Both Nazi and SPD newspapers had encouraged their readers to attend the trial, and as a result, the courtroom was packed. For once, Bauer wasn't sitting on the bench. Instead, he was at the witness stand, his back to the audience. This case revolved around him. The trial concerned allegedly libelous remarks that had been made about Bauer; in other words, it centered on his good name. This was the first time that Bauer, who had recently turned twenty-eight, had become embroiled in a political scandal. It was also the first time he seriously worried about his survival as a judge. A Nazi newspaper called *Stuttgarter NS-Kurier* gleefully observed that "the longer [the trial] lasted, the more the shadows spread across Mr. Bauer's once beaming face. By the end, these shadows had turned into dark clouds."[36]

The background to the case was as follows: On June 1, 1931, a twenty-three-year-old man named Adolf Gerlach became editor in chief of the *Stuttgarter NS-Kurier*. On June 5, Gerlach published an article about Bauer under the headline "A Jewish Local Court Judge Abuses His Position for Political Purposes." Gerlach claimed that the SPD newspaper *Schwäbische Tagwacht* had repeatedly been given access to court records containing personal information about prominent Stuttgart Nazis. The only possible explanation, according to Gerlach, was that Bauer had been passing on confidential documents to his comrades at the newspaper. "The explanation," Gerlach wrote, "consists of one word, and the word is: Jew! We have one question for the minister of justice, Mr. Beyerle: Has the ministry of justice been covering up the actions of the Jew Bauer?"[37]

The attack made Bauer nervous, and it soon became apparent he had every reason to be. He took legal measures to defend himself, filing a libel complaint against Gerlach. To put on a united front with Bauer, Württemberg's minister of justice, Josef Beyerle—a member of the Catholic Center Party—filed his own complaint. Behind closed doors, however, Beyerle viewed Bauer as a thorn in his side. Indeed, when Beyerle returned to the ministry after the fall of the Nazi regime many years later, he continued to bear a grudge against the troublemaking young Social Democrat.³⁸

Bauer admitted to the court that he had once discussed details of a trial with a *Tagwacht* journalist he had presumably met at SPD meetings. However, these details had already been disclosed in open court, Bauer insisted. Furthermore, he added, the trial in question had centered on an international conman named Siegfried; it had had nothing to do with the Nazis. In fact, Bauer hadn't been involved in any of the cases brought against Nazis. A clearly agitated Bauer concluded with a rare uncontrolled outburst, pointing out that the conman was "unlikely to be a Nazi" given that "he looks like a Jew!"³⁹

The other judges at the local court closed ranks with Bauer, but only because they were ordered to do so by the ministry of justice. They grudgingly defended their young colleague from the *NS-Kurier*'s accusation that his affiliation with the SPD had compromised the objectivity of the Stuttgart judiciary. Yet the judges presiding over Bauer's trial—two of whom were lay judges—treated Bauer himself like a layman, making him take an oath before he testified, a measure usually reserved for witnesses regarded as unreliable. Furthermore, when returning their verdict, the judges publicly rebuked him. They stated that "the court was of the opinion" that by sharing information with a correspondent from the *Tagwacht*, Bauer had failed to "comply with existing regulations." However, they added, it hadn't been proven that Bauer's actions were "politically motivated"; in other words, there was no evidence that Bauer had acted with malicious intent.⁴⁰ The court therefore ruled in favor of Bauer and against Adolf Gerlach, but it did so without entirely clearing Bauer's name. To make matters worse, the judges ignored Bauer's request that the court leave aside the fact that the *NS-Kurier* had called him a Jew. As Bauer explained, he hadn't taken offense at this—and anyway, according to established case law, the question of whether someone felt insulted should have no bearing on a case. Yet the court decided that Gerlach's "unjustified repetition four times" of the word "Jew" constituted an insult. "The phrase 'Jewish judge' is an insult," the *NS-Kurier* crowed in response.⁴¹

The court's ruling was the trigger for Bauer's demotion. At the end of 1931, the president of the local court asked employees to submit their usual annual requests for transfers. Like the year before, Bauer requested permission to remain in his current position as criminal judge.⁴² This time, however, the president removed him from his position and assigned him the politically innocuous task of handling civil cases. In his new position, Bauer no longer had the power to hand down sentences, nor indeed to rule on any matter that was of any real public interest.⁴³ Bauer felt that he had been consigned to the court's scrap heap. He spent his days in silence, poring over leases, sales agreements, and claims, until 1933. By that stage, all Jewish judges in the country had been barred from criminal justice and transferred to civil justice, where they languished for a while before being purged from the justice system entirely.[44]

Bauer and Kurt Schumacher versus the SA

Bauer suffered his crushing demotion at a time when high-profile Nazi marches were becoming regular occurrences on the streets of Stuttgart. Prompted by "an inner compulsion to do something," Bauer approached Kurt Schumacher, the head of the SPD in Stuttgart and the editor in chief of the party newspaper, *Schwäbische Tagwacht*. "We don't need intellectuals," Schumacher initially told Bauer. "Workers don't like intellectuals." Eventually, Schumacher relented and agreed to give Bauer a shot at drumming up support. He "sent me to a club for extremely radical young socialists," Bauer recalled, "where I gave a talk which went down rather well, I must admit."[45]

Even in his student days, Bauer had been admired for his ability to captivate audiences. In Stuttgart, the young judge adopted "an accessible and very appealing style of expression," a hostile observer from the SA noted.[46] As a speaker, Bauer managed to be both rousing and solemn. Many years later, the jurist and politician Jürgen Baumann recounted the following anecdote to illustrate Bauer's effect on his audiences: In the 1960s, Bauer was invited to the Bundestag to give a speech on criminal justice reform to the SPD parliamentary party. The first speaker gave his talk, then the second, and then it was Bauer's turn. "It was terrific," Baumann said. "He had such a deep, roaring voice. All the SPD's Bundestag representatives were sitting there, respectable gentlemen all of them. And then he began: 'Comrades!' That really gave them a jolt. An electrical contact placed beneath their chairs couldn't have made a greater impact. That was Fritz Bauer."[47]

Schumacher and Bauer, the Prussian and the Swabian, formed an unconventional duo. Both had doctorates in law, both came from educated middle-class backgrounds, and both were beginning to gain the support of Stuttgart's workers, whom they urged to take up armed resistance against the Nazis. Schumacher had lost an arm in World War I, and his body was riddled with shrapnel. "He had a face like a shriveled apple, thin lips that looked as if they had been slashed into his face with a razor blade, and icy green eyes," recalled Fred Uhlman, a lawyer in Stuttgart. "He was like Churchill, chain-smoking cigarettes and puffing on cigars. You could sense his resolve and unwavering belief in the absolute righteousness of his cause."[48] Schumacher's speeches were filled with passion and biting criticism. "All Nazi agitation relentlessly appeals to people's worst instincts," he said in a famous speech delivered in the Reichstag on February 23, 1932. For the first time in the history of German politics, he said, the Nazis had "managed to fully mobilize human stupidity."[49]

Bauer was now almost constantly on the road with Schumacher. He later described how they would travel together to events around Stuttgart, making appearances and delivering speeches: "He and I spoke every weekend, sometimes three, four, or five times. We were urging people to defend the Weimar Constitution but also to combat the extremism of the Weimar period."[50]

"*Frei*," shouted a man in a smoky hall in Stuttgart in April 1931. "*Heil!*" hundreds of people called back in response.

"*Frei*"—"*Heil!*"

"*Frei*"—"*Heil!*"

Repeated three times, the words "*Frei Heil!*" (hail freedom!) formed the antifascists' battle cry. With this subversion of the Nazis' infamous "*Sieg Heil*" salute, members of the Stuttgart branch of the Reichsbanner Schwarz-Rot-Gold bade farewell to their chairman, Kurt Schumacher.[51] The paramilitary Reichsbanner described itself as a "republican defense organization," and many of the workers cheering Schumacher that night were wearing military-style uniforms: puffy green breeches, long black boots, shirts made of coarse fabric, and the flat caps typically worn by factory workers. The reference to the colors black, red, and gold in the organization's name was an unequivocal statement of support for democracy. Not only were these the colors of the Weimar Republic's national flag; they were also the colors of the Hambach Festival, a major public demonstration of support for freedom and democracy that had taken place in nineteenth-century Germany. Furthermore, the black-red-gold tricolor symbolized the Reichsbanner's rejection of the colors of the former German empire: black, white, and red. Thanks to pressure from German nationalists, the black-white-red scheme had been retained as the civil ensign of the Weimar Republic, marking the beginning of a protracted "flag dispute." The Nazis called Reichsbanner members "black, red, and mustard Jew protectors" because some Jewish sports and youth clubs had joined the Reichsbanner's trade unionists in confronting the SA on the street.[52]

Within a few months, Bauer had taken over from Schumacher as leader of the Reichsbanner's Stuttgart branch.[53] Schumacher had been splitting his time between Stuttgart and Berlin since his election to the Reichstag in September 1930, but he continued to deliver fiery speeches in Stuttgart. One evening in June 1932, he shared the stage with just one other speaker: Bauer. "Comrade Bauer received a tumultuous welcome when he opened the proceedings," one journalist wrote in a report for the *Schwäbische Tagwacht*.[54]

Bauer didn't socialize much with other members in his new role as chairman of the Stuttgart Reichsbanner. He couldn't afford to neglect his work duties, and so, as his SPD comrade Helmut Mielke noted, Bauer would always leave parties early. He wasn't "terribly sociable," Mielke said; "Fritz was a bit of an outsider."⁵⁵ Reichsbanner members were nonetheless electrified by Bauer's determination and rhetorical power, and the twenty-nine-year- old bespectacled judge succeeded in galvanizing his troops. One cold Sunday afternoon in spring 1933, members of the Reichsbanner demonstrated in the streets of Ludwigsburg, a small city to the north of Stuttgart. Wearing uniforms and carrying flags, they made their way to the town square, where Bauer, the event's key speaker, addressed a packed audience.⁵⁶ As well as giving the Reichsbanner members instructions on how to behave should they be interrogated by police or in court, Bauer stoked their fighting spirit.⁵⁷ "Dr. Bauer concluded the demonstration with a rousing appeal to all Reichsbanner comrades," the *Tagwacht* reported. "The demonstrators responded with a thunderous call of 'Freedom!', their raised fists indicating that his appeal had been taken up by hearts and minds ready for battle."⁵⁸

Reichsbanner strategy meetings took place at night in Hotel Zeppelin, near Stuttgart's central station.⁵⁹ Amid thick clouds of cigar smoke, Bauer argued that, given the gravity of the situation, the time had come to establish Reichsbanner barracks.⁶⁰ In 1931, the German right had closed ranks, with the DNVP, the paramilitary World War I veterans' organization Stahlhelm (Steel Helmet), and the Nazi Party forming an alliance called the "Harzburg Front." In response, the Reichsbanner, which by now had between half a million and a million members across Germany, formed an alliance with a few independent trade unions and workers' sports clubs.⁶¹ Called the "Iron Front," this alliance was supposed to counter the Harzburg Front, but there was no hiding the reality that the German left was riven with divisions.⁶² Stuttgart's communists accused the Social Democrats of being "social fascists." "If Kurt Schumacher drank a glass of champagne at a birthday party, the communists would write that he had been spotted drunk and sick 'having eaten too many oysters and too much caviar,'" Fred Uhlman remembered.⁶³

These fatal divisions within the left were painfully apparent when Bauer summoned one last demonstration of strength just a few days before the Reichstag election of March 5, 1933.⁶⁴ Led by Schumacher and other Social Democrat leaders, a total of twenty-five thousand people marched through Stuttgart. Heading up the procession were a few thousand Reichsbanner members. These were followed first by trade union members and then by a block of a few thousand women, at which point the communists cut across the procession, thereby breaking up the last free demonstration in Stuttgart into two halves.

Tensions ran high the day before the election, the general expectation being that Hitler would triumph. Four SPD members were brought before Stuttgart's local court because two days earlier, they had sneaked into one of the city's public broadcasting studios and interrupted a live radio show, shouting "Down with Hitler! Long live freedom—vote for the SPD!"⁶⁵ Following a summary trial, one of Bauer's colleagues sentenced the men to four weeks in prison, but no one knew if the convicts would ever be set free once the election was decided. That evening, as fear of further arrests spread, Stuttgart's leading SPD members all gathered in the law offices of Fred Uhlman, who then still went by the name of Manfred Uhlmann. His office was on Archivstrasse, the same street as the local court, and so, the men hoped, it would be one of the last places where victorious Nazis would look for them. They slept on the floor, on chairs, and on the sofa, keeping their weapons close to hand.⁶⁶

One week later, the *Gleichschaltung*, or Nazification, of the German states began. A Nazi government took power in Württemberg, and Beyerle, the minister of justice, was replaced by a Nazi named Christian Mergenthaler, who also took over the ministry of education and culture. Shortly afterward, on March 23, 1933, came the rap at Bauer's office door.

Notes

1. Bauer worked at Amtsgericht Stuttgart I. Since 1924, this local court had had jurisdiction over the districts formerly known as Stuttgart-Stadt and Stuttgart-Amt as well as some southern suburbs of the city, such as Waldenbuch. Amtsgericht Stuttgart II, which is today called Stuttgart-Cannstatt, was responsible for the northern half of the city. See Helmut Borth, "Das Amtsgericht Stuttgart," in *Das Oberlandesgericht Stuttgart—125 Jahre von 1879 bis 2004*, ed. Eberhard Stilz (Villingen-Schwenningen: Neckar-Verlag, 2004), 233. During his time as a judge in Stuttgart, Bauer did not have jurisdiction over the neighborhood in which he grew up and went to school.

2. See Fred Uhlman, *The Making of an Englishman*, 125f.

3. See Markus Kienle, *Das Konzentrationslager Heuberg bei Stetten am Kalten Markt* (Ulm: Klemm & Oelschläger, 1998), 29.

4. See ibid., 32.

5. In April 1933, Württemberg's political police department became an independent police force. Only later was this political police force incorporated into the Gestapo. Günther Weinmann's assertion that Bauer was arrested by the Gestapo must therefore be erroneous; see Weinmann, "Das Oberlandesgericht Stuttgart von 1933 bis 1945," in *Das Oberlandesgericht Stuttgart*, ed. Stilz, 44.

6. See Kienle, *Das Konzentrationslager Heuberg*, 30.

7. Weinmann, "Das Oberlandesgericht Stuttgart von 1933 bis 1945," 44. In later years, Bauer rarely mentioned his persecution by the Nazis. However, he spoke in detail about his arrest when he met on one occasion after the war with young judges in Stuttgart, some of whom were colleagues of Weinmann's. Bauer emphasized the fact that his former colleagues in Stuttgart had looked on impassively as he was led away by police.

8. See Alfred Marx, *Das Schicksal der jüdischen Juristen in Württemberg und Hohenzollern 1933–1945* (N.p.: Neckar Verlag, 1965), 3ff, and "Robert Josef Bloch," Gegen das Vergessen: Stolpersteine für Stuttgart, accessed May 10, 2013, http://www.stolpersteine-stuttgart.de

/index.php?docid=251. After the war, Alfred Marx, a Jewish judge for civil cases in Stuttgart who had lost his job under the Nazis, researched the fate of other Jewish judges who had been dismissed. Robert Bloch began working as a judge in Stuttgart on September 17, 1928.

9. See Uhlman, *The Making of an Englishman*, 149. Irmtrud Wojak points out that a junior judge at Amtsgericht Stuttgart I was also a member of the SPD; see Wojak, *Fritz Bauer*, 113.

10. Quoted in Jörg Schweigard, *Stuttgart in den Roaring Twenties. Politik, Gesellschaft, Kunst und Kultur in Stuttgart 1999–1933* (Karlsruhe: G. Braun Buchverlag, 2012), 27.

11. Quoted in Gerhard Zwerenz, "Interview mit Fritz Bauer," 92.

12. See Schweigard, *Stuttgart in den Roaring Twenties*, 102–110.

13. Fritz Bauer, "Scham bei der Lektüre," *Die Zeit*, September 29, 1967.

14. Bauer, "Justiz als Symptom," 369f.

15. See the criminal files of the Amtsgericht Stuttgart I, call number F 302 II Bü 693, Staatsarchiv Ludwigsburg.

16. See Fritz Bauer, letter to the state's attorney's office in Stuttgart, August 4, 1931, call number F 302 III Bü 51, Staatsarchiv Ludwigsburg.

17. From 1931, Frauenknecht was responsible for "Verg.g.d.V.O.d.R.Pr.v. 28.3.31," as it was named in the court files: "Vergehen gegen die Verordnung des Reichspräsidenten vom 28. März 1931," or offenses against the president of the Reich's decree of March 28, 1931. This covered a range of offenses, and the judge had wide-ranging powers to "combat political disobedience."

18. See the criminal files of the Amtsgericht Stuttgart I, call number F 302 II Bü 844, Staatsarchiv Ludwigsburg.

19. See the criminal files of the Amtsgericht Stuttgart I, call number F 302 II Bü 1220, Staatsarchiv Ludwigsburg.

20. See Schweigard, *Stuttgart in den Roaring Twenties*, 105.

21. Bauer, "Scham bei der Lektüre."

22. Ibid.

23. *Simplicissimus*, no. 6 (1931), 69, reprinted in *Spott und Respekt*, ed. Eichler, 107.

24. See Michael Buchholz, "Zur Geschichte der Freien Wissenschaftlichen Vereinigung," in *Freie Wissenschaftliche Vereinigung*, ed. Voigts, 211.

25. Quoted in Claudia Schöningh, *"Kontrolliert die Justiz." Die Vertrauenskrise der Weimarer Justiz im Spiegel der Gerichtsreportagen von* Weltbühne, Tagebuch *und* Vossische Zeitung (Munich: Fink, 2000), 274.

26. Ralph Angermund, *Deutsche Richterschaft 1919–1945* (Frankfurt am Main: Fischer, 1990), 36f.

27. See Birger Schulz, *Der Republikanische Richterbund (1921–1933)* (Frankfurt am Main: Peter Lang, 1982), 22 and 206.

28. See Angermund, *Deutsche Richterschaft 1919–1945*, 41.

29. Gustav Radbruch, "Justiz und Kritik," *Vossische Zeitung*, February 16, 1926.

30. On more typical career progressions at the time, see Angermund, *Deutsche Richterschaft 1919–1945*, 29.

31. Bauer, *Als sie noch jung waren*.

32. See the schedule of responsibilities for 1931 in the files of the Amtsgericht Stuttgart I, call number F 304 Bü 6, Staatsarchiv Ludwigsburg.

33. See the criminal files of the Amtsgericht Stuttgart I, call number F 302 II Bü 369, Staatsarchiv Ludwigsburg.

34. See the criminal files of the Amtsgericht Stuttgart I, call number F 302 II Bü 1225, Staatsarchiv Ludwigsburg.
35. Bauer, letter to the state's attorney's office in Stuttgart, August 4, 1931, call number F 302 III Bü 51, Staatsarchiv Ludwigsburg.
36. *NS-Kurier.* "Die Affäre um Dr. Bauer. Der Ausdruck 'jüdischer Amtsrichter' ist eine Beleidigung," September 26/27, 1931, call number I 124 (microfilm) and Ztg. 9450 (print edition), Württembergische Landesbibliothek Stuttgart.
37. *NS-Kurier.* "Ein jüdischer Amtsrichter mißbraucht sein Amt zu Parteizwecken/Der 'Informator' der Tagwacht," June 5, 1931, call number I 124 (microfilm) and Ztg. 9450 (print edition), Württembergische Landesbibliothek Stuttgart.
38. In a letter to his friend Erwin Schöttle dated October 12, 1948, Bauer wrote that Beyerle had never forgiven him for his political involvement with the Reichsbanner Schwarz-Rot-Gold. Papers of Erwin Schöttle, file 15, Archiv der sozialen Demokratie, Bonn.
39. Bauer, letter to the state's attorney's office in Stuttgart, August 4, 1931.
40. Ruling against Adolf Gerlach of September 25, 1931, 7, call number F 302 III Bü 51, Staatsarchiv Ludwigsburg.
41. *NS-Kurier.* "Die Affäre um Dr. Bauer. Der Ausdruck 'jüdischer Amtsrichter' ist eine Beleidigung."
42. See files of the Amtsgericht Stuttgart I, requests from Department I B and II B regarding the 1932 schedule of responsibilities, call number F 304 Bü 4, Staatsarchiv Ludwigsburg.
43. See files of the Amtsgericht Stuttgart I, overview of the 1932 schedule of responsibilities of Department A for Civil Cases, call number F 304 Bü 6, Staatsarchiv Ludwigsburg.
44. See Göppinger, *Juristen jüdischer Abstammung im "Dritten Reich,"* 52, 56f.
45. Bauer, *Als sie noch jung waren.*
46. These observations were later included in a Gestapo report on Bauer, according to which, "with typical Jewish impertinence, he exploits every opportunity to agitate against the National Socialist movement." Quoted in Wojak, *Fritz Bauer,* 135. The report is available at call number R 99722, Politisches Archiv (Berlin), Archiv Auswärtiges Amt.
47. Quoted in Thomas Horstmann and Heike Litzinger, *An den Grenzen des Rechts. Gespräche mit Juristen über die Verfolgung von NS-Verbrechen* (Frankfurt am Main: Campus, 2006), 136.
48. Uhlman, *The Making of an Englishman,* 157.
49. Quoted in Schweigard, *Stuttgart in den Roaring Twenties,* 61f.
50. Bauer, *Als sie noch jung waren.*
51. *Schwäbische Tagwacht,* "Reichsbanner nötiger denn je! Hauptversammlung des Reichsbanners Schwarz-Rot-Gold Groß-Stuttgart," April 30, 1931.
52. See Jacob Toury, "Jüdische Aspekte der Reichsbannergründung," in *Deutschlands Stiefkinder. Ausgewählte Aufsätze zur deutschen und deutsch-jüdischen Geschichte,* ed. Jacob Toury (Stuttgart: Bleicher, 1997), 111.
53. See Robert M. W. Kempner, "Generalstaatsanwalt Dr. Fritz Bauer gestorben. Ein Streiter ohne Furcht und Tadel/Ein Leben für das Recht," *Das Reichsbanner,* July/August 1968. In August 1931, under the leadership of Karl Ruggaber (chairman of Württemberg's Reichsbanner branch and an SPD representative in the state's assembly), Bauer was initially only elected as one of the Reichsbanner's youth leaders in the state. See *Schwäbische Tagwacht,* "Die Gaukonferenz des Reichsbanner," August 10, 1931.
54. See *Schwäbische Tagwacht,* "Treugelöbnis der Schufo: Mitgliedversammlung des Reichsbanners," June 28, 1932.

55. Quoted in Wojak, *Fritz Bauer*, 109.
56. See Alfred Tischendorf, letter to Fritz Bauer on behalf of the mayor's office of Stuttgart, March 23, 1960, inventory 8600, number 172 (filed under "Bauer, Fritz"), Stadtarchiv Stuttgart: "On a cold Sunday afternoon a few weeks before the last Reichstag election on March 5, 1933, you were the key speaker at a large, very well-attended rally in Ludwigsburg's main square. I was the chief organizer of this impressive rally, which began with the Reichsbanner and the Iron Front parading through the city's streets."
57. See the Gestapo report on Bauer, call number R 99722, Politisches Archiv (Berlin), Archiv Auswärtiges Amt. Quoted in Wojak, *Fritz Bauer*, 135.
58. *Schwäbische Tagwacht*, "Treugelöbnis der Schufo: Mitgliederversammlung des Reichsbanners."
59. See Wojak, *Fritz Bauer*, 109.
60. See the Gestapo report on Bauer, call number R 99722, Politisches Archiv (Berlin), Archiv Auswärtiges Amt. Quoted in Wojak, *Fritz Bauer*, 135.
61. On the Reichsbanner's membership, see Benjamin Ziemann, *Die Zukunft der Republik? Das Reichsbanner Schwarz-Rot-Gold 1924–1933* (Bonn: Friedrich Ebert Stiftung, 2011), 23.
62. See ibid., 48.
63. Uhlman, *The Making of an Englishman*, 160.
64. See ibid., 161.
65. See Günther Weinmann, "Das Oberlandesgericht Stuttgart von 1933 bis 1945," 42.
66. See Uhlman, *The Making of an Englishman*, 163.

5

CONCENTRATION CAMP AND EXILE (1933–1949)

Heuberg Concentration Camp

Kurt Schumacher was sent to Heuberg, a concentration camp to the south of Stuttgart, in July 1933, just a few weeks after Bauer. "You'll never get out of here—you might as well hang yourself now!" a guard bawled at him on his arrival. "No, hanging me is your job," Schumacher replied.[1]

"I remember the camp guards lining up and beating him with nettles until he was covered in blood," Bauer later wrote. "The camp commandant jeered, 'Why are you here, Schumacher?' Without hesitation, Schumacher said, 'Because I'm a member of the defeated party.' This frank answer rendered the commandant speechless, interrupting his stream of invective."[2]

At Heuberg, Schumacher behaved as if something far more important than his life was at stake. The one-armed World War I veteran was a provocative figure for the guards, who found various ways to torment him, including forcing him to pick up pebbles in the yard, collect them in a bucket, empty the bucket when full, and then start all over again.[3] Once a guard told Schumacher that he'd been badly injured when a brawl had broken out at one of Schumacher's political events. Schumacher expressed regret—but "only that the guy hadn't been finished off there and then," according to Schumacher's biographer, Peter Merseburger.[4]

Both Bauer and Schumacher faced long stretches of imprisonment, and Bauer would often seek out Schumacher for conversation. Bauer later wrote: "I don't mind admitting, I was counting down the hours to freedom. But [Schumacher] said to me, 'I'll be here until Nazism is gone, and Nazism won't be gone until war breaks out, which it inevitably will. I reckon it will take ten, eleven years; that's how long I'll be here.' I must say, never again in my life—not even now as a jurist—have I come across someone who imposed a sentence on himself—ten, eleven years—with such clarity, such unflinching resolve."[5]

The SA wreaked brutal revenge on their opponents at Heuberg. The Nazis hadn't yet developed the diabolically efficient system of humiliation, violence, and murder that would later be established at camps such as Auschwitz. In 1933, it was the Württemberg police, not the SS, who were nominally in charge of Heuberg. In reality, though, thousands of SA members, hastily kitted out with auxiliary police uniforms, ran the camp.[6] These were the same men who had previously clashed with Reichsbanner members in street fights and barroom brawls. Now they were intent on settling old scores—with Schumacher; with Karl Ruggaber, the regional leader of the Reichsbanner; and with Bauer, the local Reichsbanner chairman, who was still wearing the suit he had been arrested in at the courthouse.[7] The camp commandant of Heuberg was Karl Buck, a burly SA member from Stuttgart with a toothbrush moustache. After the war, Buck was sentenced to death by a French court for crimes committed while he was in charge of the concentration camp in Schirmeck, Alsace. He was later pardoned, however, and in the decades following his release from prison in 1957, he led a placid existence in the countryside near Stuttgart.

Bauer and his fellow SPD leaders were separated from the other Heuberg inmates and incarcerated in barracks 19 and 23, where they were regularly subjected to brutal interrogations involving various kinds of blunt instruments.[8] "Prisoners were divided into three groups," recalled another inmate, Ernst Plank, who after the war would become a judge at the higher regional court of Stuttgart:

> The first class was made up of defectors and people on the road to rehabilitation; they received better treatment. The second class comprised functionaries—prisoners they had no concrete evidence against and on whom they tried out their nationalist regeneration strategies. Second-class prisoners received similar treatment to first-class prisoners, except that it was stricter, the food was worse, and they didn't enjoy any of the privileges granted the first class. The third class comprised so-called leaders, including Buchmann from the Communist Party of Germany, the local court judge Dr. Bauer from the Reichsbanner, the Social Democrat Engelhardt, and the editor Max Hammer from the Communist Party of Germany [Opposition]. This class was subjected to the worst treatment; the aim was nothing less than physical and psychological annihilation.[9]

"Third-class" prisoners would be forced to stand in a long line facing a wall while guards kicked them in the hollows of their knees and banged their heads against the wall. Sometimes the SA would attack them with scissors. One former inmate described how prisoners would be "forced to squat while SA men cut off their hair. If prisoners collapsed in exhaustion or could no longer maintain the squatting position, lumps of their scalps would end up dangling from the scissors."[10]

Bauer was subjected to eight months of abuse in the concentration camp, but in later years he only ever mentioned one small detail: the fact that he had been forced to clean the "twelve-cylinder," slang for the filthy pit beneath the camp's latrine. Bauer only shared this detail because he wanted to illustrate how the camp debased both sides: not just the inmate (as was intended) but also the young guard charged with supervising Bauer's work for hours on end. Bauer recounted this story in the 1960s to two friends who were left lost for words, discomfited by the philosophical insight at its heart.[11]

For the rest of his life, Bauer was unwilling to discuss what happened at Heuberg. A certain logic underpinned his reluctance to talk publicly about the concentration camp in postwar Germany. After all, as a prosecutor who brought Nazi criminals to trial, Bauer always insisted that he was pursuing justice, not revenge. Publicizing his own personal experiences of Nazi brutality would only have provided his political opponents of the 1950s and 1960s with ammunition. But this doesn't explain why Bauer also maintained his silence in private. His friends Gisela and Heinz Meyer-Velde said that he was "very reluctant" to talk about Heuberg.[12] You just knew not to bring it up, another friend, Wolfgang Kaven, said.[13] Bauer probably felt it wasn't right to talk about his own suffering, friends thought; it wasn't in his nature to complain.

The paths of Schumacher and Bauer, the two comrades in arms who had taken on Stuttgart's Nazis, eventually diverged, because whereas Schumacher was incarcerated at Heuberg until 1943, Bauer was released after eight months. By September 1933, the main camp at Heuberg had become overcrowded, and so Bauer was transferred along with several other "particularly dangerous" SPD and Communist Party functionaries to a former garrison prison on Frauenstrasse in the city of Ulm.[14] There, Bauer was locked into a single cell behind thick steel doors, where he was supposed to be kept under stricter detention conditions. The transfer turned out to be an unexpected stroke of luck. The prison was run by long-serving Württemberg police officers, not SA auxiliaries, and their chief was a senior police officer named Gnaier, who "couldn't understand . . . how a judge could be put in prison simply because of his affiliation with the Social Democrats and his leadership of the Reichsbanner Schwarz-Rot-Gold," according to Bauer.[15] The chief made Bauer an unlikely offer. "As he couldn't keep up with all the paperwork, he put me to work processing clemency appeals and censoring letters," Bauer explained. "This gave me the chance to steal my passport out of my file and send it home along with the censored letters."[16]

To make space for new barracks, Württemberg's Nazi government ordered the release of several "protective custody prisoners," one of whom was Bauer, in November 1933. Bauer told his family that his release came about thanks to friends in the judiciary who had put in a word for him.[17] It may well be the case that acquaintances tried to help Bauer out. On the very same day Bauer was arrested, a tip-off from a judge enabled Fred Uhlman, a fellow SPD member, to narrowly avoid being sent to a concentration camp. The Stuttgart-based judge Gottlob Dill, who had attended the same high school as Uhlman and Bauer, told a go-between, "If you see my friend Uhlman, tell him Paris is supposed to be very nice right now. Tell him: right now."[18] Similarly, in 1942, the president of the regional court of Stuttgart, Martin Rieger, intervened to stop the Gestapo from deporting Robert Bloch—the Jewish judge who had worked with Bauer at the local court—to Auschwitz.[19]

It is therefore entirely possible that Bauer's former colleagues, prompted by some sense of solidarity, stepped in to help. Such an intervention alone wouldn't have secured Bauer's release, however. In 1933, political "protective custody prisoners" could only be released if they declared their loyalty to Germany's new rulers.[20] Some prisoners had to write out these self-abasing declarations by hand, while others signed preprinted declarations. On November 13, 1933, a declaration of submission signed by eight Social Democrats incarcerated in Ulm's garrison prison was published in one of the city's newspapers, the *Ulmer Tagblatt*. Appearing under the headline "Pledge of Loyalty from Former Social Democrats," the declaration took the form of an open letter addressed to the Nazi leaders of the government of Württemberg. The declaration included the following statement: "We believe in the government's commitment to providing the German people with work and bread; we know that there is no place for militant activities when the battle for German people's lives is going on. . . . In the fight for honor and peace, we are unreservedly on the side of the Fatherland."[21] The first two signatures at the bottom of the letter, which concluded with a profession of the signatories' "loyalty and esteem," were those of the Reichsbanner leaders, Karl Ruggaber and Fritz Bauer. Bauer would never again speak about this letter, a humiliation he endured so as to avoid even more egregious abuse.

The unyielding Kurt Schumacher was one of the few prisoners in Württemberg who refused to sign a declaration of submission.[22] Bauer and Schumacher therefore went their separate ways, with Schumacher remaining incarcerated long after Bauer was released. Years later, Bauer would continue to speak of Schumacher in reverent tones. While he himself "timidly counted down the hours to freedom," Bauer said, he was "amazed by [Schumacher's] unshakeable conviction and courage . . . in the days of the Weimar Republic, later after the collapse of the Nazi regime, and, most of all, in the concentration camp."[23]

Bauer's open admiration of Schumacher's resolve stands in stark contrast to his reticence about the suffering he himself endured at the hands of the Nazis.

Denmark 1936: Like a Criminal on Parole

Returning to life as a free citizen was out of the question for Bauer after his release from the concentration camp. When the humiliated Social Democrat went back to Stuttgart, he was treated like a criminal on parole. He had to report regularly to the police, pay fines amounting to 2.60 Reichsmarks per day of imprisonment to cover the costs of "meals, accommodation, and surveillance," and generally keep his head down.[24] Thanks to a new law introduced by the Nazis to purge Jews from the civil service, Bauer had been removed from judicial office while he was still incarcerated.[25] His dismissal was followed by that of the remaining six Jewish judges in Stuttgart, who were fired in August 1933.[26] Earning a living as an attorney was now also out of the question, as Jewish lawyers had been banned from courthouses since spring 1933 and their licenses had been revoked in summer 1933.[27] Bauer's only option, then, was to help out in his father's textile firm; this marked the beginning of "a terrible period for him," his sister, Margot, recalled.[28]

From 1935 onward, it was the Nuremberg Reich Citizenship Law, and not one's faith, that determined who was a Jew in Germany. This new law defined anyone with at least three "fully Jewish" grandparents as a Jew and anyone with one or two "fully Jewish" grandparents as a *Mischling*, or mixture. As a result of this redefinition of Jewishness, yet another judge was removed from office in Stuttgart.[29] As boycotts of Jewish businesses and discriminatory decrees mounted, one thousand Jews—one-fifth of Stuttgart's Jewish population—left the city during the first two years of the Nazi regime.[30] One of those to leave was Bauer's sister, Margot, who in 1936 set off for a new life in Copenhagen with her husband, the textile salesman Walter Tiefenthal. Not long afterward, Bauer—now officially also a textile salesman by profession—followed them.

Dense clouds hovered over the entire country as Bauer's train pulled off from Stuttgart's main station on March 15, 1936.[31] Bauer would have seen the remilitarized Rhineland roll past his window as the train made its way northward to Denmark; just a few days previously, in a show of Germany's renewed military might, the zone had been reoccupied by Hitler's Wehrmacht. For the sum of 150 Reichsmarks, Bauer had sent ahead his furniture, and his friend Carlo Schmid—a lawyer who would go on to have a successful political career after the war, eventually running as the SPD's presidential candidate—came to the station to see Bauer off. Schmid did his best to cheer Bauer up, telling him it would all blow over eventually.[32] Not long before his departure, Bauer had been arrested in Stuttgart and locked up for a day.[33] "We're watching you," the police warned him on February 1, 1936. "If we catch you involved in anything remotely resembling political subterfuge, we'll throw you back into the concentration camp." Since his release from the camp, Bauer had kept in touch with his Social Democrat comrades and continued to frequent their old haunts. The final straw came when his former colleagues in the courthouse launched criminal proceedings against him—Bauer never explained why—making "it senseless to stay at home any longer," Bauer later explained.[34]

But Bauer would soon find that he was treated like a convicted criminal in Copenhagen, too. Whereas Mr. and Mrs. Tiefenthal managed to build a new life for themselves, the Danish authorities viewed Bauer as a troublemaker right from the start and kept him under strict surveillance. He had to report to immigration officials every Thursday, and, unbeknownst to him at the time, he was constantly shadowed by the police as he strolled around the city.[35] They were looking for incriminating material—and they soon found it.

During his first month in Copenhagen, the police confronted Bauer after he had spent the night with a Danish man. Homosexual intercourse was legal in Denmark. However, the Danish police questioned Bauer about whether he had been involved in homosexual prostitution, which was illegal. Bauer didn't deny having (legal) intercourse with the man, but he did deny (illegally) paying for it. "From the street, one could see that the German did not put on pajamas after getting undressed," wrote the police officer who observed Bauer's window until 2:30 a.m.[36] The immigration police clearly committed considerable resources to monitoring Bauer, but in the end, they weren't able to pin anything on him, and proper criminal proceedings were never launched.

Nevertheless, the police continued to harass Bauer, later accusing him of taking part in a second homosexual encounter. Bauer, who emphatically denied that the encounter took place, tried to use this new attack to his tactical advantage, seizing the opportunity to remind the police about his application for a Danish work permit. "If I were allowed to work, I would be able to suppress my urges," he argued.[37]

Did Bauer mean what he said? Did he identify as gay, and if so, did he really view homosexuality as a shameful "urge"? The context is significant: Bauer uttered these words during a legal row with hostile officials. It is therefore impossible to determine whether he was being honest, strategic, or both. There's no record of Bauer ever making any other statements to the effect that he was gay, there's no evidence he was involved in the gay scene in Germany prior to 1936, and the Danish police didn't observe any further homosexual "liaisons" after 1936.[38] Was this just an isolated incident, then? Bauer seems to have been a lifelong loner as far as romantic relationships went. The only thing his ignominious encounter with the police makes clear is that right from the beginning of his exile in democratic Denmark, he was subjected to the vagaries of the authorities. There can be little doubt that his run-ins with the law in Denmark—run-ins experienced by very few other noteworthy German criminal lawyers and judges—profoundly shaped Bauer's outlook on the justice system.

A Life Put on Hold

Bauer was anxious to move on from Denmark as soon as possible, but his many attempts to obtain a visa for the United States, where many of his mother's relatives were now living, failed.[39] In articles for the German Jewish newspaper *C.V.-Zeitung*, Bauer wrote warmly about his country of exile: "The Danes enjoy their good fortune with easy-going cheer."[40] In private, however, he vented his frustration: "I live on the periphery here.... Given that I do not have a proper passport, I fear I will be largely chained to Denmark."[41]

"Esteemed Professor," Bauer wrote to the philosopher Max Horkheimer in a letter dated September 21, 1937.[42] He hoped to get a foot in the door of Horkheimer's Institute of Social Research, which had relocated from Frankfurt to New York.

For one and a half years, Bauer had been keeping his head above water by writing innocuous articles for the arts and culture section of the *C.V.-Zeitung*, for which he was the Scandinavian correspondent, and by selling shirts and fabric for drapes. Bauer's attire in later years gives a sense of how little interest he had in clothes: he never wore expensive shirts, just practical, very crumpled ones, many of them speckled with cigarette ash.[43] Fritz Bauer, a textile salesman? He was more of a bookworm, unsuited to a practical life, his brother-in-law, Walter Tiefenthal, believed.[44] But Bauer wasn't eligible to work as an attorney, as he hadn't sat the Danish bar exams, and he didn't have the right background for a job at the university. His area of legal expertise—which centered on Gustav Radbruch and Franz von Liszt's modern theories of resocialization and prevention—was certainly of great interest to the academic world, particularly in Scandinavia. Stephan Hurwitz, a Jewish professor of criminal law in Copenhagen, responded positively when Bauer got in touch with him.[45] But even in peacetime, sovereign states were loath to take advice on criminal law from outsiders. Professor Hurwitz therefore had to explain to Bauer that there was no point in applying for a job as a lecturer. A German had no chance of being appointed.

So Bauer wrote to Horkheimer instead. The two men already knew of each other, having both grown up in Stuttgart's small Jewish community. Horkheimer's father had manufactured synthetic wool while Bauer's father had sold fabric. In the Bauer family home, Fritz had often heard about Max, who was eight years his senior and had left home at an early age to pursue an academic career in Frankfurt.⁴⁶ By the same token, Max Horkheimer's parents spoke with admiration about Fritz, the son of a textile salesman who went on to become a judge.⁴⁷ Bauer was hoping to benefit from this shared background when he contacted Horkheimer in 1937.

Bauer certainly wasn't lacking in self-confidence: "Perhaps you've already been ambushed by friends of mine in New York," he wrote jovially. "If not, this dubious pleasure awaits you!"⁴⁸ Bauer was encouraged by the fact that his doctoral thesis had been cited by one of Horkheimer's employees, Friedrich Pollock.⁴⁹ "I assume the books listed in the references were actually read!" Bauer snapped after receiving Horkheimer's rejection letter.⁵⁰ The institute didn't have the funds to hire Bauer, the professor explained. In his offhand reply, Bauer misspelled Pollock's name; after that, Horkheimer stopped writing to Bauer personally. Instead, one of the institute's employees sent a response inviting Bauer to recommend Scandinavian books for review in the institute's journal.⁵¹ With that, the matter was closed. It was yet another humiliation for the restless exile.

The German Army Approaches

It was a sunny day in a Copenhagen park in 1936, a few weeks into Bauer's exile.⁵² Summer had just arrived; far away in Berlin, elaborate preparations were underway to host the Olympic Games. By turning a blind eye to Hitler's remilitarization of the Rhineland in blatant violation of the Treaty of Versailles, the international community had recently given the Nazi regime a boost. Bauer had been chatting for hours with Richard Schmid, a left-wing Stuttgart-based lawyer who had just arrived in Copenhagen. Bauer was in low spirits, according to Schmid, for while he was relieved to have escaped the Gestapo, he found his life in exile absurd. In Denmark, Bauer told his visitor, people were constantly asking him, "What have you got against Hitler, anyway?"

Bauer sent many pleading letters to the Danish authorities requesting asylum for his parents, but to no avail. The Danes didn't take the threat facing the Bauer family seriously, not even after Stuttgart's synagogue went up in flames on the night of November 9 to November 10, 1938. The fire had been expertly started by the chief of Stuttgart's Fire Station II to foment even further the "spontaneous public anger" that erupted on *Kristallnacht*. That night, Jewish homes and business were destroyed, and several hundred Jews were arrested in Stuttgart and deported to the concentration camps at Welzheim and Dachau.⁵³ One of those arrested was Bauer's uncle Leopold Hirsch, the new head of Tübingen's synagogue. Hirsch, followed by a few other members of his community, eventually managed to escape to South Africa in 1939.⁵⁴ Like Bauer's father, who had lost his textile business, Hirsch had lost his clothing store in Tübingen—the same store Bauer had loved playing in as a child—some years previously when it was confiscated and "Aryanized."

Months passed before anything was done. Eventually, in 1939, Denmark granted Bauer's parents, now aged sixty-nine and fifty-nine, the right to seek refuge in the north. It then took another few months for the German authorities to grant their approval: "It is hereby confirmed that Ludwig Israel Bauer and his wife, Ella Sara, née Hirsch, Stuttgart-W, 9 Gustav Siegle Strasse, are not in arrears for taxes, penalties, fees, or charges," the Stuttgart North tax office certified on December 1, 1939. "The Jewish Assets Tax and the Reich Flight Tax have been paid or guaranteed."[55] On January 1, 1940, Bauer met his parents at Copenhagen's central station. He hadn't seen them in five years.

"I myself and many other emigrants had heard about the liquidations in Poland and so on," Bauer recalled years later. "It was difficult to persuade people in Denmark, even political people, that these rumors, reports, etc., were true. People generally found them implausible."[56] On April 9, 1940, just a few weeks after his parents' arrival, the Nazis caught up with the Bauer family again when the Wehrmacht marched into Denmark.

Hoping that Denmark would be an ally, the Nazis allowed the Danish government to remain in office. However, the new rulers wanted to eradicate all opponents of the Nazi regime, and so a German soldier and a Danish police officer soon came knocking on the Tiefenthal family's door. They had come to arrest Bauer, who, sensing what was in store, had already gone to ground. Hiding between his parents' legs, the Tiefenthals' four-year-old son called out to the men in uniform. He knew where Uncle Fritz was, he said. Fortunately, though, the child spoke in Danish. The German soldier couldn't understand, and the Danish soldier pretended not to hear.

"They caught him on a street in Korsør," Margot Tiefenthal remembered.[57] Following his arrest in September 1940, Bauer was locked up in Copenhagen's Vestre Prison. Then, along with other German opponents of the Nazis, he was sent to Horserød, a prison camp on the island of Zealand, eight kilometers from the coast. The camp consisted of primitive barracks surrounded by barbed wire. As the wind whistled through the wire, prisoners could see neutral Sweden in the distance, but it remained unreachable. Bauer's family visited him at the camp every Sunday for two and a half months.[58] Right up to his release in December, Bauer lived in constant fear that, like one in every two Horserød prisoners, he would be deported to a concentration camp in Germany.[59]

Sweden 1943: At Willy Brandt's Side

Bauer made one last bid to secure a safe future for himself in Copenhagen, according to his sister, Margot. On June 4, 1943, he entered into a marriage of convenience with a Danish friend, a kindergarten teacher named Anna Maria Petersen, whose father came from the northern German region of Holstein.[60] In their registry office wedding, both bride and groom stated that they were members of the Lutheran Church of Denmark.[61] Just a few months later, in October 1943, Bauer wrote Petersen a farewell letter: "Dear Anna Maria, Thank you for your letter and for everything else. Lis will let you know how I'm getting on. You'll hear from me again. All the best, Fritz."[62] This perfunctory note gives a sense of how distant their relationship was. Bauer and Petersen never lived together, they never introduced each other to their families, and their marriage didn't even serve its purpose for very long, as in fall 1943, the Nazis decided to deport all Jews from Denmark. By now, the subtleties of Danish immigration law were immaterial, as was Bauer's marriage. The only option was to flee.

As soon as Bauer heard about the leaked German plan to round up Denmark's Jews, he went into hiding in a cellar along with his parents, sister, brother-in-law, and two young nephews. On the night of October 13, 1943, having spent eight days in the cellar, Bauer and his family took off for Sweden in a motorboat belonging to a Danish fisherman.[63] Getting out of Denmark was the only way to avoid the Nazi killing machine, to which family members who had stayed behind in Stuttgart had already fallen victim. Bauer's aunt Paula Hirsch and his cousin Erich Hirsch had been rounded up during the first big wave of deportations in December 1941. Together with 1,013 other Stuttgart Jews, they had been sent to Riga, where they were murdered.[64]

"There is an atmosphere of jealousy here, and a toxic struggle for the few available jobs has been going on for years."[65] This is how Bauer described the socialist emigrant milieu he encountered in Stockholm in 1943.[66] The city was an important center for German-speaking emigrants. Around 120 SPD politicians and activists lived there, including the future German chancellor Willy Brandt and the future Austrian chancellor Bruno Kreisky. Innumerable societies, groups, and labor movement "internationals" argued over their plans for the post-Hitler era; like an agitated, amorphous swarm of bees, they were constantly splitting, reforming, and overlapping. In their midst was Fritz Bauer, who had left his family in the city of Gothenburg before moving farther north to Stockholm, where he could keep up with the "toxic" debates that were raging.

Bauer joined several groups at once: the International Economic Policy Working Group, the Free German Cultural Association, and the Working Committee of German Anti-Nazi Organizations.[67] Financially, Bauer managed to get by on a grant from Stockholm University's Institute for Social Research, which an SPD acquaintance had secured for him.[68] Bauer quickly gained a reputation as an eloquent orator, and when Stockholm's entire swarm of bees eventually came together to elect a joint executive committee in December

1944, Bauer was one of the nine members appointed.[69] Bauer, together with the young leftist Willy Brandt, was also charged with launching a magazine for German exiles entitled *Sozialistische Tribüne* (Socialist Tribune). Brandt served as one of the magazine's two co-publishers, while Bauer assumed the role of editor in chief. Bauer found Brandt, who was ten years his junior, to be likable, capable, and exceptionally gifted: "He is a man who has no difficulty making friends in international circles," Bauer wrote to his old friend Kurt Schumacher. "Some people in the party think he's a rogue because he can be as crafty as an American. They are right about one thing: As an emigrant, he has adapted to the West, particularly America. Party members who criticize him tend to be second- and third-rate journalists who would like to emulate him but unfortunately lack the talent."[70]

Brandt would keep in touch after the war. In early 1946, he visited Bauer in Denmark, where Bauer had returned in the hope of building relationships with the Americans.[71] When Brandt became president of the state parliament of Berlin in 1955, he contacted Bauer again, this time to invite his friend to take up the position of attorney general of Berlin.[72]

Bauer Tears Up His Doctoral Thesis

Whenever Bauer flicked through his old doctoral thesis on commercial law—a work he described in his 1938 letter to Max Horkheimer as an "opus that has been ravaged by time"—he felt like he was taking a journey back to a more innocent time.[73] Never again would he demonstrate such a lenient attitude toward the captains of industry; too much had happened since he completed the thesis in 1925.

Bauer returned to economic themes during his time in exile. He had little other choice, given that his background in German criminal law was no longer of any use to him. If he was to find work as an academic, he would have to specialize in another field. And he gradually realized that his work within the field of economics would entail radically rethinking some of his earlier theories.

In 1941, when Bauer was still in Copenhagen, he published an academic textbook entitled *Penge* (Money). In this almost three-hundred-page work, Bauer wanted to prove that he could do more than sell textiles; he could also teach and research—in Danish. A study of monetary policy, the textbook was expertly structured, encyclopedic, and descriptive: the kind of book that could be used as the core text in an undergraduate economics course. Beginning with a bang, the introduction drew together quotes from the giants of world literature, from Sophocles through Shakespeare to Goethe's *Faust*. "Money rules the world," Bauer announced at the outset.[74] Many of the world's most brilliant authors have written about "gold and golden things," but, Bauer explained, what really concerns them is the power such things embody.[75] The book explained how money came into being, why it's "not metal but belief" that determines the significance of "golden things," and why the value of money goes up and down.[76] Bauer refrained from advancing any particular thesis. The most he offered was a suggestion, right at the end of the book, for an alternative to the gold standard, a suggestion that seems rather cursory compared to the lengthy bibliography that directly follows. *Money* is a painstaking piece of work that appears to have been motivated more by Bauer's desperate need to find a job than by a burning desire to communicate ideas. As soon as he arrived in Sweden in 1943, Bauer arranged for the textbook to be translated into Swedish.[77]

Once surrounded by other socialists in Sweden, Bauer wrote a book with an altogether different, more strident tone. Published in 1945, *Ökonomisk Nyorientierung* (Economic Reorientation) argued that by 1932, the crisis was almost over in Germany. Having passed the peak of its popularity, Bauer claimed, the Nazi Party's coffers were empty. However, "property magnates and major industrial and banking representatives" bailed the party out and pushed for Hitler to be appointed chancellor, thereby "putting power in the hands of the man who had so openly championed war and German expansionism."[78] At the instigation of IG Farben, German industrialists donated a total of 3 million Reichsmarks to fund the Nazi Party and DNVP election campaigns. IG Farben itself made the highest single donation: 400,000 Reichsmarks. American observers had noted that "the cartels made Hitler, and Hitler made war," Bauer wrote. With the privilege of hindsight, his book set out to examine how this came about.

Economic Reorientation offered a Marxist critique that Bauer would reiterate in a later article.[79] It argued that in colluding to maintain artificially high market prices, trusts and cartels always ended up facing the same problem sooner or later: if they wished to sell more products, they had to either lower their prices or increase their employees' wages. Understandably, neither of these options was appealing to companies.[80] The only way to increase sales, then, was to tap new markets abroad: "They have to look for consumers outside their own country. This situation inevitably arises in all capitalist countries." This led to conglomerates from various states fighting for spheres of influence: "There is a scramble for colonies, for industrially underdeveloped countries, South America, China, India, the Middle East, the Balkans. Capitalists from various countries end up battling each other, scrapping over the same bones." According to Bauer, Hitler's 1939 demand for *Lebensraum* (living space) was in fact a demand for "markets and capital investment abroad."[81] Bauer cited the steel corporation Thyssen and the Rhenish-Westphalian Coal Syndicate as examples of Hitler's industrial backers.[82] He did not mention IG Farben, however, the conglomerate that established its very own Auschwitz subcamp, Buna, in the Polish village of

Monowice in late October 1942. Between then and 1945, around thirty thousand prisoners, most of them Jewish, died there.

People were mistaken in believing that all that needed to be done was to remove Hitler and his henchmen from power, Bauer wrote. Instead, the system that gave rise to Nazism needed to be transformed; global industry—and not just German industry—needed to be "pacified."[83] Germany was just the most recent country to wage war as a means of solving the problems facing its industries, but similar problems were to be found throughout Europe:[84]

> We are not fighting the capitalists, but the entire capitalist system, which is like a machine that is not working satisfactorily, and which we believe can be replaced with a better, more efficient machine. The main objection to socialism is that it suffocates the individual's initiative and restricts freedom. There is no doubt that socialism limits freedom. It is similar to road traffic regulations. Once one-way streets, speed limits, and right-hand traffic are introduced, one can no longer drive around however one pleases. But while these restrictions may be bothersome for the individual driver or pedestrian, they benefit others.[85]

Bauer went even further in *Monopolernes Diktatur* (The Monopolies' Dictatorship), published in 1948. Here, he argued that the concentration of economic power—no matter what form it takes, and even if it is the result of international agreements—is always malign. Bauer illustrated this idea by drawing a picture of his desk. He then went through the items on the desk, identifying the "monopoly capitalists"—in other words, cartels—responsible for the production and sale of each one.[86] For example, when describing the books stacked beside his Underwood typewriter, Bauer lambasted the Danish publishing conglomerate that controlled the book market by dictating minimum prices and limiting supply. He then pointed out that the paper on his desk was the product of various Scandinavian paper cartels. The electric lamp on Bauer's desk was also produced by a cartel, he pointed out, as were the brass in the lamp's base, the base's ornate casting, the lampshade, the dye used in the lampshade's fabric, and the bulb. Indeed, Bauer added, the desk itself was a typical product of the "international wood cartel," which set wood export quotas. Even Bauer's pencil eraser reminded him of the abuse of market power, as in 1934, the United Kingdom, India, the Netherlands, and France had signed the International Rubber Regulation Agreement, which controlled rubber prices by limiting the production of rubber and banning the planting of new rubber trees. According to Bauer, this agreement had near-disastrous consequences, as "the shortage of natural and synthetic rubber almost led to the war being lost after Pearl Harbor."[87]

"The socialist answer is a planned economy," Bauer acknowledged in 1947. If economic power was to be concentrated anywhere, he said, then it ought to be concentrated in the hands of the state: "We do not allow motorists, cyclists, and so on, to ride through the streets however they please. By the same token, we cannot allow a country's economic players to manufacture products however they like, set whatever prices they want, and send capital and products abroad however they choose."[88]

Bauer even saw a positive side to the Soviet Union's efforts to establish a planned economy in East Germany: "In the long run, the situation in Germany will necessitate the establishment of a planned economy, regardless of whether one is a proponent of the planned economy or free initiative." When deciding how much butter, livestock, and crops East German farmers had to supply, the state would "obviously" take into account demand and crop failures, Bauer wrote as the rubble of the war was being cleared away. "Germany as a whole will learn a great deal from East German planning experiences, as will many other countries," he added.[89]

Bauer applauded the Allies' decision to start breaking up German cartels and trusts. In the exile newspaper *Deutsche Nachrichten* (German News), he accused "international monopoly lords"—whom he derisively referred to as "limited liability patriots"—of "collusion throughout the wars. During the First World War and to an even greater extent the Second one, they joined forces abroad."[90] Under pressure from the United States, Konrad Adenauer's government set about prohibiting most cartels in 1952. Bauer responded in an article for *Geist und Tat* (Intellect and Action), a theoretical journal published by the SPD's left wing, in which his only criticism was that the government's actions were not drastic enough. The article was entitled "The Land of Cartels."[91]

Bauer never referred to his doctoral thesis of 1925 again. The industry-friendly views he had espoused as a young middle-class student were now alien to him.

"Inopportune": No Room for Jews in Postwar German Politics

When the Nazis capitulated on May 8, 1945, Bauer was ready for action. After nine years in exile, he was keen to say goodbye to his fellow émigrés and return to Germany. On May 9, 1945, he delivered a farewell speech in front of a large audience gathered in Stockholm's trade union headquarters. In his speech, Bauer argued that the task of rebuilding a democratic Germany, a task that had hitherto been discussed by emigrants in Sweden in purely theoretical terms, now required decisive action.[92] He then set off for Germany, leaving his parents and his sister behind him in Sweden. By this stage, his father had been diagnosed with leukemia and would die a few months later, in December 1945. Bauer's first port of call on his homeward journey was Copenhagen, where he immediately informed the Americans of his desire to assist in Germany's reconstruction. He was determined to return to Germany with a mission. What followed in Copenhagen, however, were four more excruciatingly long years of waiting and watching from the sidelines. It was during this waiting period that Bauer, having already lost almost a decade, came to a painful realization.

As reconstruction began, former colleagues, friends, and political allies of Bauer's were appointed to important positions throughout Germany. In October 1945, for example, Bauer learned that the Americans had appointed his urbane, liberal doctoral supervisor, Karl Geiler, as the nonaffiliated state premier of Hesse. In Tübingen, the French military government made Bauer's old friend Carlo Schmid the first head of government of the newly created state of Württemberg-Hohenzollern. Another friend, the socialist lawyer Richard Schmid, became attorney general in Stuttgart. In Hanover, Kurt Schumacher became leader of the federal SPD. The Allies invited Bauer's former fellow exile, Willy Brandt, to become mayor of his hometown, Lübeck, at the age of just thirty-three, but Brandt turned down the offer because he was poised to move to a larger political stage, joining Schumacher in the Bundestag. Why, then, was there no position for Bauer?

When Schumacher was elected SPD leader in May 1946, Bauer wrote to him from Copenhagen, where he felt like he was in limbo:

> Needless to say, I'm very keen to see the lay of the land in Germany. In May and June of last year [i.e., right after Germany's capitulation, RS], I discussed the prospect of going back to Stuttgart with the Americans. They had me fill out a dozen forms (they were interested in jurists), but they never got back to me. I don't know why. I suspect, however (based on several private discussions with gentlemen from the legation), that they don't want Jews, or—to be precise—they believe it would be inopportune for Jews to undertake work that is in any way public. This is one of the things I'd like to investigate for myself.[93]

Bauer reached out to various people and offered his services. He made it clear that he wanted to "put an end to [his] personal state of uncertainty" and that he was looking for a role in public service: "What I have in mind is a position in the judiciary or in a ministry such as the ministry of justice or economic affairs."[94] But all of his efforts remained fruitless. Foisting Jewish politicians on the defeated Germans seemed too risky a move to the Allies with whom Bauer spoke; they feared it would jeopardize their efforts to win over the Germans and gain their support for the new system.

This must have been a hard blow for Bauer, the patriot who had been waiting for so many years for the horror to pass. The man who, back in his student days, had called on other Jewish students to "embrace" their Germanness. The man who, in his speech in Stockholm on May 9, 1945, repeatedly used the word "we" to refer to the entire German nation: "We recognize Germany's duty to atone for the war crimes perpetrated in its name. . . . None of us expects any sympathy for the German people. We know that the German people will have to work for years and decades to earn respect and sympathy."[95] These words weren't directed at wrathful young Jews like the writer Ralph Giordano, who wandered the razed streets of his native Hamburg in 1945, plotting revenge on the Germans, "caught in the web of the past, in the countless images they created, none of which he would ever be able to forget."[96] No, when Bauer said "we," he meant "we Germans."[97]

Countries that had been invaded by Germany, like Poland, the Netherlands, and the Soviet Union, had far higher mountains of rubble to clear away, Bauer reminded his compatriots in an article published in *Deutsche Nachrichten* in 1945. "These people's optimism should be a model for us all," he wrote in an attempt to buoy readers' spirits.[98] With Germany forced to surrender territory to neighboring countries, Bauer urged his readers to remember the sentence that had helped Danes in the same predicament a century previously: we must make up for external losses through internal gains. "The same motto must be adopted in Germany today. . . . The new Germany must become a Reich of social justice. . . . Its workers and farmers, its engineers and architects can put into action Schiller's line: 'And new life blossoms in the ruins'!"

Yet Bauer continued to be regarded as too Jewish.

In the summer of 1949, a Cologne-born Jewish doctor named Dr. Lewin was elected chief physician of the municipal gynecology clinic in Offenbach. At the behest of the deputy mayor, however, and with the approval of the city's Social Democrat head mayor, Lewin was promptly removed from the position, as it was felt that Offenbach's women wouldn't be safe in the hands of a Jewish doctor whose family had been murdered by the Nazis and who was himself a concentration camp survivor. It was claimed that the doctor would bring to his role "the resentment of his race and the concentration camp inmate's desire for revenge."[99] At the very least, it was said, this would be the public's perception. An appalled Kurt Schumacher issued his SPD colleagues a stinging rebuke: "This new Social Democratic form of opportunistic racial ideology cannot be tolerated."[100] In 1949, Schumacher saw a real danger that "in view of the supposed 'political ill breeding of the German people,' certain people will claim that candidates of Jewish descent make less attractive election candidates or even repel voters. Leaving aside the fact that this is not true—people with anti-Semitic views would never vote for the Social Democrats anyway—one can never quite get to the real motives of such apparently concerned, upright citizens."[101]

The chasm between Jewish and non-Jewish Germans didn't disappear with the collapse of the Third Reich; in fact, it was now wider than ever. There was a widespread perception that, after the events of the previous twelve years, the few surviving Jews in Germany were bent on revenge, or at least that their interests were at odds with those of their non-Jewish compatriots. A Jewish foreign minister like Walter Rathenau or a Jewish state premier of Bavaria like Kurt Eisner now seemed inconceivable.

Lewin and Bauer weren't the only Jewish figures to learn from their experiences of rejection and mistrust. Three Jewish politicians joined the first German Bundestag, whose members—almost five hundred in total—convened for the first time in 1949. One of these three Jewish men, Jakob Altmaier, had been specifically selected by Kurt Schumacher to serve as a link to the Jewish communities and the state of Israel.[102] The second Jewish member of parliament, Peter Blachstein, was more ambitious than Altmaier, and so he decided not to draw attention to his Jewish heritage at all. A Hamburg-born member of the SPD, Blachstein had played an active role in Jewish associations when he was younger, yet in the parliament handbook he described himself as having "no religion" and as having been "persecuted for political reasons."[103] Finally, the Social Democrat Rudolf Katz, who had turned his back on the Jewish community in his youth, now described himself as Protestant. Katz would go on to become minister of justice of the state of Schleswig-Holstein in 1947 before being appointed to the Federal Constitutional Court in 1951; in his obituary, the news magazine *Der Spiegel* paid tribute to a man who, "surrounded by the ethereal prima donnas of the courthouses in Karlsruhe, seemed almost like a tribune of the plebs, ... strident, affable, tough."[104]

Like Blachstein, Bauer claimed to have "no religion." Moreover, he was keen to emphasize that during his years in exile, he had had nothing to do with the Jewish community or German Jewish emigrants.[105] He kept quiet about his work as Scandinavia correspondent for the Jewish *C.V.-Zeitung*, a job that had entailed developing contacts in the Jewish community. Similarly, Bauer never mentioned his friendship with Erich H. Jacoby, a Jewish lawyer from Berlin who had planned to get married in a traditional Jewish ceremony in Denmark just before the Wehrmacht invaded.[106] Now, Bauer maintained a cool distance from other Jews.

Rudolf Katz offered Bauer the politically insignificant position of president of the administrative court of Schleswig-Holstein. However, as Bauer told a friend, "I didn't pursue [the offer] as I have absolutely no experience in administrative law and I suspect that people expect a person in this position to have the kind of presidential gravitas that I lack."[107]

In Hanover, some of Bauer's Social Democrat friends encouraged him to apply for a position in judicial administration, such as attorney general or president of one of the court's criminal divisions. Yet within the party, there was palpable mistrust of Bauer. When he urged his comrades to comply with Allied directives, he drew the ire of right-leaning members of the party. It was a disgrace, this support for "atonement and the Potsdam Agreement," one detractor wrote in a letter attacking Bauer and his ilk. "They're serving as train-bearers for the worst kind of nationalism—the nationalism of foreigners."[108] It was time to "fight tooth and nail . . . with these rootless heathens, who don't want to be Jews . . . , aren't German, and don't have the guts to openly be Bolshevists," Hans Reinowski, a former Reichsbanner member from Braunschweig, wrote to Kurt Heinig, a former member of the Reichstag.[109] Heinig, for his part, called Bauer a "Russian quisling."[110] When Bauer tried to persuade his fellow Germans to accept the territorial losses sustained as a result of Germany's defeat, another SPD member grumbled, "It makes me sick, the way he's always kissing the Russians' asses."[111]

In response to Bauer's job application, a representative of Hanover's SPD government informed him that the most important posts within the attorney general's office had already been filled.[112] Bauer suspected that the government intended to offer him "a lower and therefore more closely supervised position."[113]

Notes

1. Quoted in Peter Merseburger, *Der schwierige Deutsche. Kurt Schumacher* (Stuttgart: Deutsche Verlags-Anstalt, 1995), 169.
2. Bauer, "Im Kampf um des Menschen Rechte," 39.
3. See Merseburger, *Der schwierige Deutsche*, 170.
4. Ibid., 174.
5. Bauer, *Als sie noch jung waren*.
6. See Markus Kienle, *Das Konzentrationslager Heuberg*, 30.
7. On Ruggaber's imprisonment, see ibid., 69.
8. See ibid., 64, 73, 82f.
9. Ernst Plank, "Bericht des Genossen E. P." (three undated typewritten pages that were among Plank's papers), copy available at call number Rep. 2, 76, archives of Dokumentationszentrum Oberer Kuhberg, Ulm. (The copy is also labelled "Gedenkstätte Dachau, 20.518".) On Plank, see Kienle, *Das Konzentrationslager Heuberg*, 120.
10. Quoted in Kienle, *Das Konzentrationslager Heuberg*, 81.
11. Meyer-Velde, interview by author.
12. Ibid.
13. Kaven, interview by author.
14. According to Kienle, these transfers took place in May and September 1933; see Kienle, *Das Konzentrationslager Heuberg*, 38. Given that Bauer was present when Kurt Schumacher arrived at Heuberg in July 1933, we can deduce that he was transferred in September. It has been claimed elsewhere that Bauer was moved to the concentration camp at Oberer Kuhberg before being transferred to Ulm. However, the Oberer Kuhberg camp wasn't established until

November 1933. According to the memorial and museum that now exists at the site, Bauer didn't spend time there before being imprisoned in the garrison prison in Ulm.

15. According to Silvester Lechner, the police officer sometimes spelled his name "Gneier." Neither "Gnaier" nor "Gneier" appear in the telephone book of the time. See Lechner, *Das KZ Oberer Kuhberg und die NS-Zeit in der Region Ulm/Neu-Ulm* (Stuttgart: Silberburg-Verlag, 1988), 63.

16. Bauer, interview by Leni Yahil. Transcript (handwritten and initialed by Yahil on March 9, 1962) available at call number 0-27/13-5, Yad Vashem Archives.

17. Tiefenthal, interview.

18. Quoted in Uhlman, *The Making of an Englishman*, 163f.

19. See Weinmann, "Das Oberlandesgericht Stuttgart von 1933 bis 1945," 44.

20. See Kienle, *Das Konzentrationslager Heuberg*, 114f.

21. Facsimile of the *Ulmer Tagblatt*, November 13, 1933, reprinted in ibid., 115. The "Pledge of Loyalty from Former Social Democrats" is dated October 22. The signees are listed in order of importance rather than alphabetically, with Bauer's name appearing directly after Karl Ruggaber, the chairman of the Württemberg branch of the Reichsbanner, and before Erich Roßmann, the state chairman of the SPD. Close examination of the facsimile reveals that Bauer's name is spelled "Fritz Hauer." In old German typeface, "B" and "H" are often mixed up, and in any case, there are no records of the existence of a prominent figure named Fritz Hauer. Bauer's release around the time of the publication of this "pledge" further indicates that his name was simply misprinted.

22. See ibid., 115.

23. Bauer, "Im Kampf um des Menschen Rechte," 39.

24. See Kienle, *Das Konzentrationslager Heuberg*, 68.

25. On May 25, 1933, Bauer was dismissed on the basis of the Nazis' Law for the Restoration of the Professional Civil Service; see Bauer's judiciary personnel file, call number NL-08/03, page 41, Fritz Bauer Institute Archives, Frankfurt am Main. In later years, Bauer himself named various dates for his dismissal: March, April, and May 1933.

26. See Weinmann, "Das Oberlandesgericht Stuttgart von 1933 bis 1945," 43; and Borth, "Das Amtsgericht Stuttgart," in *Das Oberlandesgericht Stuttgart–125 Jahre von 1879 bis 2004*, ed. Stilz, 235.

27. See Göppinger, *Juristen jüdischer Abstammung im "Dritten Reich,"* 90f.

28. Tiefenthal, interview.

29. See Göppinger, *Juristen jüdischer Abstammung im "Dritten Reich,"* 77f.

30. See Roland Müller, *Stuttgart in der Zeit des Nationalsozialismus* (Stuttgart: Konrad Theiss Verlag, 1995), 295; and Sauer and Hosseinzadeh, *Jüdisches Leben im Wandel der Zeit*, 135.

31. See the date on the cover sheet of the police files on Bauer, Udl. number 53.658–113.954, Copenhagen City Archives.

32. Bauer recalled this episode in a birthday card he sent to Schmid on December 4, 1961; see Carlo Schmid's papers, file 972, Archiv der Sozialen Demokratie, Bonn.

33. See the police files on Bauer, Udl. number 53.658–113.954, Copenhagen City Archives.

34. Bauer to Horkheimer, September 21, 1937, call number I/2 230, Max Horkheimer Archive, Stadt-und Universitätsbibliothek Frankfurt am Main.

35. See the reports of August 4, 1943, and June 5, 1936, in the police files on Bauer, Udl. number 53.658–113.954, Copenhagen City Archives.

36. See report of April 18, 1936, ibid.

37. See report of October 21, 1936, ibid.
38. Report of March 3, 1939, ibid.
39. Hirsch, interview; and Wojak, *Fritz Bauer*, 129.
40. Bauer, "Die glückliche Insel Dänemark," *C.V.-Zeitung*, December 24, 1936. Steffen Steffensen's claim that Bauer really did feel at home in Denmark is based on this single article; see Steffensen "Fritz Bauer (1903–1968). Jurist und Volkswirt," in *Exil in Dänemark. Deutschsprachige Wissenschaftler, Künstler und Schriftsteller im dänischen Exil*, ed. Willy Dähnhardt und Birgit S. Nielsen (Heide: Westholsteinische Verlagsanstalt Boyens & Co., 1993), 171–177.
41. Bauer to Horkheimer, September 21, 1937.
42. Ibid.
43. Warlo, interview with author; and Wiese, interview with author, October 17, 2012.
44. Statement in police report of October 21, 1936, police files on Fritz Bauer, Udl. number 53.658–113.954, Copenhagen City Archives.
45. See Bauer, interview by Yahil, 2f.
46. See Bauer to Horkheimer, February 15, 1965, call number I/2 230, Max Horkheimer Archive, Stadt-und Universitätsbibliothek Frankfurt am Main.
47. See Horkheimer to Bauer, October 9, 1937.
48. Bauer to Horkheimer, September 21, 1937.
49. See Bauer to Horkheimer, February 1, 1938.
50. Ibid.
51. One of Horkheimer's employees (signature illegible) to Bauer, March 7, 1938.
52. See Richard Schmid, "Nachruf auf Fritz Bauer 1903–1968," *Kritische Justiz* 1 (1968): 60f.
53. See Sauer and Hosseinzadeh, *Jüdisches Leben im Wandel der Zeit*, 139.
54. See E. Guggenheimer, "Aus der Geschichte des Synagogenbaus," in *Festschrift zur Einweihung der Synagoge in Stuttgart*, ed. Israelitische Kultusvereinigung Württemberg und Hohenzollern (Stuttgart: Israelitische Kultusvereinigung Württemberg und Hohenzollern, 1952), 30.
55. Finanzamt Stuttgart-Nord, "Unbedenklichkeitsbescheinigung," December 1, 1939, call number EL 350 I Bü 23925, Staatsarchiv Ludwigsburg.
56. Bauer, interview by Yahil, 4.
57. Tiefenthal, interview by Fabian. In the original interview, Tiefenthal refers to "Kossör," a Germanized version of the Danish name "Korsør." In the transcript of the interview, Tiefenthal's error has been corrected without comment.
58. See ibid.
59. See the police files on Fritz Bauer, Udl. number 53.658–113.954, Copenhagen City Archives.
60. Tiefenthal, interview by Fabian.
61. See marriage register 2092/1943, Copenhagen City Archives.
62. See Wojak, *Fritz Bauer*, 154. Wojak came across Bauer's farewell to Petersen in the personal archive of Bauer's nephew, Rolf Tiefenthal, in Denmark.
63. See ibid.
64. See ibid, 539.
65. Bauer to Kurt Schumacher, May 23, 1946, Fritz Bauer's papers, call number 1/FBAB 000001, Archiv der sozialen Demokratie, Bonn.
66. Tiefenthal, interview by Fabian.
67. See Wojak, *Fritz Bauer*, 166, 169.

68. See ibid., 166.
69. See ibid., 177.
70. Bauer to Schumacher, May 23, 1946.
71. See Brandt to Schumacher, January 13, 1946, Kurt Schumacher's papers, file 64, Archiv der sozialen Demokratie, Bonn.
72. See Wojak, *Fritz Bauer*, 280f.
73. Bauer to Horkheimer, February 1, 1938.
74. Bauer, *Penge* (Copenhagen: Martins Forlag, 1941), 5.
75. Ibid., 5.
76. See ibid., 9–39.
77. Bauer, *Pengar i går, i dag och i morgon* (Money Yesterday, Today, and Tomorrow; Stockholm: Bokförlaget Natur och Kultur, 1944).
78. Bauer, *Ökonomisk Nyorientering* (Copenhagen: Martins Forlag, 1945), 28.
79. See Bauer, "Sozialismus und Sozialisierung," *Deutsche Nachrichten*, May 12, 1947.
80. Bauer, *Ökonomisk Nyorientering*, 19.
81. Bauer, "Sozialismus und Sozialisierung."
82. Bauer, *Ökonomisk Nyorientering*, 7, 27.
83. Ibid., 28.
84. Ibid., 22.
85. Bauer, "Sozialismus und Sozialisierung."
86. Bauer, *Monopolernes Diktatur* (Copenhagen: Forlaget Fremad, 1948), 5–8.
87. Ibid., 9.
88. Bauer, "Sozialismus und Sozialisierung." Bauer had considered the advantages and disadvantages of interventions in a planned economy in an earlier work, *Ökonomisk Nyorientering* (see 158f.).
89. Bauer, "Die Wirtschaftsgesetzgebung in der Ostzone," *Deutsche Nachrichten*, April 14, 1947.
90. Bauer, "Ein bisschen Arsenik. Blick hinter die Kulissen der Wirtschaft," *Deutsche Nachrichten*, April 28, 1947.
91. Bauer, "Das Land der Kartelle," *Geist und Tat. Monatsschrift für Recht, Freiheit und Kultur*, (June 1952): 167–171.
92. See the transcript of the speech, published in *Politische Information*, May 15, 1945, 11f., Fritz Bauer Institute Archives, Frankfurt am Main.
93. Bauer to Schumacher, May 23, 1946.
94. Bauer to Erwin Schöttle, October 12, 1948, Erwin Schöttle's papers, file 15, Archiv der sozialen Demokratie, Bonn.
95. Transcript of speech published in *Politische Information*, May 15, 1945, 11f.
96. Ralph Giordano, *Die Bertinis* (Frankfurt am Main: Fischer, 1982), 712.
97. Bauer, "Wiedergutmachung und Neuaufbau," *Deutsche Nachrichten*, September 4, 1945.
98. Ibid.
99. *Neuer Vorwärts*, September 24, 1949, 10.
100. Schumacher to Peter Blachstein, November 26, 1949, published in *Kurt Schumacher. Reden–Schriften–Korrespondenzen, 1949–1952*, ed. Willy Albrecht (Bonn: Dietz, 1985), 990–992.
101. Ibid.
102. See Willy Albrecht, "Jeanette Wolff, Jakob Altmaier und Peter Blachstein. Die drei jüdischen Abgeordneten des Bundestags bis zum Beginn der sechziger Jahre," in *Leben im*

Land der Täter. Juden im Nachkriegsdeutschland (1945-1952), ed. Julius H. Schoeps (Berlin: Jüdische Verlagsanstalt Berlin, 2001), 243.

103. Ibid., 246.

104. *Der Spiegel*, "Nachruf auf Rudolf Katz (30. September 1895–23. Juli 1961), August 2, 1961. Walter Strauß has been cited as another example of a prominent Jewish postwar politician; see, for example, Thomas Horstmann and Heike Litzinger, *An den Grenzen des Rechts*, 166. However, Strauß—who cofounded the Berlin CDU after the war and served as an undersecretary in the federal ministry of justice from 1950 to 1963—was Protestant from birth. He was considered Jewish only according to the Nazis' criteria. The title of Friedemann Utz's biography—*Preuße, Protestant, Pragmatiker* (Prussian, Protestant, Pragmatiker, 2003)—is a more accurate reflection of Strauß's identity.

105. See Bauer, interview by Yahil.

106. See Wojak, *Fritz Bauer*, 133; and Corinna Waffender, "Porträt einer erfolgreichen Weltbürgerin. Ruth Jacoby, Schwedens Botschafterin in Berlin," *Jüdische Zeitung*, April 2007. (Ruth Jacoby is Erich H. Jacoby's daughter.)

107. Bauer to Schumacher, September 14, 1948, file 165, Archiv der sozialen Demokratie, Bonn.

108. Letter from one unnamed party member to another, November 22, 1945, quoted in Wojak, *Fritz Bauer*, 201.

109. Hans Reinowski to Kurt Heinig, May 26, 1946, quoted in ibid., 211.

110. Heinig to an unnamed party member, December 22, 1946, quoted in ibid., 205.

111. Letter from one unnamed party member to another, August 21, 1946, quoted in ibid., 201.

112. See Bauer an Schöttle, October 12, 1948.

113. Bauer to Schumacher, September 14, 1948.

6

REHABILITATING THE PLOTTERS OF JULY 20, 1944

The Returned Emigrant Takes on West Germany's Resurgent Nazis: The Remer Trial of 1952

Around eight hundred people were crammed into the small hall in Lower Saxony on a spring evening in 1951. Another four hundred waited outside, where they were entertained by a red sound truck decorated with the party's logo. At the entrance to the building, wearing red armbands, black pants, and boots, stood stewards from the Socialist Reich Party (Sozialistische Reichspartei Deutschlands, or SRP). The party's paramilitary wing—troops armed for skirmishes with political opponents—was known as the "Reichsfront," while the youth wing, whose members wore olive-green shirts and shorts, was called the "Reichsjugend." Thick tobacco smoke billowed up from the crowd gathered in the hall, and out of the loudspeakers thundered the "Badenweiler-Marsch" (the music played when the Waffen-SS paraded in front of Hitler) followed by "Preussens Gloria," another rousing military march.

"What the Prussians were in the twentieth century, the Lower Saxons are today," the thirty-nine-year-old Otto Ernst Remer bellowed into the hall.[1] Remer was wearing a "messianic loden ensemble" topped off with a green felt hat, an observer from *Der Spiegel* noted.[2] The imperial eagle was embroidered on Remer's lapels, its wings spread to reveal thirty black feathers. "We are at the heart of a future pan-German empire," Remer continued, gesticulating wildly as the crowd cheered.

"The atmosphere resembled that of Nazi gatherings in 1931/1932," a reporter from *Die Welt* wrote.[3] The SRP's chairman, Fritz Dorls, who was known to praise the "revolutionary technology" used in the gas chambers, was based far away in Bonn. He was one of two SRP representatives in the first German Bundestag, which had not yet introduced the "5 percent hurdle" that today prevents splinter parties from entering parliament. However, the true stronghold of resurgent Nazism was Lower Saxony, where Remer, one of the SRP's cofounders, campaigned on a platform of ending "discrimination" against former Nazi Party members. The international press therefore tended to refer to the SRP as "Remer's party." It won 11 percent of the vote in the state election of May 6, 1951, and an absolute majority in thirty-five of Lower Saxony's districts. As a result, the SRP secured sixteen seats in Lower Saxony's parliament.

The German chancellor, Konrad Adenauer, was concerned by the SRP's growing popularity, and his government filed an application with the Federal Constitutional Court to ban the party. Yet Adenauer also hoped to persuade the party's elected representatives, including those in Lower Saxony, to join his own party, the conservative Christian Democratic Union (Christlich Demokratische Union Deutschlands, or CDU). Ultimately, Adenauer's plan was never brought to fruition, because the Federal Constitutional Court banned the SRP on October 23, 1952, thereby rescinding its mandate.

Remer, a gangling man with a high forehead, was revered as a hero by Nazi nostalgists because of the role he had played in foiling the attempted military coup of July 20, 1944. Remer, then a low-ranking major, had been commander of the Berlin guards' battalion when word spread that Hitler had been killed in a bomb attack on his "Wolf's Lair" headquarters in East Prussia. Remer was ordered to seal off the government buildings in Berlin, but as he was doing so, he realized he had become caught up in a plot to overthrow the regime. When it emerged that Hitler was still alive, Remer shared the good news with Joseph Goebbels, who was waiting anxiously inside the government buildings. "Little Goebbels felt like flinging his arms around the giant," wrote the Nazi propagandist and future *Spiegel* correspondent Wilfred von Oven, who celebrated the moment in a book published in Buenos Aires entitled *With Goebbels to the End* (1950). Oven's panegyrical account transforms the weedy Remer into a "lean, tan officer as tall as a tree with the Knight's Cross with Oak Leaves pinned to the collar of his field tunic."[4] Declaring Major Remer to be the hero of the hour, Hitler promoted him to the rank of major general and put him in charge of the *Führer-Begleitbrigade* (Führer Escort Brigade) as a token of his gratitude. Meanwhile, Goebbels's propaganda machine made Remer the star of the *Deutsche Wochenschau* newsreel. The regime was determined that the humble major-turned-hero, and not the chief conspirator, Claus von Stauffenberg, would be the face of July 20.

"He is one of hundreds, a speck of dust among thousands," one observer of Remer's career wrote in 1952. "A beam of light flashed over him, and suddenly this speck of dust became visible. Coincidence illuminated the major and distinguished him from the dark masses. He became caught up in major historical events by accident. Now he wants to remain in the spotlight."[5]

Remer continued to brag about his deed after the war and appealed to the solidarity of his former brothers in arms by inveighing against the plotters of July 20, 1944. "The conspirators were traitors to their country and were paid by foreign powers.... I promise that a German court will one day bring these traitors to justice," Remer ranted in the packed clubhouse in Brunswick on May 3, 1951, just a few days before his spectacular electoral victory in Lower Saxony.[6]

Brunswick: this is where Bauer comes into the story, as he had been serving as state's attorney general there since 1950.

Robert Lehr, Adenauer's minister of the interior, filed a complaint about Remer's comments with Bauer's office. A former member of the resistance himself, Lehr argued that Remer had defamed the resistance fighters by calling them "traitors." Initially, one of Bauer's clerks tried to put Lehr off, urging him to withdraw the complaint because there was "no chance of success."[7] However, Lower Saxony's ministry of justice had ordered staff to report any issues relating to Remer to their superiors. As a result, Bauer became aware of Lehr's complaint before it disappeared into the court's files, and he immediately took the matter in hand.

Bauer spurred his little team of jurists into action, causing a good deal of agitation as he did so. Warning that time was of the essence, he demanded that Remer be charged "as soon as possible." Years later, when Bauer was transferred to the city of Frankfurt, his former Brunswick colleagues sent sarcastic congratulatory messages to his new team in Hesse: now it's your turn to put up with Dr. Bauer, they wrote.[8] "Even today, just thinking of Fritz Bauer makes my hackles rise," a former Brunswick prosecutor later said.[9]

Bauer dictated the indictment to a senior prosecutor named Erich Günther Topf. Topf, an erstwhile SA *Rottenführer*, baulked at transcribing Bauer's accusation that, in calling the July 20 conspirators "traitors," Remer hadn't merely used defamatory language but had lied outright. Topf made sure his reservations were recorded in the case file, jotting down the word "questionable" in the margins. On discovering this, Bauer decided to don the prosecutor's robe himself. "Given the significance of the trial," he said, he felt it was best to prosecute the case personally.[10]

A State's Attorney General in Brunswick in 1950

In 1952, Bauer held a rather humble, low-profile position within the German judicial system. However, his success in turning the Remer trial into a major public event is testament to the scale of his ambition after his return to Germany.

Bauer had resettled in Germany in April 1949 after finding a job in a provincial court close to the East German border. Shortly afterward, Bauer was appointed to a post he ironically described as a "sinecure," an untaxing position with little real responsibility.[11] Brunswick's town center had been completely destroyed during the war, and there was still rubble everywhere. Blocks of concrete buildings were beginning to spring up from the mountains of debris, but it would be decades before the rubble was entirely cleared. In a 1954 letter to Max Horkheimer, whom he had invited to Brunswick to give a talk, Bauer joked, "You write that you are looking forward to seeing the beautiful city of Brunswick. Evidently someone has sent you brochures from the Middle Ages; as far as I know, Henry the Lion passed away a few years ago."[12]

A "sinecure": Bauer was one of nineteen state's attorney generals scattered across the young West German republic. He was like a provincial prince in the country's federal-style prosecution system, and from his base in the Higher Regional Court of Brunswick, he oversaw all the prosecutors in his judicial district. The prosecutors worked independently; as attorney general, Bauer could intervene wherever he wanted to, but he was also entitled to take a hands-off approach. He could provide the prosecutors with guidelines and urge them to be tougher or more lenient in specific cases. Even prosecutors in the farthest-flung village courts within his jurisdiction were obliged to follow his directions. The principle of judicial independence applied to judges but not to prosecutors, who followed a strict chain of command. Bauer was therefore permitted to issue them with instructions on how certain laws should be interpreted. He could also personally prosecute major cases if he wished to provide his subordinates with examples of good practice—or if he wanted to send a message to the rest of the country.

Bauer reported to Lower Saxony's minister of justice, Otto Krapp. Krapp was the leader of the state's German Center Party (Deutsche Zentrumspartei), which was in coalition with the SPD. A former lawyer and SA member, Krapp had completed his law studies three years after Bauer. On April 1, 1950, he welcomed Bauer back into the judiciary with a rather bizarre gesture, presenting him with a certificate commemorating twenty-five years of service.[13] To ensure that Bauer wouldn't be at a disadvantage compared to those whose careers had continued during the Nazi era, Krapp ignored the fact that Bauer hadn't held a judicial position since 1933.

Very few of Bauer's colleagues suffered similar career disruptions during the Nazi regime. In 1949, Lower Saxony's ministry of justice admitted that it employed largely the same staff as "before the collapse."[14] Bauer was clear-eyed about the situation: "It is safe to assume," he wrote in reference to Germany's higher courts, "that between two-thirds and three-quarters of these judges previously worked in the judiciary of the illegitimate Nazi state, and that almost all of them were either party members or military judges (military judges not being permitted to join the Nazi Party)."[15] As he hadn't worked as a jurist for fourteen years, Bauer had to prove he had the necessary expertise for the attorney general position in Brunswick by first serving a year as the presiding judge of a criminal court.

"For the time being," Bauer wrote to his friend Kurt Schumacher two weeks after his return to Germany, "I feel at home—more so than I expected. The people here, and indeed my colleagues, are very friendly and obliging."[16] Bauer was too polite to elaborate on the qualifying phrase "for the time being." Having suffered repeated rejections over the past four years, he was grateful to Schumacher for helping him secure the position in Brunswick. But years later, Bauer provided a little more insight into his reservations: It was immediately apparent to him on starting his new job that returned emigrants weren't welcome, he said: "Emigrants reminded people of things they wanted to repress. People were afraid of the questions emigrants might ask."[17]

When the West German constitution came into force on May 23, 1949, Bauer had a cause for celebration. "Looking at the tricolors of black, red, and gold flying today," he wrote to Schumacher, "makes me think of our old Reichsbanner."[18] But there was hardly anyone he could celebrate with. Not one member of Bauer's extended family lived in Germany now: his immediate family had stayed in Scandinavia; many uncles, aunts, and cousins were in the United States; some family members had immigrated to Latin America and South Africa; and others had been murdered. The same went for many of his old friends, colleagues, and allies. Robert Bloch, his Jewish colleague at the local court in Stuttgart, had been deported to Auschwitz on July 13, 1942, as part of a *Vernichtungstransport* (extermination transport) and had never returned.[19] Many members of Bauer's old Jewish fraternity, the FWV, had been murdered too. Hardly any of the few survivors returned to Germany. Leo Herz, for example, the "gynecologist with a carrot-colored goatee beard" whose drinking habits had so annoyed the pacifist writer Kurt Hiller, now lived in London, where he went by the name Leo Hart.[20] Others made it to New York, Los Angeles, Buenos Aires, and Palestine.[21] Bauer learned what had happened to them because one of his former fraternity brothers, Ernst Rosenthal, was trying to revive the old network from his new home in London.[22]

Through Rosenthal's newsletters, Bauer learned that the paths of many of his old college friends had crossed in the concentration camp in Theresienstadt. "There was some excitement when . . . Karl-Wolfgang Philipp (AKA 'Dash') and his young wife, who had arrived on a transport from Holland, joined us in Theresienstadt," recalled a fraternity brother named Erich Simon.[23] Like Bauer, Philipp had been an active fraternity member in Heidelberg in 1922 and 1923; in fact, Philipp had served as chairman of Heidelberg's FWV.[24] Bauer read that "old FWV-style" meetings were regular occurrences in Theresienstadt, where "we upheld the FWV's values . . . in opposition to those espoused by the KC, to which the vast majority of university graduates in the camp belonged."[25] (The KC, or Kartell-Convent, was the national association of dueling Jewish fraternities.)

Theresienstadt even had its own jurisprudence discussion group, which was "always attended by around 100 people, [and] where the most complex problems in international jurisprudence were debated." Eventually, however, most of Theresienstadt's fraternity members died of starvation or illness or were deported to killing centers. In a 1948 report for Rosenthal's newsletter, Simon recalled one FWV brother in Theresienstadt standing by a coffin containing the body of another fraternity member and whispering, "Sleep well, my loyal old beer-swilling friend!" Simon also reported that the brother known as "Dash" had been deported to a killing center shortly after his arrival in Theresienstadt. "It remains to be seen whether the FWV will ever be revived at a university," Simon concluded. "But we must keep the memory of the FWV and its Theresienstadt branch alive."

The newsletters also informed Bauer that just one of his brothers at Heidelberg, Richard Neumann, had managed to secure a job in the West German public service, having been appointed attorney general of Berlin by the Allies.[26] The sprawling city of Berlin seemed very far away from Brunswick. Located in the south of Lower Saxony, the landscape surrounding this razed town was dominated by turnip fields and stud farms. The SRP campaigned vigorously in this area from 1949 onward, as it knew that statements such as the following, which comes from a draft SRP speech, were likely to receive a warm response from voters there: "Do people really think that anti-Semitism disappeared when emigrants with distinctive noses wearing American and English uniforms flooded back into the country in 1945?"[27]

Bauer's jurisdiction covered only a small part of this conservative rural region. Each state's attorney general in West Germany was responsible for the judicial district of a higher regional court. As several higher regional courts were scattered across large states such as Bavaria, North Rhine-Westphalia, and Lower Saxony, Bauer shared responsibility for his state with two other attorney generals. From his office in Brunswick, Bauer oversaw the smallest, most sparsely populated, and most poorly resourced district.

When Bauer took up his position, Brunswick prosecutors had made a few isolated efforts to bring Nazi criminals to justice. For example, the trial of Dietrich Klagges had begun one winter morning in early 1950. Journalists eager to catch a glimpse crowded into the neon-lit courtroom as Klagges, who had been premier of the state of Brunswick between 1933 and 1945, was escorted into the courtroom by two uniformed men. Some months later, at the end of a long, grueling trial involving testimony from 250 witnesses, the three judges sentenced Klagges to life imprisonment. Klagges later lodged an appeal, and Bauer was faced with the difficult task of defending the conviction. A few other, lower-ranking Nazi officials had also been tried in Brunswick in the immediate postwar years. Bringing such cases before the court was a hit-and-miss affair. A range of factors came into play, such as whether the Western Allies applied sufficient pressure (which they did only in the early days), whether there was enough public interest in the case (and such interest tended to subside quickly), and whether the state's attorney's office had the political will to initiate proceedings. The Allies had demanded that Klagges be prosecuted back in 1945, but Bauer's predecessor, Curt Staff, only managed to bring the case to trial by issuing official warnings that forced his team into action.[28]

Prosecutors who looked the other way were more likely to have successful careers than those who tried Nazi criminals. The judiciary's reluctance to prosecute Nazis was evident in 1958, when the Federal Constitutional Court (Germany's highest court) claimed that not one of the verdicts of the Nuremberg trials was legally valid.[29] Hans-Joachim von Merkatz—a member of the German Party (Deutsche Partei), a Bundestag representative, and the federal minister of justice from 1956 to 1957—insisted that refusing to recognize the Nuremberg verdicts was a matter of "German honor."[30] Merkatz spoke of "alleged" war criminals; similarly, the Federal Constitutional Court used the word "alleged" when referring to figures the Nuremberg trials had found guilty of war crimes.[31] On the few occasions when former members of the SS and Gestapo did stand trial, it became apparent that they were among thousands of former Nazis who had by now returned to positions of power within the police force and government ministries. Some of them would soon enjoy successful careers with the newly established army, the Bundeswehr.

Looking back on this period some years later, Bauer wrote:

> Public servants, from judges and prosecutors right up to the Federal Constitutional Court, saw themselves as the one constant in an ever-changing world. They believed their rootedness and irremovability would provide German history with continuity. One of Kant's famous lines states that to every jurist, the legal constitution in force at any time is the best, but when it is amended from above, this amendment always seems the best too. By following this philosophy, the German public servant has become an interchangeable functionary. [He has been] degraded to a legal handyman lacking convictions or a conscience, someone who, provided he has lived long enough, and depending on the oaths he has taken, has carved out a comfortable existence "conscientiously" serving his Kaiser and king until 1918, an official republic until 1933, a gangster regime until 1945, and, after that regime's collapse, a democratic, social, and constitutional state that enshrines human rights.[32]

"The Question Had an Electrifying Effect":
A Nation Debates the Resistance

One morning in 1952, a long queue had already formed an hour before the regional courthouse on Brunswick's Münzstrasse opened.[33] The court had printed tickets for members of the public eager to watch Bauer, the returned Jewish emigrant, take on Remer, the star of Germany's resurgent Nazi scene. Twenty-five SRP members, including the party leaders at state and national levels as well as all sixteen members of the Lower Saxon parliamentary party, took their places in the gallery. "In the dock, Otto Ernst Remer frowned, smiled, and whispered to his lawyers behind his raised hand," one observer noted.[34] Given any chance, Remer would stand up and make a short speech, casually leaving one hand in his jacket pocket and gesturing energetically with the other. Parts of the courthouse still lay in ruins, and the sound of hammering echoed through the halls.[35] In the courtroom itself, the presiding judge repeatedly called for order, warning spectators not to applaud.[36]

The legitimacy of the July 20 attempt on Hitler's life was on trial, at least according to the newspapers reporting on the case throughout the country. Remer had been charged with the relatively minor offense of defamation, but the trial was set to raise far more serious issues, press commentators believed. For a statement to be judged defamatory, as opposed to merely offensive, it had to be demonstrably false. The court would therefore have to discuss whether in calling the plotters of July 20 traitors, Remer had made a factually false statement. It was this key question that gave the trial its significance.

At the time, the young republic—whose armed forces Adenauer was planning to rebuild—was in urgent need of heroes and traditions untainted by the Nazi era. In representing the voice of the military's conscience, the July 20 plotters appeared to be good candidates. Throughout the country, however, there were millions of former Wehrmacht soldiers who had adhered to their oath of allegiance to Hitler right to the end. The more glowing the terms in which a figure such as Stauffenberg was remembered, the more culpable these millions of Germans appeared. The center-left SPD party wanted the Bundestag to legalize "conscientious" disobedience within the military, but their conservative counterpart, the CDU, was concerned that such legislation would enable its smaller coalition partners, the Free Democratic Party (Freie Demokratische Partei, or FDP) and the German Party, to position themselves as the parliamentary voice of Germany's powerful soldiers' associations.[37]

Bauer wasn't the first jurist to take on Remer against this context, and he wasn't the first to address in court the events of July 20, 1944.[38] But he was the first to do so in such a high-profile manner and the first to ensure that the

Figure 6.1. Brunswick, 1952: As the state's attorney general, Bauer (seen here with a prosecutor) charges the leader of the Socialist Reich Party. Credit/Source: *Deutsches Historisches Museum*.

arguments presented in court were debated throughout the country. Bauer invited the press, with whom he had built up a good relationship since his arrival in Brunswick, as well as an array of major German figures, including the federal minister for displaced persons, refugees, and war victims; the president of the Federal Office for the Protection of the Constitution; and members of the clergy and the military.[39] As a result, the brief one-week trial had a far-reaching impact.

Shortly after Bauer made his widely reported closing argument, the mayor of Berlin, Ernst Reuter, unveiled a monument to Stauffenberg. In rehabilitating Stauffenberg, this gesture brought an end to the ostracism suffered by his widow, who had hitherto been denied an officer widows' pension. Before an audience of students in Berlin, the West German president, Theodor Heuss, professed his admiration for the coup against Hitler, referring to the "heroes" of July 20, 1944, as men whose blood had "wiped away the shame . . . Hitler brought on us Germans."[40] However, the 1960s were well underway by the time

Stauffenberg's face appeared on a stamp and regular commemorative services were held in his honor, and it took far longer for other German resistance fighters to be rehabilitated.[41] Due to opposition within the conservative CDU and its sister party, the Christian Social Union (CSU), the convictions of tens of thousands of German soldiers executed by Wehrmacht tribunals for "military treason" weren't overturned until 2010. In the Bundestag, the CSU politician Norbert Geis explained, "Even in an unjust war, the rules of law must apply. The crime of treason cannot simply be dismissed as justified." Nevertheless, 1952 marked a clear turning point in attitudes toward the July 20 plotters. A survey conducted shortly before the Remer trial found that only 38 percent of Germans supported the actions of the plotters. By the end of 1952, a politically turbulent year, this figure had increased to 58 percent.[42]

The strong reaction provoked by the Remer trial was palpable within the courtroom itself, as one observer noted: "There was a great deal of discussion about whether the July 20 conspirators had abandoned troops in order to carry out their coup, leaving soldiers to bleed to death on the front due to a lack of men. One could see that this question had triggered debate among the spectators. Even the policemen in the courtroom started sharing their wartime memories. The question of whether 'sabotage' had taken place had an electrifying effect."[43] The court aimed to find a legally binding answer to this question. If Bauer won the case, German citizens would no longer be able to refer to the military's resistance fighters as "traitors" with impunity.

Bauer's case had a significant weakness, however, insofar as Remer's use of the term "traitors" to describe Hitler's would-be assassins was open to interpretation. It was possible to argue that Remer had used the term in a loosely colloquial or moral sense rather than a strictly legal one. In 1950, Wolfgang Hedler, a German Party Bundestag member, had stood trial in Kiel on similar charges. The judge in Kiel rebuked Hedler—who had called the resistance fighters "blackguards" and "traitors"—for his insensitivity. Nevertheless, the judge concluded that the defendant had expressed a political view and that it was not the court's task to pass judgment on people's political opinions, or indeed on the actions of the resistance fighters themselves. Hedler was acquitted, the judge ruling that in a democracy, the purpose of the heavy "sword" of criminal justice was not to adjudicate on differences of opinion.[44] Theodor Heuss echoed the judge's view in 1952 when he stated that "regardless of how objective their proceedings may be, and no matter how fair their efforts to administer justice are, [the courts] are not responsible for judging history."[45]

When asked by Bauer for an expert opinion, a prominent historian, Hans Rothfels, expressed a similar view. Remer's claim that Hitler's attackers had committed "treason" need not necessarily be characterized as an objective lie, Rothfels wrote:

> I believe it is well known that preserving the memory of the resistance fighters is extremely important to me and that I deeply regret the tendentious manner in which these men have been vilified. As a layman, I can offer no opinion on the legal aspects. But if the defense counsel asks me about the facts, which no doubt they will, I cannot possibly deny that, from the perspective of positive law [in other words, the law of the time, RS] the men behind July 20 were traitors, and that indeed some of them committed high treason.[46]

To make matters even more difficult, official documents from the courts of Lower Saxony supported Remer's view that the resistance fighters had committed treason. "It cannot be disputed that the death penalties" imposed by the Nazi naval judge Manfred Roeder on fifty-six resistance fighters "were legitimate," a prosecutor from the Lower Saxon town of Lüneburg had written. After all, the prosecutor explained, the military opposition shouldered "a huge burden of guilt" because "the blood of innocent German soldiers" had been "pointlessly spilled as a result of their treasonous actions."[47] The name of this prosecutor was Erich Günther Topf—the former SA *Rottenführer* who had questioned the charges brought against Remer in Brunswick in the first place and whom Bauer had transferred to Lüneburg as a disciplinary measure.

Bauer's charge against Remer rested on the premise that there was one single historical truth and only one legally valid perspective on the German resistance. The judges didn't accept this premise, however. In fact, they didn't take any side in the debate on whether the July 20 plotters had committed treason, nor did they consider it a punishable offense, as petitioned for by Bauer, to advocate a position in this debate. Instead, they ruled that the debate went beyond black-and-white legal issues, involving moral values that vary from individual to individual. In other words, whether the July 20 plotters were traitors was to some extent a matter of opinion, and Otto Ernst Remer was entitled to his view, the judges concluded, though they ruled that the manner in which he had expressed this view was overly drastic. Thus, while they cleared him of defamation, which involves telling an objective lie, they sentenced him to three months' imprisonment for "insulting" the resistance fighters. Later, the Federal Constitutional Court took a similarly cautious approach—and an approach that favors freedom of speech—in its ruling on the matter.[48]

Ultimately, the subtleties of the Brunswick court's verdict had little influence on German attitudes toward the July 20 plotters. Instead, it was scenes from the trial that played a critical role in changing people's perceptions in 1952. Bauer therefore didn't view the lenient sentence imposed on Remer as a defeat. He had presented testimony from respected experts supporting his argument that the conspirators' actions were not just legitimate but legal too. This helped bring about a shift in the public debate, a shift that went far beyond the legal discussion taking place within the courtroom itself. As soon as planning for the trial had got underway in the summer of 1951, Bauer had issued a series of public statements designed to fuel this debate.

In one of these statements, Bauer said that resistance fighters within the military hadn't broken their oath of allegiance to Hitler, as this oath was "immoral" in the first place. "Before Hitler, swearing absolute obedience to a person—rather than to God, the law, or one's fatherland—was legally unprecedented in Germany, not to mention immoral," he later explained.[49] According to the German Civil Code, agreements *contra bonos mores* are invalid. The Hitler oath therefore had no legal validity, Bauer argued, and no one should feel bound to it. Bauer's aim here was to encourage the millions of people in Germany who had remained loyal to their oath to break it now, years later. But his comments were misunderstood and triggered widespread outrage. The headline "Germany Debates the Oath Issue" appeared in the *Neue Zeitung* newspaper in November 1951.[50] Just a few days previously, a correspondent for the *Süddeutsche Zeitung* wrote, "Going by the sheer volume of words uttered on the topic, one would think that the German people were interested in nothing last weekend but the status of the soldier in the world."[51]

Bauer didn't seem perturbed by the "deluge of letters" pouring into his office, nor indeed by the fact that these letters contained some of his first death threats.[52] After years of exile, of feeling cut off and consigned to the periphery, he was invigorated by the controversy. His extraordinary quick-wittedness was on full display in the courtroom; one reporter described him as an "animated" prosecutor who "responded with gusto to the defense counsel's constant digs."[53] Meanwhile, back in his office, Bauer read every letter he received and responded personally to many of them. One letter, written on official Bundestag paper and signed "A Member of the Bundestag," stated, "If one swears an oath, one may never break it. Anyone [who breaks an oath] is a perjurer, a traitor, and a public enemy. . . . If, calling God as my witness, I swear allegiance to the constitution or the sovereign, I must adhere to this oath no matter what happens, otherwise I violate my oath and commit high treason."[54] In another outraged letter, the father of a fallen Wehrmacht soldier accused Bauer of dishonoring the dead. Bauer replied as follows:

> In order to show you, [a father] who lost your son in the war, how Hitler and his soldiers' oath dragged young people into conflict, please allow me to quote from a letter written by a simple farmer to his parents. . . . It is dated February 3, 1944. "Dear Mother and Father, I am writing to share with you the sad news that I have been sentenced to death together with Gustav G. We refused

to sign up to the SS, so they sentenced us to death. . . . We would both rather die than besmirch our conscience with such terrible deeds. I know what kind of things the SS has to do. My dear parents, although it is difficult for me and you, . . . please forgive me and pray for me. If I were to die in the war with a bad conscience, you would be just as sad."[55]

Another member of the public wrote, "Dear Attorney General, I have no idea how the court will rule in the case against Mr. Remer. I ask that Mr. Remer not be judged at all for fulfilling his soldierly duty to his countrymen and leaders on July 20, 1944. Any such judgment would be unfathomable to any former soldier."[56]

Of course, Bauer had no intention of prosecuting Remer for being obedient on July 20; rather, he wanted to defend the disobedience of Hitler's attackers and put an end to their vilification. To convince the Germans that it had been morally right to resist the Nazis, Bauer invoked a palatable figure with whom they would be able to identify: Claus Schenk Graf von Stauffenberg, the nationalistic German aristocrat who had been loyal to Hitler for many years before joining the resistance.

"My Schoolmate Stauffenberg": A Closing Argument That Made History

"Your honors."[57] So began Bauer's final address to the court, a closing argument that made its audience almost forget about Remer, according to a reporter from *Die Zeit*.[58] This grave, superbly crafted speech was carefully tailored to Bauer's real audience: the Germans listening to their radios and reading their newspapers at home. Using the word "we" repeatedly and invoking the "fatherland" five times, Bauer continued as follows:

> The prosecution has not put the former Major Remer on trial for thwarting the resistance on July 20, 1944. Mr. Remer, one of the leaders of the SRP, is being tried for defaming and insulting the July 20 resistance fighters by calling them traitors.
>
> What seemed opaque to many on July 20, 1944, has now become transparent, and what was then seen as an understandable mistake has now revealed itself as sheer spite, malicious intent, and deliberate sabotage of our democracy.
>
> The aim of this trial is not to sow discord, but rather to build bridges and foster reconciliation, not by making lazy compromises, but by having a democratic, independent court answer the question "Were the July 20 conspirators traitors?" The Federal Republic of Germany and the state of Lower Saxony have entrusted this criminal court in Brunswick with the task of providing an independent and just answer to this question.
>
> The question of whether the July 20 resistance fighters were traitors was answered once before. By abusing judicial procedures, Mr. Freisler—who presided over the Nazi's supreme court in Berlin until "Providence," if you will

excuse the expression, struck Freisler dead, thereby ending his activities as executioner—provided the answer "Yes." [Here, Bauer was referring to the fact that Freisler, Hitler's top judge, died when a beam fell on top of him during an American bombing of his courthouse, RS.]

Today, we wish to "resume" this trial. It now falls to the prosecutors and judges of our constitutional democracy to unreservedly rehabilitate the heroes of July 20. [We must do this] based on the facts known to us today, and based on the law, which applied yesterday, applies today, and will apply forever.

The prosecution calls on the court to convict the defendant of the crimes of defamation and of disparaging the memory of deceased persons within the meaning of Articles 186 and 189 of the Criminal Code.

Bauer's first argument was that disobedience to inhumane laws is Christian. "I could make things easy for myself," he told the packed courtroom, "and simply remind you of the opinions expressed by three experts in theology. They all agree that from the perspective of Protestant and Catholic moral theology, the men of July 20 are not guilty of treason, as their intention was to save their country, not betray it." The matter wasn't quite as straightforward as Bauer made it out to be, however. In fact, it took Bauer a long time to find three theologians he could call to the witness stand. Eventually, he decided on Professor Hans Joachim Iwand and Professor Ernst Wolf—both of whom were members of the Confessing Church, a Protestant anti-Nazi movement—as well as Professor Rupert Angermair, who came from a Catholic seminary in Freiburg. All three held minority views within their churches. Just a few years previously, in 1946, the leaders of the Protestant Church in Hanover had tried to justify its failure to rebel against the Nazis. According to Luther's two kingdoms doctrine, they said, the National Socialist state was an authority the church was obliged to respect. Nazism may have been un-Christian and even anti-Christian, they added, but "we nonetheless demonstrated the necessary external obedience. . . . We . . . believe we have thereby followed Holy Scripture and the teachings of Martin Luther."[59] Bauer deliberately ignored such statements from the clergy. He wanted to promote the opposite view, even if this entailed an arduous search for theologians who would support it.

Bauer's second argument was that disobedience is patriotic. In 1944, the *mens rea* of treason (in other words, the intent a court had to prove in order to secure a conviction) was the intent to "endanger the welfare of the Reich" or "cause grave harm to the Reich." However, Bauer said, addressing the court,

> I don't think anyone in this courtroom would deny that each and every resistance fighter was motivated by the honorable intention of serving his German fatherland. Stauffenberg's dying words were "Long live blessed Germany!" By July 20, the war had been well and truly lost. By July 20, the German people had been completely and utterly betrayed, betrayed by their government, and

the crime of treason can no longer be perpetrated on people who have already been completely and utterly betrayed, just as a dead man can no longer be stabbed to death. It would be pointless to even try. The war had been lost long ago, and the resistance fighters knew it.

To support this argument, Bauer called on testimony from Percy Schramm, a professor from Göttingen University who had been responsible for keeping the Wehrmacht High Command's war diary between 1943 and 1945.

"Any attempt to avert the war, any attempt to shorten the war was an attempt to spare German lives and German homes while improving Germany's standing in the world," Bauer told his audience. In fact, he added, the resistance fighters hadn't even violated the law. The Enabling Act of 1933 had been unconstitutional, Bauer said, as the government had only managed to secure the two-thirds majority required to pass the act in the Reichstag by unconstitutionally rescinding the Communist Party's mandate. Thus, Bauer continued:

> The Nazi state was inherently illegitimate. This will not be news to the jurists of our constitutional democracy. Since 1945, several courts, including this very criminal court, the Regional High Court in Cologne, and the Federal Court of Justice, have declared the Third Reich to be a system of violence and despotism.
>
> Unfortunately, it must be pointed out that Hitler usurped his way to becoming not only the world's foremost warlord, but also the world's foremost war criminal, and, based on our Criminal Code, the worst criminal we have ever had. I refer you to the Federal Court of Justice's Judgments in Civil Matters, Volume 3, page 107, which presents our highest court's most recent judgment on this matter. Here, we read that "a positive law reaches its limits when it runs counter to the generally recognized rules of international or natural law, or when it runs counter to justice to such an unacceptable extent that as an improper law, it must give way to justice. If a positive law in any way denies the principle of equality, then the law lacks legal status and cannot be considered a law at all." These words from the Federal Court of Justice apply to all legislation enacted by the Third Reich. I therefore argue that it is not possible to commit treason against an illegitimate state such as the Third Reich.
>
> According to Article 53 of the Criminal Code, everyone has the right to defend himself against an illegitimate state that kills tens of thousands of people a day. Everyone had the right to defend Jews or foreign intelligentsia who were in danger. All acts of resistance are therefore covered by Article 53 of the Criminal Code.

Bauer's most compelling argument was his third one: the argument that disobeying a tyrant is a quintessentially German act. This argument was directed in particular at the blustering German nationalists on the rise again in Lower Saxony:

> The defense has stated that in this courtroom, we administer German justice. That is absolutely true; we administer German justice here. And that is

precisely why I feel obliged to discuss what exactly ancient Germanic justice was. I am reminded of the following lofty passage from the *Sachsenspiegel* [a law book dating to the Holy Roman Empire, RS]: "One must resist one's king if the latter does wrong, or help oppose him in every way, even if he is one's relative or lord. Doing so does not mean one has abandoned one's duty of allegiance."

In the debate surrounding July 20, it is time to recall ancient German democracy and the Germanic right of resistance. Snorri Sturluson tells us the following bloody story: "When, ignoring the wishes of his people, the king refused to make peace with the Norwegians, the old lawspeaker from Tiundaland spoke: This king refuses to speak to anyone and hears only what he wants to. Therefore, we, the farmers, want you, King Olaf, to make peace. If you do not carry out our wish, we will kill you, and we will refuse to tolerate strife and unlawfulness any longer. This is what our forefathers did. They threw five kings into a well at Mulathing because these kings demonstrated the same arrogance as you do toward us." This is the pithy language of the German past. In German law, the oath of allegiance was a pledge of subjects' loyalty, but obedience and certainly unconditional obedience were alien concepts to the Germans. The Germanic peoples said that while slaves had to be obedient, free men are obliged only to be loyal, and loyalty requires reciprocity.

The principles of German law correspond to what our theologians have told us about the theological situation. The right of resistance evolved by way of the *Magna Carta* to eventually be enshrined by the corporate state. In the *Magna Carta*, the people's right of resistance was concentrated and monopolized in the hands of twenty-five English barons, who were the precursors to the corporate state, the constitutional monarchy, and parliamentary democracy. The people's and the individual's right of resistance was suspended here because the rights of the people and the individual were well protected by the estates and by parliament. The right of resistance goes into abeyance in a state under the rule of law—as long as human rights are protected, as long as there are opportunities to express opposition, as long as parliament is allowed to pass legislation, as long as independent courts are allowed to do their work, and as long as there is a separation of powers. However, the right of resistance comes back into play if any of these prerequisites is no longer in place.

Germany's constitutional monarchy and democracy held the right of resistance in abeyance. In an irony of fate, Adolf Hitler's *Mein Kampf* reminded the German people of this right. One of our witnesses, Mr. Kleffel, provided an exceptionally dramatic description of how Goerdeler [one of the anti-Nazi conspirators of July 20, RS], when asked about the legality of the resistance, went to his bookcase and quoted directly from *Mein Kampf*: "Authority of the state can never be an end in itself; for, if it were, all kinds of tyranny would be inviolable and sacred."

But I have no intention of letting Hitler have the last word. The most eloquent words on the people's and the individual's right of resistance are to be found in Schiller's *William Tell*:

> Nay, there are bounds unto oppression's power;
> For when its victim nowhere finds redress,

> And when his burden may no more be borne,
> With hopeful courage he appeals to Heaven,
> And grasps from thence his everlasting rights,
> Which still inalienable hang on high,
> Inviolable as the stars themselves.
> Then nature's primal state returns once more,
> When man in conflict meets his fellow-man;
> And at the last, when nothing else avails,
> The sword's fierce surgery must cure his ills.
> Our dearest treasures we can yet defend
> 'Gainst tyranny.[60]

"Your honors," Bauer concluded, "as I recite these words from [*William Tell*] here today, . . . I am transported back many, many years to a humanist high school in Stuttgart." As a young pupil at the school, Bauer had helped stage a production of this classic play, he explained. Also working on the production was none other than Claus Schenk Graf von Stauffenberg, a boy four years younger than Bauer.[61] Bauer still felt a personal connection to "my schoolmate" Stauffenberg, he said, when he recalled the proud spirit of Schiller's play and the ancient tradition of "our venerable German law."

The closing words of Bauer's speech to the court were somewhat economical with the truth, giving the misleading impression that the young Fritz Bauer had been a fully integrated member of a community of equals at his high school in Stuttgart. Bauer conveniently avoided mentioning the fact that his aristocratic schoolmate Stauffenberg would one day cheer on Germany's dictator. Moreover, he avoided mentioning his Jewishness, thereby heeding the advice given to him by the Americans back in 1945.

Bauer didn't petition for a specific sentence for Remer, further indication that he regarded the latter as a figure of secondary importance. It's unlikely that Bauer was particularly troubled by the meager three months imposed on Remer for insulting the July 20 conspirators, or by the fact that Remer, who managed to flee overseas soon after the trial, never even served this sentence. Of far greater importance to Bauer was the vigorous debate he managed to trigger from his little courtroom in Brunswick, a debate that had a profound impact throughout the country.

Notes

1. See *Der Spiegel*, "Remer-Partei. Schickt deutsche Maurer," May 2, 1951; and Ernst Riggert, "Das letzte Aufgebot," *Die Welt*, April 26, 1951.

2. See Norbert Frei, *1945 und wir. Das Dritte Reich im Bewußtsein der Deutschen* (Munich: C. H. Beck, 2005), 137.

3. Ibid.
4. Quoted in Michael Freund, "Der Angeklagte aus Versehen. Der Prozess gegen Remer," *Die Gegenwart*, March 15, 1951, 166.
5. Ibid., 167.
6. Quoted in Frei, *1945 und wir*, 138.
7. See ibid.
8. Warlo, interview by author.
9. Kramer, interview by author.
10. See Claudia Fröhlich, *"Wider die Tabuisierung des Ungehorsams." Fritz Bauers Widerstandsbegriff und die Aufarbeitung von NS-Verbrechen* (Frankfurt am Main: Campus, 2006), 37f.
11. Bauer to Schöttle, October 12, 1948.
12. Bauer to Horkheimer, March 2, 1954, call number I/2 230, Max Horkheimer Archive, Stadt-und Universitätsbibliothek Frankfurt am Main.
13. See duplicate of certificate, Hanover, March 24, 1950, in Fritz Bauer's judiciary personnel file, call number NL-08/03, Fritz Bauer Institute Archives, Frankfurt am Main.
14. See minutes of a meeting in the ministry, January 27, 1949, quoted in Fröhlich, "Wider die Tabuisierung des Ungehorsams," 61.
15. Bauer, "Justiz als Symptom." (Parenthesis in the original.)
16. Bauer to Schumacher, April 24, 1949, Kurt Schumacher's papers, file 165, Archiv der sozialen Demokratie, Bonn. In this letter, Bauer writes that he has been in the country for two weeks.
17. Sender Freies Berlin, ed., *Um uns die Fremde. Die Vertreibung des Geistes 1933–45* (Berlin: Haude & Spener, 1968), 69.
18. Bauer to Schumacher, May 23, 1949, Schumacher's papers, file 71, Archiv der sozialen Demokratie, Bonn.
19. See Alfred Marx, *Das Schicksal der jüdischen Juristen in Württemberg und Hohenzollern 1933–1945*, 3f; and "Robert Josef Bloch," Gegen das Vergessen: Stolpersteine für Stuttgart, accessed May 10, 2013, http://www.stolpersteine-stuttgart.de/index.php?docid=251.
20. Kurt Hiller, *Leben gegen die Zeit*, vol. 1 (Reinbek: Rowohlt, 1969), 61–63.
21. See typewritten membership list of 1948, papers of the FWV member Rudolf Zielenziger, Leo Baeck Institute, New York. Accessible at: http://archive.org/details/rudolfzielenziger.
22. See circular from the Bund der Freien Wissenschaftlichen Vereinigungen, August 1948, papers of the FWV member Rudolf Zielenziger, Leo Baeck Institute, New York. Rosenthal signed off the circular with the words "warmest FWV wishes," describing himself as the "first president of the revived A. H. Association" (A. H. stands for "Alte Herren," or "Old Gentlemen"). The author of the typewritten membership list of 1948 already knew that "Fritz Bauer (born 7.16.1903)" lived at "Maltagade 15, Copenhagen" following his return from Sweden, which indicates that Bauer had been in touch. The FWV was never revived at universities after 1945.
23. "Erich Simon, FWV Theresienstadt. Zum Gedächtnis der Toten, Rundschreiben des Bundes der Freien Wissenschaftlichen Vereinigungen, August 1948," papers of Rudolf Zielenziger, Leo Baeck Institute, New York. Erich Simon studied in Berlin. It is possible but not certain that he and Bauer met each other during their studies at a national FWV convention.
24. See *Monatsbericht des Bundes Freier Wissenschaftlicher Vereinigungen*, May/June 1923, 6.

25. "Erich Simon, F.W.V. Theresienstadt. Zum Gedächtnis der Toten, Rundschreiben des Bundes der Freien Wissenschaftlichen Vereinigungen."
26. The typewritten membership list of 1948 (see above) listed members' professions.
27. Quoted in file 1 Bv 1/51-H6-Urkunde Nr. 237, December 28, 1951, Landesinformationsdienst des Landes Schleswig-Holstein.
28. See Hans-Ulrich Ludewig, "Nazi-Verbrecher Klagges ohne Einsicht. Der ehemalige Braunschweiger Ministerpräsident erhielt–nach vorzeitiger Haftentlassung–600 DM Rente monatlich," *Braunschweiger Zeitung*, May 8, 2012.
29. See *Entscheidungen des Bundesgerichtshofs in Strafsachen*, vol. 12, 36 (Cologne: Carl Heymanns Verlag, 1959), 40f.
30. Quoted in ibid., 41f.
31. Ibid., 40f.
32. Bauer, "Justiz als Symptom," 367f.
33. See Fröhlich, "Wider die Tabuisierung des Ungehorsams," 104.
34. Michael Freund, "Der Angeklagte aus Versehen," 168.
35. Guido Zöller, "Rehabilitierung der Widerstandskämpfer," *Rhein-Neckar-Zeitung*, March 14, 1952.
36. See Fröhlich, "Wider die Tabuisierung des Ungehorsams," 105.
37. See Frei, *1945 und wir*, 135f.
38. While on the campaign trail, Remer had accused the German government of securing "alternative quarters" it could retire to should war break out. The state's attorney's office of Verden—a town within the jurisdiction of one of Lower Saxony's other attorney generals—therefore prosecuted Remer and succeeded in having him sentenced to four months in prison. See Frei, *1945 und wir*, 135.
39. Meyer-Velde, interview by author.
40. Theodor Heuss, speech delivered at the Freie Universität Berlin, June 19, 1954, quoted in Olivier Guez, *Heimkehr der Unerwünschten. Eine Geschichte der Juden in Deutschland nach 1945* (Munich: Piper, 2011), 131.
41. See Peter Steinbach, "Einführung," in Eberhard Zeller, *Oberst Claus Graf Stauffenberg. Ein Lebensbild*, XVIII.
42. See "Report No. 114 (5 December 1951)," in *Public Opinion in Semisovereign Germany: The HICOG Surveys, 1949–1955*, ed. Anna Merrit and Richard Merrit (Illinois: University of Illinois, 1980), 147; and "Report No. 167" (January 12, 1953), in ibid., 198.
43. Michael Freund, "Der Angeklagte aus Versehen," 168.
44. See Frei, *1945 und wir*, 135; and Fröhlich, "Wider die Tabuisierung des Ungehorsams," 49f.
45. Theodor Heuss, "Zum 20. Juli 1944," *Bulletin des Presse-und Informationsamtes der Bundesregierung*, July 19, 1952, 927.
46. Rothfels to Bauer, December 13, 1951, quoted in Fröhlich, "Wider die Tabuisierung des Ungehorsams," 48.
47. Cited in Fröhlich, "Wider die Tabuisierung des Ungehorsams," 56–61.
48. See the Federal Court of Justice's ruling of May 8, 1952, published in *Neue Juristische Wochenschrift* (1953): 1,183: "Anyone who refers to those who resisted the Nazis as 'traitors' or 'traitors to the Fatherland' cannot intend these designations to be interpreted as statements of fact." The Federal Court of Justice's ruling of May 6, 1958, came to a similar conclusion: "Anyone who refers to members of the resistance as 'traitors' is guilty of insulting [the resistance fighters] but not of defaming [them]" (see *Entscheidungsband* 11, 329). The court's ruling of May 22, 1959, on the use of the word "traitor" as a term of abuse reiterates this view; see file

number 1 StE 3/58. Decades later, this liberal attitude was again evident in the German judiciary's response to left-wing statements, most notably in the case of a man arrested for displaying a bumper sticker with a famous line by Kurt Tucholsky: "Soldiers are murderers." In 1994, the Federal Constitutional Court ruled that in this case, "a conviction for incitement to hatred and offensiveness" limited freedom of speech, because "its interpretation of a sticker's message" was "based solely on the [German Criminal Code] and failed to take into account the colloquial meaning of the contested statement." See the Federal Constitutional Court's chamber decision of August 25, 1994, file number 1 BvR 1423/92, Archive of the Federal Constitutional Court, Karlsruhe.

49. Bauer, "Eine Grenze hat Tyrannenmacht. Plädoyer im Remer-Prozess" (1952), published in *Die Humanität der Rechtsordnung*, ed. Perels and Wojak, 176.

50. Quoted in Fröhlich, "Wider die Tabuisierung des Ungehorsams," 78.

51. Quoted in ibid.

52. Bauer to Margarethe von Hase, March 21, 1952, call number 61 Nds. Fb. 1, Nr. 24/4 Niedersächsisches Staatsarchiv, Hanover.

53. Michael Freund, "Der Angeklagte aus Versehen," 168.

54. Anonymous letter to Bauer, February 6, 1952, quoted in Fröhlich, "Wider die Tabuisierung des Ungehorsams," 79.

55. Bauer to Walther V., March 19, 1952, call number 61 Nds. Fb. 1, Nr. 24/3, Niedersächsisches Staatsarchiv, Hanover; quoted in ibid., 80.

56. Paul A. to Bauer, March 15, 1952, quoted in ibid.

57. The closing argument is not quoted in its entirety here; instead, the quotations that follow comprise key excerpts. The full speech was published with the title "Eine Grenze hat Tyrannenmacht. Plädoyer im Remer-Prozess" in *Die Humanität der Rechtsordnung*, ed. Perels and Wojak, 169–179.

58. See Jan Molitor (pseudonym used by Josef Müller-Marein, who later became editor in chief of *Die Zeit*), "Die Schatten der Toten vom 20. Juli. Ehrenrettung der Widerstandskämpfer–Der Remer-Prozeß in Braunschweig," *Die Zeit*, March 13, 1952.

59. Quoted in Fröhlich, "Wider die Tabuisierung des Ungehorsams," 89.

60. Translation of *Wilhelm Tell* by Maj. Gen. Patrick Maxwell (London: Walter Scott, Ltd., n.d.), 69.

61. All the major biographies of Stauffenberg confirm that he took part in theater productions in his youth. Wolfgang Venohr and Eberhard Zeller mention that he played the role of Stauffacher in *William Tell*. See Wolfgang Venohr, *Stauffenberg. Symbol des Widerstands. Eine politische Biographie*, 3rd edition (Munich: Herbig, 2000), 29f.; and Eberhard Zeller, *Oberst Claus Graf Stauffenberg*, 6.

7

"MURDERERS AMONG US"

The Psychology of a Prosecutor

What's the Point of Punishment?

Philosophically, he was an antiauthoritarian defender of reform and reintegration and an opponent of retribution and revenge. In postwar legal debates, he argued that if a perpetrator no longer poses a risk to others, then there's no point in punishing him or her. During the Weimar period, this view had been attacked for being soft on crime. Bauer responded to such criticism in his polemical book *Das Verbrechen und die Gesellschaft* (Crime and Society, 1957), where he contended that "no sensible person inflicts punishment because wrong has been done, but to prevent wrong from being done again."[1] In the 1950s and 1960s—a defining period in West Germany's legal development—he championed this view more vociferously than any other German jurist.

Bauer didn't shy away from strident tones, pouring scorn on a justice system that had been claiming since 1945 to be committed to preventing crime yet at the same time continued to exact retribution. The "dual-track" model upon which the German Criminal Code was based—whereby judges are expected to both punish those who are guilty and deter those who are dangerous from causing harm—was "a sphinx," he wrote, "half-lion, half-human."[2] As chairman of the SPD's postwar working group on criminal justice reform, Bauer demanded that the entire system be radically overhauled so that it no longer sought any form of retribution for past actions. Prisons should have one objective and one objective only, he argued: to reform prisoners. Similarly, preventing future harm should be a judge's only concern when deciding how long a criminal was to spend behind bars. This would mean imposing very short sentences on perpetrators who posed no risk of reoffending and long ones on those who seemed likely to commit crime again. Criminal judges should look forward and not back: This was Bauer's basic philosophy.

In practice, though, Bauer's work centered on looking to the past.

How are we to make sense of this paradox? What was the point of the Frankfurt Auschwitz trial if not to exact retribution for past crimes, to make Nazi criminals atone, to get some sense of payback? These former Nazis no longer posed any threat to society. They were inherently obedient people who were as compliant to the new system as they had been to the old one. They had certainly demonstrated many failings in their lives, but they could never be accused of failing to follow the rules. There was no reason to be concerned about their *Resozialisierung* (resocialization)—their reintegration into German society—after 1945.

Thousands of murderers slotted back into German society after the war, going on to lead apparently unobjectionable lives as pharmacists, postal workers, and the like. Not all scholars consider the postwar conduct of such former Nazis to be beyond legal reproach, however. "In fact," argues the political scientist Joachim Perels, "the behavior of almost all Nazi perpetrators during the Auschwitz trial gives the lie to the notion that they became law-abiding citizens after 1945. Most of those convicted of serious mass crimes and individual acts of sadism professed their innocence in their closing statements."[3] The apparent absence of any sense of guilt on the part of many Nazi criminals is certainly problematic. Under the rule of law, however, defendants are presumed innocent until they are proven guilty, and they have a legal right to protest this innocence. One can hardly impugn their current or future lawfulness simply because they exercise this right. If one defines "resocialization" as reintegration into a life that outwardly abides by the law—and the state can't demand any more than this—then one must acknowledge that most Nazi perpetrators had already been successfully resocialized by the 1960s. In working to ensure that the criminal pasts of these men caught up with them, in uprooting them from their unremarkable lives and destroying their now harmless existences, didn't Fritz Bauer contradict his own progressive philosophy of punishment, which was predicated on looking forward, not back?

Many people—and by no means just reactionary jurists—criticized Bauer for this apparent inconsistency.[4] It didn't help that Bauer was so intransigent. In August 1963, he told a reporter that there was never any place for retributivism, not even in the trials of those who oversaw the terror of the concentration camps. "Most of the state prosecutors who have been dealing with this horrific subject matter for years [aren't seeking revenge]," he added, "because they know, of course, that vengeance and retribution can neither bring millions of people back from the dead nor stop the tears from falling."[5] In any case, who could honestly believe that it's possible to exact retribution for the Nazis' heinous crimes? What kind of earthly punishment could adequately compensate for the genocidal acts perpetrated in Auschwitz? Surely not the paltry "ten minutes of jail time per victim," the average sentence for Nazi murderers, according to a rumor that went around in 1962.[6] And ultimately, what would it change now, Bauer asked, "if forty more men went to prison?"[7]

Bauer's apparent failure to take his own words to their logical conclusion vexed several observers. Even Herbert Jäger, a young admirer of Bauer's who worked as a junior law professor at the time, claimed that in practice, and especially in the trials that were most important to him, Bauer abandoned his radical philosophy of prevention as the only legitimate purpose of punishment.[8] The philosopher and sociologist Theodor W. Adorno also believed that there was an intractable discrepancy between Bauer's thinking and practice. "Justice that is based on theoretical reflection" ought not to "shy away" from accepting this discrepancy, Adorno wrote in a text that otherwise praises Bauer.[9]

But in fact, in practice as a prosecutor, Bauer did remain committed to the principle of prevention—just not in the obvious sense of the word. When seeking convictions for concentration camp guards, for example, his aim wasn't to prevent those specific individuals from committing the same crimes again. Rather, he hoped that subjecting the dark Nazi past to the courtroom's harsh glare would help the wider German public learn from the mistakes of history. He vigorously, and often bluntly, insisted that this was the ultimate objective of his criminal trials.[10] Such trials "can and must open the German people's eyes to what happened and teach them how to behave," he said.[11] On other occasions, Bauer's choice of words was a little more understated: by examining genocidal horrors, he said, the trials could provide valuable "historical, legal, and moral lessons."[12]

Germany was in dire need of such lessons, Bauer believed. "You can draft clauses, you can write articles, you can create the best constitutions," he told a group of students in 1964. "But what you really need are the right people putting these things into action." He divided the Germans who had supported the Nazi regime into three categories: obedient types who followed the rules, those who supported the Nazis because it was advantageous for them to do so, and true devotees who willingly embraced an "antihuman" ideology. The latter was "probably the largest group, which people tend to forget in today's discussions," Bauer claimed. "The question is, what do we do with these people? And this question doesn't just concern the twenty-two [defendants in the Frankfurt Auschwitz trial]; it also concerns fifty million, or to be more accurate, seventy million other Germans." (Seventy million was the approximate population of West Germany and East Germany combined.) Bauer maintained that the real purpose of criminal trials, which always centered on individual cases, was to share lessons with the wider populace. The more observers learned, the less often the lessons would have to be repeated, until eventually such trials would no longer be necessary, he believed. "We wouldn't need to extend statutes of limitations if we just learned the right lessons from the few trials that have already taken place," Bauer insisted.[13]

He thereby managed to reconcile the apparent contradiction between his philosophy and his work as a prosecutor. At the same time, he revealed that his antiauthoritarian views on punishment had a tough, uncompromising side. The twenty-two defendants in the Auschwitz trial were "really just scapegoats," he admitted; a few of them needed to be put in the dock in order to help the people sitting in the gallery learn their lessons.[14] The defendants were therefore "little more than a means to an end."[15]

"I Knew What Company I Wanted to Keep": Bauer's Vision of a Humane Justice System

Bauer's fascination for legal theory was first awakened by his discovery of a revolutionary idea promoted by left-wing jurists and criminal lawyers in the early years of the twentieth century. At the heart of this idea was the belief that punishment in all its forms needed to pursue a new objective: preventing crime. In the early years of the Weimar Republic, the legal system was the subject of intense debate, not just in parliament but also among scholars. Germany had experienced a population explosion over the previous decades. Small towns had transformed into teeming industrial cities with a new social class: the workers. As these workers' living and working conditions deteriorated, crime rates soared. The state responded by erecting more and more prisons, houses of correction, and workhouses. Franz von Liszt, a professor of criminal law in Berlin (and a cousin of the famous composer), called these institutions "breeding grounds for vice" and "colleges of crime." At the turn of the century, Liszt delivered a blistering attack on the traditional German criminal justice system. "Punishment that promotes crime ... is the final, ripest fruit" of the "retributive righteousness" at the heart of this system, he argued.[16]

Long before Bauer's student days, Liszt had been a member of the FWV fraternity. He later sent notes bearing messages like "Keep moving forward—that is our solution" to subsequent generations of FWV brothers, writing "FWV EM," the acronym reserved for honorary fraternity members, after his signature ("EM" standing for *Ehrenmitglied*, or honorary member).[17] The SPD politician Gustav Radbruch—a close friend of Bauer's doctoral supervisor, Professor Geiler—had studied under Liszt.[18] When Bauer took up his own studies, Radbruch had just been appointed as minister of justice, and the newspapers carried daily reports on his attempts to put Liszt's calls for radical transformation into practice. As a student, Bauer followed these developments with excitement.

Bauer devoured Radbruch's books over the course of his studies. "The *Corpus Juris* was too heavy for me to take out into Heidelberg's blooming spring landscapes," he explained, but "in the woods surrounding the palace, I read with great emotion and excitement" *Introduction to Jurisprudence* (1910), a work demonstrating Radbruch's exceptional skills as a writer.[19] Bauer heavily underlined the book's strongest arguments. (Throughout his life, Bauer treated books in a manner "any bibliophile would consider sacrilege," his friend Manfred Amend once said.[20]) Bauer later recalled, "I knew what company I wanted to keep."[21]

Radbruch and Liszt broke with a powerful tradition in German jurisprudence. For conservative adherents of philosophers such as Immanuel Kant and Georg Wilhelm Friedrich Hegel, the justice system's only objective should be to exact retribution for crimes committed. This retribution should take the form of ceremonial, symbolic acts detached from questions of purpose or social consequences, they believed. Kant and Hegel saw the act of punishment as a clear, logical, and strict "restoration" of the law. Crime, they argued, repudiates the law, and so punishment symbolically cancels out this repudiation. According to Hegel's well-known articulation of this idea, crime is the "negation" of the law, and punishment is the "negation of the negation." Pragmatic concerns should play no role in judges' decisions, even if a country's workhouses are overflowing and the penal system is destroying lives, the argument went. Public opinion should be disregarded, as should the social and individual circumstances that may have driven someone to a crime and may indeed drive him or her to it again. Would a sentence result in fewer crimes being committed in future? Or would it further exacerbate a criminal's circumstances, thereby driving him or her to even more criminal acts? It didn't matter. Such questions ought to have no bearing on the ceremonial act of retribution, Kant and Hegel believed, because this act serves a higher, "metaphysical" cause: the law itself.[22]

In the first year of his studies, Bauer gave a speech so critical of Kant that some of his fraternity brothers felt compelled to jump to the philosopher's defense.[23] In the speech, Bauer expressed anger at how "Kant's leap into metaphysics" had paved the way for the conservatism of the German criminal justice system, which took "pride in its lack of realism, a lack it calls 'idealism.'"[24] Later, Bauer would illustrate his point by recounting a satirical short story by the English essayist G. K. Chesterton featuring a judge who says, "I sentence you to three years' imprisonment, under the firm, and solemn, and God-given conviction, that what you require is three months at the seaside."[25]

Liszt and Radbruch argued that there was only one sound reason for the state to get involved when citizens committed unlawful acts against each other, and that was to prevent such acts from being committed again in the future.[26]

Prevention rather than retribution: this was the idea that sparked Bauer's passion for criminal law. "Franz von Liszt coined the phrase, 'Social policy is the best criminal policy,'" Bauer wrote, "and Radbruch criticized the justice system's dubious task: to make the criminal pay the price for [the state's] failed social policies. The sad truth is that if the amount of money it costs to hold a trial had been invested before the crime, it would very often have prevented the crime from being committed in the first place!"[27]

As justice minister, Radbruch encouraged judges to examine the individuals behind the crimes with the aim of "edifying" or at least "containing" these criminals. This didn't necessarily mean perpetrators would get lighter sentences, but it would result in greater benefits for society as a whole, Radbruch believed. Had the individual in question simply lost his way, or was he a dangerous serial offender who had to be locked away until he no longer posed a threat? According to Liszt, crime statistics "show that each new conviction increases the likelihood that more crimes will be committed. I would also argue that the more severe a sentence is, . . . the faster recidivism occurs. I would put it like this: If a youth or adult commits a crime and we let him walk, it is less likely that he will reoffend than if we were to punish him. If what I have said is true, . . . it clearly exposes the utter failure and bankruptcy of our entire criminal justice system."[28]

Liszt's statistical analysis finds little credence among contemporary criminologists. Experts no longer see the correlation between severe sentences and high rates of recidivism as proof that tougher sentences directly lead to more recidivism. In fact, the opposite may be true; it's possible that judges impose tougher sentences on precisely those criminals they (accurately) identify as being highly likely to reoffend. But despite such shortcomings, Liszt's contribution to the discipline of criminology is widely recognized today, particularly as he was one of the first scholars to examine empirical data on how the justice system impacts on society.

The principle of prevention didn't begin to have a major impact on German legislation until the 1960s, long after Radbruch's death. In that decade, Bauer, by now a high-profile attorney general, took up Radbruch's mantle to become one of the principle's foremost advocates. Bauer didn't add any new philosophical insights to the ideas advanced by pioneers such as Liszt and Radbruch, but he did communicate these ideas in eloquent, politically astute, and often witty ways.

Kant and Hegel believed that every crime is an act of free will driven by ill intent and that the state is therefore entitled to unleash its full wrath in avenging such crimes. Bauer, however, found no evidence to support this belief in real life. "All the great tragedies and novels understand the influence exerted by age and sex, by background and character," he wrote. "They portray the passions that grip human beings and the environments people get trapped in. [Life is] one inescapable blow followed by another inescapable counterblow, and what is tragic is the inexorability and ineluctability, the unbending logic of fate."[29]

The German justice system had taken the easy route, Bauer argued, in ignoring the role played by society in determining the individual's actions. "The concept of free will is appealing to a civilization that has for millennia been driven by the desire for revenge," he wrote. The concept "is practically an addiction, one that is sustained with great zeal. It is an ideology designed to legitimize retributive justice and ease the guilt humans feel about their aggressive thirst for revenge."[30] To support his point, Bauer quoted Nietzsche, who saw the entire concept of free will as the product of the desire to find other people guilty and punish them.[31] Bauer warned judges not to philosophize about guilt and atonement; ultimately, he said, criminal justice should focus on its therapeutic function, not on "metaphysical speculation and self-righteous hypocrisy. Morals and moralizing are none of its business."[32] However, Bauer wrote elsewhere, "Even if it's true that every action is determined, it doesn't follow that human beings are entirely governed by fate. Genetics and our environment predispose us to behave in certain ways, but that doesn't mean that certain people are predestined to commit crime. The environment can always be changed. The environment is made up of people who can help."[33]

Bauer saw social inequality, frustration, and breakdown as the real causes of crime: "An unlawful act is a symptom pointing to deeper problems. At most, it is the tip of an iceberg towering out of the sea."[34] To illustrate this point, he cited the German philosopher and scientist Georg Christoph Lichtenberg: "It's questionable whether, when we break a murderer on the wheel, we aren't lapsing into precisely the mistake of the child who hits the chair he bumps into."[35] Bauer also invoked Radbruch's well-known aphorism that to be a good jurist, one must have a bad conscience. This bad conscience was probably caused by the fact that German judges had to operate on the premise that the thief, beggar, or pickpocket standing in front of them acted of their own free will, Bauer believed.[36] Most judges knew better than to believe this premise, he said, but they were required to follow the "inhumane rationalism of Kant and Hegel, a rationalism divorced from reality and human nature."[37]

Bauer also drew on the nineteenth-century English writer Samuel Butler to reinforce his critique of retributive justice:

> In *Erewhon: or, Over the Range*, a novel in the style of Swift's *Gulliver*, Samuel Butler describes with quintessential Anglo-Saxon sarcasm a land called "Erewhon" ("nowhere" spelt backwards). In this land, ill people are treated as criminals for being ill. For example, a young man is tried for the crime

of being emaciated. The man is in fact a reoffender, as he had bronchitis the previous year and was a sickly child. The defendant pleads that his parents had also suffered from ill health and that he had recently been involved in a bad accident, but the court refuses to recognize these mitigating circumstances, claiming that examining the many excuses submitted by defendants would divert the court's attention, preventing it from ever arriving at a verdict.[38]

On the Cutting Edge of Justice: Bauer's Experience as a Juvenile Court Judge (1928)

In Stuttgart in the late 1920s, a boy appeared before the judge. "No respectable person wants to waste their time on me," the boy said, looking miserable.

"You think I'm a respectable person?" Judge Bauer asked.

"Yes, I do."

Bauer responded by taking the boy out to Stuttgart's finest café.[39]

On another occasion, Bauer was sitting in his office smoking one of his filterless cigarettes when a teenage boy was brought to him from prison. Bauer's favorite cigarette brands were Roth-Händle and Reval, both of which were manufactured in the southern state of Baden. "If you can smoke Revals, you can eat little children," went a saying at the time, since this was the strongest brand available. When the boy asked if he could have a cigarette too, Bauer reached into his shirt pocket and handed over the entire packet. "Just don't get caught," he said; smoking was forbidden in the prison.[40]

Bauer's sense of pride was evident whenever he recounted these stories to friends. He was particularly proud that juvenile courts had brought to the justice system of the 1920s a belief in the good in people. The idea of special courts for juveniles was very new, having been introduced by Radbruch in 1922. The German judiciary's response to the SPD's progressive reforms was less than enthusiastic, and at Stuttgart's local court, responsibility for juveniles was given to the least-experienced member of staff: Bauer. But Bauer relished his role, first as a juvenile prosecutor and then, from the end of 1928, as a modestly paid assistant juvenile court judge.[41]

The establishment of juvenile courts was the first victory in Radbruch's drive to revolutionize the entire criminal justice system by replacing retribution with prevention. In 1922, Radbruch had tried to reform the adult criminal justice system. He had wanted to abolish workhouses and the death penalty, decriminalize adultery, and liberalize morality laws, but his proposed reforms had been crushed by the parliament. In 1923, Radbruch sent a list of *Reichsgrundsätze*, or "Basic Principles of the Reich," to prison directors throughout the country, informing them that their task was not just to deter prisoners from reoffending by instilling fear but also to resocialize prisoners.[42] However, the prisons failed to put these principles into practice. The only area where Radbruch achieved some degree of success was in juvenile justice.

Juvenile courts were a radical departure for the German justice system. Inspired by Radbruch's modern ideas, the young Bauer saw them as a chance to win over his skeptical colleagues to the new preventive approach. Juvenile courts, he claimed, had already realized what he and other advocates of preventive justice "wish[ed] to put in place for all perpetrators, regardless of age."[43] Juvenile judges didn't see themselves as wrathful avengers. They were more like doctors, reaching a diagnosis and considering a wide range of treatment options before deciding on the best medicine. They could impose any form of punishment they believed would have an edifying effect, whether this be a reprimand, probation, a work order, or detention. The judges' task, Bauer said, was "not so much to tackle the problems young people cause, but rather to identify and treat the problems [young people] have."[44]

Many older judges dismissed this as a cowardly approach to crime—"Softening of the bones is a modern sickness," a prominent retired judge complained in 1928—and even as shoddy jurisprudence.[45] It had long been held that clarity, predictability, and logic were more important in criminal justice than in any other area of the law, but now Radbruch wanted to provide scope for flexibility and creativity. In legal journals of the time, experts explained that juvenile judges should no longer view the law as an unbending set of rules. Instead, juvenile justice ought to be seen as a set of tools. Using their own wisdom and experience to select the tools that work best in specific contexts, judges should bear in mind Radbruch's vision of the ideal judge as someone who adds "a hundredweight of life experience and human insight to a pound of jurisprudence."[46] This new area of law was regarded as infinitely flexible, and as a result, many people doubted the expertise of the young jurists who embraced it. Years later, when Bauer was searching for a position in postwar Germany, he avoided mentioning his work in juvenile justice. When he sent his résumé to a long-serving court president in 1948, for example, he simply made a vague reference to having "worked as a criminal judge."[47]

The vocabulary used in the early days of Germany's juvenile courts—which divided teenage defendants into two categories: "good-natured" and "bad-natured"—may not seem very enlightened by today's standards.[48] Furthermore, the path taken by the juvenile justice system under the Nazis illustrates that the border between rehabilitation and political reprogramming can be troublingly porous.[49] Nevertheless, Bauer remained a lifelong proponent of preventive justice. During a discussion with students in the 1960s, he cited the United States as a paragon of preventive justice in action. In progressive US penal institutions, he said, "There's a period of three or four months between sentencing and punishment when people are thoroughly examined, when twenty-five young men and women walk around in white coats as if they're in a hospital. They carry out all manner of tests to find out what the real cause of a crime is. Is it misanthropy? Could it really be down to an individual's innate sadism, etc.? And in the end, of course, the punishment contains the treatment."[50]

Few progressives today would consider the scenario described by Bauer a humane one. For some time now, the preventive principle has been seen as a double-edged sword. In *Discipline and Punish* (1975), the French philosopher Michel Foucault emphasized the authoritarian nature of prisons that attempt to resocialize their inmates. In fact, he argued, such prisons subjugate their inmates to an even greater degree than other penal institutions, because as well as applying the usual physical constraints, they attempt to remold each prisoner's psyche and character.

Foucault's analysis prompted a phase of self-reflection and self-criticism, causing many on the left of the political spectrum to question the humaneness of the preventive approach promoted by figures such as Radbruch.[51] Bauer didn't live long enough to witness this change in attitude or contribute to the debate. Perhaps the most controversial example of preventive justice in action in Germany is "preventive detention," a form of custody that became increasingly common from the 1990s. Preventive detention allows the state to continue to detain prisoners it deems particularly dangerous after these prisoners have served their sentences. Such detainees can be kept behind bars indefinitely, and potentially for the rest of their lives. The more suspicious of an inmate a prison authority is, the less likely it is that psychiatric and criminological experts will recommend the inmate be released. The controversy surrounding such extreme forms of preventive justice has led many left-wing critics to call for fixed, clearly delimited prison sentences. The Humanist Union, for example, a German civil liberties organization, became highly critical of preventive detention in the 1990s, long after the death of Bauer, who in 1963 had sat on the organization's board of directors.

The Nuremberg Trial (1945): A Shining Example and a Cautionary Tale

In 1945, Bauer was observing closely as the Allies set about the task of turning a courtroom in Nuremberg into the nation's classroom. It was fall, and Europe was by now a colossal cemetery. As propaganda battles between various regimes and political groups raged, millions of people were displaced, confused, traumatized, and alone. Amid this chaos, the Allies knocked down a wall in the main courtroom of Nuremberg's largest courthouse, the Justizpalast, to make room for the international press and prepare a stage for their efforts to uncover not just individual guilt but also the historical processes that led to Nazi atrocities.

Twenty-four defendants had been chosen to stand trial before the International Military Tribunal in Nuremberg—"just enough to fill two rows," Benjamin B. Ferencz, one of the American prosecutors, later joked. There could just as easily have been thirty-three or seventy-seven defendants; given the vast scale of the horror, the number was arbitrary.[52] But the Allies made a virtue of necessity, using the small number of defendants as a means of providing the world with a clear, comprehensible account of what had taken place in Europe. Bauer would later borrow this technique for the Frankfurt Auschwitz trial.

The twenty-four men represented a cross section of the Nazi regime's elite, and so, from the prosecutors' point of view, they stood for the forces that had plunged Europe into the abyss.[53] The defendants had been carefully chosen from a range of political, social, military, and economic domains. They therefore included old national conservatives and people who had helped Hitler rise to power as well as major Nazi leaders. After long discussions, the American, British, Soviet, and French prosecutors also decided to put two bankers and an industrialist in the dock as representatives of those who had bankrolled and profited from the Nazi regime.[54] The presence of these financiers and captains of industry was deemed of such importance that when the industrialist Gustav Krupp fell ill, the prosecutors proposed replacing him with another industrialist: his son, Alfried.[55] The judges rejected this proposal on procedural grounds. Nevertheless, the idea that defendants could simply be swapped reveals a great deal about the primarily symbolic value they held for the prosecutors.

While the number of defendants brought to trial was small enough to create a coherent narrative, the stories that emerged were powerful enough to leave a lasting impression on German collective consciousness and memory. It is no coincidence, writes Mark Drumbl, an American professor of international law, that "sixty years later, the Nuremberg judgment remains a fixed anchor of our children's education."[56] Indeed, the Nuremberg trial had a far greater public impact than the mammoth UN tribunal for the former Yugoslavia, which decades later tried a selection of 164 individuals for war crimes. In contrast to the lengthy, rambling tribunal in The Hague, the tight focus of the Nuremberg trial allowed prosecutors to deliver a clear, stark message from the outset.[57]

Bauer had been eagerly awaiting the trial for some time. He was still in exile in Sweden when he first heard about the Allies' plan to bring the Nazi leadership before a tribunal once the war was over. In anticipation of the tribunal, he wrote a book in Swedish with the programmatic title *Krigsförbrytarna inför domstol* (The War Criminal on Trial, 1944).[58] By providing a sober, legally precise analysis, the book aimed to persuade skeptics in Europe of the importance of bringing Nazi war criminals to trial. It was published in German in October 1945, just before the indictments were read out in the Justizpalast in Nuremberg; Bauer wanted to help a wide readership understand the Allies' objectives.[59] At the time, some critics were accusing the Allies of serving victors' justice: "It is often claimed that the Allies are judging crimes they themselves are implicated in, and indeed that they are a party in the trial," Bauer wrote.[60] There was some truth in this, he acknowledged, but added that such a scenario is by no means uncommon. After all, a thief is judged not by other thieves but by those who have possessions. Some sections of the book provide detailed explanations of the intricacies of international law. Bauer's aim here was not to inform the Allies' legal experts about technicalities they may have been unaware of but to help his German and Scandinavian readers understand the legal framework: "Is it permissible to take hostages and kill them?" for example.[61] And, given that the retreating Wehrmacht had systematically destroyed civilians' food reserves and blown up their stoves with hand grenades, "Are scorched-earth tactics legal?"[62]

Reading Bauer's book, it's easy to imagine how dismayed he must have been when it emerged in 1945 that the Holocaust was not going to be the focus of the Nuremberg trial. "No crime committed during the war can possibly have been worse than this mass extermination, which epitomizes [the Nazis'] cynical contempt for human life," he wrote as he described a massacre he had read about in a Russian memo dated January 6, 1942:[63]

> A large number of Jews, including several women and children of all ages, were rounded up in a Jewish cemetery in Kiev. Before they were gunned down, they were stripped naked and brutally beaten. The first group of Jews was forced to lie down in a grave with their faces facing down into the earth, whereupon these unfortunate victims were shot dead with machine guns. The Germans then shoveled a thin layer of earth over the bodies, made the next batch of victims lie down on top, and the machine gun fire started all over again.[64]

In the German edition of the book, Bauer included a report by Alaric Jacob, the *Daily Express*'s Moscow correspondent, describing the Majdanek extermination camp, which had been liberated on July 23, 1944. Fifty corpses, which the Germans had obviously attempted to incinerate before fleeing, were still lying in the crematorium, Jacob wrote. "Some of the bodies had been dismembered so that they could be squeezed into the ovens more easily. Beside these ovens there was a table made of zinc, which provided running water. This is where the gold fillings were pried out of the corpses."[65]

But the Nuremberg trial focused on battlegrounds rather than concentration camps, as the Allies' central charge was that the defendants had led a war of aggression. World War II had differed from the previous world war in that it wasn't just another power struggle between rival forces, the prosecutors maintained. Instead, they argued, this had been a unilateral crime perpetrated by one state and eventually halted by other states. When a few Eastern European states protested the absence of Holocaust atrocities in the charges, the American chief prosecutor, Robert Jackson, responded: "It is probably very difficult for those of you who have lived under the immediate attack of the Nazis to appreciate the different public psychology that those of us who were in the American government dealt with. The thing that led us to take sides in this war was that we regarded Germany's resort to war as illegal from its outset, as an illegitimate attack on the international peace and order."[66]

One of the Allies' main reasons for setting up the tribunal in the first place was "to give meaning to the war against Germany," Taylor Telford, Jackson's key adviser, explained in a memo in June 1945: "To validate the casualties we have suffered and the destruction and casualties we have caused. To . . . make the war meaningful and valid for the people of the Allied Nations and, it is not beyond hope, for at least some people of the Axis Nations."[67] The Americans argued that if Nazi crimes were punished without trial, "Germany will simply have lost another war," as a US government official named Murray Bernays put it: "The German people will not know the barbarism they have supported, nor will they have any understanding of the criminal character of their conduct and the world's judgment on it."[68] To the British prime minister's astonishment, it was this emphasis on the courtroom's potential to shape future perspectives on history that ultimately won Stalin's support for the trial.

For the most part, the history lessons taught at Nuremberg were restricted to ones that the British, American, Soviet, and French governments wanted to share.[69] Britain pushed for German war crimes against British cities to be examined.[70] The Soviet Union made sure that Hitler's and Stalin's regimes were portrayed as polar opposites, both militarily and morally; the Nazi-Soviet pact of August 1939, which had carved Poland up into German and Soviet spheres of influence, was never mentioned.[71] Due to public pressure in the United States and Great Britain, the Holocaust was eventually referred to in the list of indictments, but it played a marginal role in the trial itself.[72] "The complexities of the concentration camps . . . didn't fit into the plan," Bauer complained some years later.[73]

Bauer had a second criticism. In the following commentary, published in the emigrant newspaper *Deutsche Nachrichten* at the height of the Nuremberg trial, he wrote:

> German anti-Nazis are disappointed that Allied rather than German courts will convict Nazi criminals. They are disappointed not because they think Allied judges lack objectivity or fairness, or because they think [the trial] is an affront to German prestige. There are more important things than national

prestige. They are disappointed because German courts have been denied the opportunity to show the world clearly that the new Germany has reinstated the rule of law, broken with its lawless past, and rejected the Nazi idea that power and the law are the same thing. A state under the rule of law does not control the law; instead, it upholds the law and its citizens' rights.[74]

The above passage shows that Bauer stayed true to his ideal of preventive, future-oriented justice. For him, it was important to confront the past not because the old Germany deserved to be punished but because this confrontation would help build a solid foundation for the new Germany.

Commenting on the Nuremberg verdicts, which were issued on September 30 and October 1, 1946, Bauer wrote: "We have no doubt that the healthy, decent segments of the German population abhor and condemn without reservation the collective crimes of mass murder, the gas chambers, Gestapo torture, and all the barbarism of Hitlerism. The defendants Frank and Schirach [i.e., Hans Frank, governor general of occupied Poland, and Baldur von Schirach, head of Hitler Youth and Gauleiter of Vienna, RS] represent the most shameful events in the history of Germany and the world.... The German people share the judgment of the Nuremberg tribunal and of the world."[75]

It would soon emerge that Bauer was a little premature in vouching for the German population's support for the Nuremberg verdicts. Nevertheless, he was convinced that it would have been preferable for Nazi criminals to have been tried by a German court under German law: "It would be better if the German people administered justice themselves, if the people, and not some learned scholar, replaced the sword of war with the sword of justice. An honest German 'J'accuse' would not 'foul our own nest.' (Our nest has already been fouled, and showing solidarity with the criminals would only foul it even more.) In fact, it would express a commitment to creating a new Germany."[76] In other words, as far as Bauer was concerned, there was still a great deal of work to be done.

"You Should Have Said No": The Prosecutor Who Encouraged People to Break the Law

Criminal proceedings against Nazi criminals "should give us much to think about," Bauer once told a radio interviewer. He continued:

> One of the most important tasks of these trials is not just to present us with the dreadful facts, but to teach us something we completely lost sight of here in Germany over the past century as we contravened the laws and morals of the states around us. Quite simply, it is the principle that has been with us throughout history but was excised from German law in the nineteenth and twentieth centuries. A principle that goes back to Socrates and the Bible: You must obey God rather than man. That is the alpha and omega of every

law. This sentence means that above every law and every command, there is something unshakeable and indestructible: the clear realization that there are certain things on earth that one just cannot do. Firstly, because they are forbidden in the Ten Commandments, and secondly, because they go against all religions and all moral principles.[77]

Arguing that a defendant should have broken the law is a problematic position for a state prosecutor to take. Bauer realized that appealing to the German Criminal Code, which dated back to the German Empire and had been amended by the Weimar Republic, would be of little help when prosecuting Nazi criminals. Though the code had nominally remained in force during the Nazi period, the murder of specific groups had been ordered and legalized by the state. But the fact that the Nazis were powerful enough to turn the law on its head shouldn't prevent a democratic criminal justice system from pursuing prosecutions, Bauer wrote in an article for the *Sozialistische Tribüne* in February 1945.[78] The courts had to call a crime a crime, he argued, and to do so, they couldn't allow themselves to be restricted by the laws that had been in force under the Nazi regime. Freeing themselves of these restrictions might involve performing legal contortions and applying the law in a "revolutionary," retroactive manner, he suggested.[79] This would mean departing from the basic principle of *nullum poena sine lege*, or no punishment without a law (a law in force at the time of the offense, that is), but Bauer believed the end result would be worth it: "If it wishes to flourish and be respected, the new Germany cannot allow its judges to return to being the accomplices of murderers. The line from Goethe's *Faust* is as relevant as ever: 'A judge who cannot punish associates himself in the end with the criminal.'"[80]

Bauer's old hero Gustav Radbruch provided an elegant solution to this legal problem in an essay published in 1946. Here, Radbruch argued that Nazi laws legalizing the Holocaust had been invalid right from the start. These laws demonstrated no fundamental "desire for justice" and refused to recognize the principle of human equality before the law, a principle that forms the very basis of justice. As such, they were never binding, Radbruch argued; as "'flawed laws,' they must yield to justice."[81] Claiming that one had simply obeyed such flawed laws was no excuse and ought to offer no protection from punishment. "And that," Bauer added, "means quite simply that one should have followed the path of passive resistance." In a radio interview, he explained:

> This was taken for granted throughout the German Empire from the Middle Ages, through the early modern period, and well into the modern period. People were taught that if you are told, whether by a statute or an order, to do something unlawful—in other words, something running counter to cardinal principles such as the Ten Commandments, principles that everyone ought to

know—then you must say no. Let me put it rather bluntly: The heroism of the men on the front was celebrated in Germany. There was plenty of evidence of valor and courage against the external enemy. But what was forgotten was that civil courage—courage in the face of the enemy within one's own people—is just as impressive, perhaps even more impressive, and no less important. It was forgotten that it is honorable, that it is one's duty, to stand up for what is right within one's own state. That's why it's imperative to emphasize in these trials: You should have said no.[82]

Notes

1. Fritz Bauer, *Das Verbrechen und die Gesellschaft* (Munich and Basel: Ernst Reinhardt Verlag, 1957), 135.
2. Ibid., 251f.
3. Joachim Perels, "Zur rechtlichen Bedeutung des Auschwitz-Prozesses. Eine kritische Intervention," in *Gesellschaft und Gerechtigkeit. Festschrift für Hubert Rottleuthner*, ed. Matthias Mahlmann (Baden-Baden: Nomos, 2011), 494.
4. See, for example, Paul Bockelmann, "Straflosigkeit für nicht mehr gefährliche Schwerverbrecher?" *Frankfurter Allgemeine Zeitung*, January 23, 1964. The publication of Bockelmann's article was followed by a weeks-long debate in the newspaper's letters page between Bockelmann (a criminal law professor), Bauer, and other readers; see the Fritz Bauer Institute Archives. Bauer was on the defensive in this discussion, and he presented his philosophy in a far less radical manner than in press interviews. For a more recent discussion of the putative contradiction between Bauer's philosophy and his practice, see Gerd Roellecke, "Aber wehe, wenn ihr euch diesmal nicht bessert! Volksaufklärung durch Strafrechtstheater: Vor hundert Jahren wurde Fritz Bauer geboren," *Frankfurter Allgemeine Zeitung*, July 16, 2003. According to Roellecke, a legal philosopher, "Bauer's thesis that punishment by the state ought to protect legal interests and reintegrate criminals into society collapses in the very cases he was most committed to."
5. *Zu den Naziverbrecher-Prozessen. Das politische Gespräch*, radio interview with Bauer, first broadcast on April 25, 1963, by NDR. Transcript published in Joachim Perels and Irmtrud Wojak, ed., *Die Humanität der Rechtsordnung*, 116.
6. Dieter Strothmann, "Ein Toter gleich 10 Minuten Gefängnis," *Die Zeit*, May 25, 1962.
7. Bauer, interview by the *Frankfurter Neue Presse*, December 22, 1964.
8. See Jäger to Just-Dahlmann, August 9, 1962, quoted in Annette Weinke, *Eine Gesellschaft ermittelt gegen sich selbst*, 63.
9. Theodor W. Adorno, *Negative Dialektik. Jargon der Eigentlichkeit. Dritter Teil: Modelle. Gesammelte Schriften*, vol. 6, ed. Rolf Tiedemann (Frankfurt am Main: Suhrkamp, 1986), 282.
10. See Bauer, *Die Kriegsverbrecher vor Gericht* (Zürich and New York: Europa Verlag, 1945), 21.
11. Ibid., 211.
12. Bauer, "Im Namen des Volkes. Die strafrechtliche Bewältigung der Vergangenheit" (1965), republished in *Die Humanität der Rechtsordnung*, ed. Perels and Wojak, 78. See also Werner Renz, "Fritz Bauer zum Zweck der NS-Prozesse. Eine Rekonstruktion," *Einsicht 07. Bulletin des Fritz-Bauer-Instituts*, spring 2012.

13. Bauer, *Heute abend Kellerklub. Die Jugend im Gespräch mit Fritz Bauer.*
14. Ibid. See also Bauer's correspondence with Melitta Wiedemann, published to mark Bauer's death in *Gewerkschaftliche Monatshefte*, issue 19 (August 1968).
15. Bauer, *Die Kriegsverbrecher vor Gericht*, 205.
16. Franz von Liszt, *Zeitschrift für die gesamte Strafrechtswissenschaft* 9 (1889), 743, 749.
17. Franz von Liszt, "Organisation und Organisationsformen im studentischen Leben" (1908), republished in *Freie Wissenschaftliche Vereinigung*, ed. Manfred Voigts, 30.
18. See Stefanie Weis, *Leben und Werk des Juristen Karl Hermann Friederich Julius Geiler (1878–1953)*, 133.
19. Bauer, "Im Kampf um des Menschen Rechte," 41.
20. Amend, interview by author.
21. Bauer, "Im Kampf um des Menschen Rechte," 41.
22. The following drastic example from *The Metaphysics of Morals* illustrates just how rigidly Kant adhered to the principle of retributive justice: "Even if a civil society were to be dissolved by the consent of all its members (e.g., if a people inhabiting an island decided to separate and disperse throughout the world), the last murderer remaining in prison would first have to be executed, so that each has done to him what his deeds deserve." In other words, Kant believed that punishment is meaningful for the sake of the law itself, even when punishing an individual is of no benefit to others. See Immanuel Kant, *The Metaphysics of Morals*, ed. Lara Denis and trans. Mary Gregor (Cambridge: Cambridge University Press, 2017), 116.
23. See *Monatsberichte des Bundes Freier Wissenschaftlicher Vereinigungen*, December 1921/January 1922, 7.
24. Bauer, *Das Verbrechen und die Gesellschaft*, 21.
25. Ibid., 147.
26. For a clear overview of the so-called clash of the schools, see Arnd Koch, "Binding vs. v. Liszt. Klassische und moderne Strafrechtsschule," in *Der Strafgedanke in seiner historischen Entwicklung*, ed. Eric Hilgendorf and Jürgen Weitzel (Berlin: Duncker & Humblot, 2007). Hinrich Rüping and Günter Jerouschek provide a shorter synopsis in *Grundrisse der Strafrechtsgeschichte*, 5th edition (Munich: C. H. Beck, 2007).
27. Bauer, *Das Verbrechen und die Gesellschaft*, 134.
28. Quoted in Olaf Miehe, "Die Anfänge der Diskussion über eine strafrechtliche Sonderbehandlung junger Täter" (1966), republished in *Weg und Aufgabe des Jugendstrafrechts*, ed. Friedrich Schaffstein and Olaf Miehe (Darmstadt: Wissenschaftliche Buchgesellschaft, 1968), 2.
29. Bauer, *Das Verbrechen und die Gesellschaft*, 27.
30. Bauer, "Die Schuld im Strafrecht" (1962), republished in *Die Humanität der Rechtsordnung*, ed. Perels and Wojak, 252.
31. Ibid., 254f.
32. Bauer, "Straffälligenhilfe nach der Entlassung" (1957), republished in *Die Humanität der Rechtsordnung*, ed. Perels and Wojak, 324.
33. Bauer, *Das Verbrechen und die Gesellschaft*, 193.
34. Bauer, "Straffälligenhilfe nach der Entlassung" (1957), republished in *Die Humanität der Rechtsordnung*, ed. Perels and Wojak, 320.
35. Bauer, *Das Verbrechen und die Gesellschaft*, 23; Georg Christoph Lichtenberg, *The Lichtenberg Reader*, trans., ed., and introduced by Franz H. Mautner and Henry Hatfield (Boston: Beacon Press, 1959), 90.

36. See Bauer, "Die Schuld im Strafrecht" (1962), republished in *Die Humanität der Rechtsordnung*, ed. Perels and Wojak, 268. See also Bauer's discussion of free will in ibid. 264ff.
37. Bauer, *Das Verbrechen und die Gesellschaft*, 235.
38. Ibid. 173; parenthesis in the original.
39. Bauer recounted this anecdote to his friend Manfred Amend; Amend, interview by author.
40. Carl Bringer, a journalist and a personal friend of Bauer's, shared this story with the filmmaker Ilona Ziok.
41. According to his résumé, Bauer worked for "a few months as a prosecutor in Stuttgart" before becoming an assistant judge at the local court Amtsgericht Stuttgart I. See Bauer's résumé, signed and dated September 3, 1948, in Copenhagen, in Bauer's judiciary personnel file, call number NL-08/03, Fritz Bauer Institute Archives, Frankfurt am Main. Bauer told Amend that he had also worked as a juvenile prosecutor; Amend, interview by author. Bauer told Bringer and Amend that he had worked as a juvenile judge. In the eulogy he delivered at Bauer's funeral, Richard Schmid also mentioned Bauer's experience as a juvenile judge. See Schmid, "Fritz Bauer 1903–1968," *Kritische Justiz* 1 (1968): 60f. Before his appointment as a local court judge in 1930, Bauer's official position was "assistant judge."
42. See Ralph Angermund, *Deutsche Richterschaft 1919–1945*, 36.
43. Bauer, *Das Verbrechen und die Gesellschaft*, 155.
44. Ibid., 27.
45. Dr. Baumbach, "Der Bankrott der Strafjustiz," *Deutsche Juristen-Zeitung* 1 (1928): 42.
46. Radbruch, *Einführung in die Rechtswissenschaft*, 7th/8th edition (1929), republished in *Gustav Radbruch Gesamtausgabe*, vol. 1, ed. Arthur Kaufmann (Heidelberg: C. F. Müller, 1987), 317.
47. Bauer's résumé, signed and dated September 3, 1948, in Copenhagen.
48. See Bernd-Dieter Meier, Dieter Rössner, and Heinz Schöch, *Jugendstrafrecht* (Munich: C. H. Beck, 2007), 39.
49. See ibid., 38–40; and Klaus Laubenthal and Helmut Baier, *Jugendstrafrecht* (Berlin: Springer-Verlag, 2006), 17.
50. Bauer, *Heute abend Kellerklub. Die Jugend im Gespräch mit Fritz Bauer.*
51. More recent examples include Tobias Singelnstein and Peer Stolle, *Die Sicherheitsgesellschaft. Soziale Kontrolle im 21. Jahrhundert*, 3rd edition (Wiesbaden: VS-Verlag für Sozialwissenschaften, 2011); and Peter-Alexis Albrecht, *Der Weg in die Sicherheitsgesellschaft. Auf der Suche nach staatskritischen Absolutheitsregeln* (Berlin: Berliner Wissenschafts-Verlag, 2010).
52. See also *Zu den Naziverbrecher-Prozessen. Das politische Gespräch*, radio interview with Bauer, first broadcast on August 25, 1963, by NDR; republished in *Die Humanität der Rechtsordnung*, ed. Perels and Wojak, 105.
53. See Telford Taylor, *The Anatomy of the Nuremberg Trials* (Boston: Back Bay Books, 1992), 85, 89f.
54. See ibid., 81.
55. See ibid., 151–161; and Walter T. Schonfeld, *Nazi Madness* (London: Minerva, 2000), 24.
56. Mark A. Drumbl, *Atrocity, Punishment, and International Law* (Cambridge: Cambridge University Press, 2007), 175.
57. See Ronen Steinke, "Aus Schwarz und Weiß wird Grau. Die letzte Anklage vor dem Jugoslawien-Tribunal ist auch das letzte Kapitel einer Wahrheitssuche," *Süddeutsche Zeitung*, July 30, 2011.

58. Bauer, *Krigsförbrytarna inför domstol* (Stockholm: Natur och kultur, 1944).
59. Bauer, *Die Kriegsverbrecher vor Gericht*.
60. Ibid., 84.
61. Ibid., 115.
62. Ibid., 132.
63. Ibid., 212.
64. Ibid., 126.
65. Ibid., Appendix.
66. Quoted in Gary J. Bass, *Stay the Hand of Vengeance: The Politics of War Crimes Tribunals* (Princeton: Princeton University Press, 2000), 176.
67. See Taylor, *The Anatomy of the Nuremberg Trials*, 50.
68. Murray Bernays (colonel in the US War Department), memorandum, September 15, 1944; quoted in Bradley F. Smith, *The American Road to Nuremberg* (Stanford: Hoover Institution Press, 1982), 23.
69. See Ronen Steinke, *The Politics of International Criminal Justice: German Perspectives from Nuremberg to The Hague* (Oxford: Hart Publishing, 2012), 40ff.
70. See ibid., 191–194.
71. See ibid., 200.
72. See ibid., 178–180; and Annette Weinke, "Von Nürnberg nach Den Haag?" in *Leipzig-Nürnberg–Den Haag. Neue Fragestellungen und Forschungen zum Verhältnis von Menschenrechtsverbrechen, justizieller Säuberung und Völkerstrafrecht*, ed. Helia-Verena Daubach (Düsseldorf: Justizministerium des Landes NRW, 2007), 28.
73. Bauer, interview in *Weltbild*, January 13, 1961, 3.
74. Bauer, "Recht oder Unrecht . . . mein Vaterland," *Deutsche Nachrichten*, June 24, 1946.
75. Bauer, "Nürnberg," *Deutsche Nachrichten*, October 14, 1946.
76. Bauer, *Die Kriegsverbrecher vor Gericht*, 211; parenthesis in the original.
77. Bauer, *Zu den Naziverbrecher-Prozessen. Das politische Gespräch*, 113f.
78. See Bauer, "Die Abrechnung mit den Kriegsverbrechern," *Sozialistische Tribüne*, February 1945, 12.
79. Ibid.
80. Bauer, "Mörder unter uns," *Deutsche Nachrichten*, January 20, 1947.
81. Radbruch, "Gesetzliches Unrecht und übergesetzliches Recht," *Süddeutsche Juristenzeitung*, 1946, 107.
82. Bauer, *Zu den Naziverbrecher-Prozessen. Das politische Gespräch*, 113f.

8

BAUER'S GREATEST ACHIEVEMENT

The Auschwitz Trial (1963–1965)

A Cola during the Recess

Traffic was bumper-to-bumper as the young writer Horst Krüger drove across the city in a convertible with the top down. The sound of honking horns surrounded him. Frankfurt had been expanding rapidly since 1960. As the commercial center of West Germany, it had become somewhat frenetic and seedy, Krüger thought, like "a mixture of Old Sachsenhausen" (the quaint historic center of Frankfurt) "and Little Chicago."[1] It was Thursday, February 27, 1964, the sun was shining in a bright blue sky, and in Frankfurt's city hall, the horrors of Auschwitz were being discussed.

There was no parking available anywhere nearby, so Krüger was late by the time he got to city hall. It felt like arriving in the cinema after a movie has already started, fumbling in the dark as you try to find your seat, and then desperately trying to catch up on the plot.

When he entered the wood-paneled plenary chamber—a hall that had been temporarily vacated by the city council to make room for the proceedings—the trial had already been running for twenty days. Soon after his arrival, the presiding judge called for a ten-minute recess. Around 120 people filed out of the chamber. The men, sporting almost identical suits, glasses, and haircuts, gathered together in small groups and lit their cigarettes. Krüger was reminded of a theater intermission as he watched the people standing around and sharing their opinions on the action so far. Some stood in line to retrieve their jackets from the cloakroom and give the cloakroom assistant a few coins in exchange for a cola. Krüger eventually asked a friend, "So where are the defendants?" With a grim smile, his friend replied, "The defendants? They're right here in our midst."

Fourteen of them were at liberty, some of them on bail. They weren't segregated, guarded by soldiers like the twenty-four war criminals in Nuremberg or

Figure 8.1. Dossiers on prominent Nazi figures pile up on Bauer's desk in 1966. Credit/Source: *Alexander Kluge*.

kept in a glass booth like Adolf Eichmann in Jerusalem. In fact, there was nothing to mark them out from the other participants and observers. A couple of them were now sitting on leather seats by a wall in the foyer, drinking cola and German soda pop and smoking. They were fat, jovial figures. One of them was standing right beside the unknowing Krüger. Within the courtroom, too, the seating plan did nothing to differentiate the defendants from everyone else. The small stand in front of the judge could only accommodate one defendant at a time. Thus, whoever happened to be the focus of a particular sitting would take the stand while the other defendants would simply sit in the first few rows of the gallery, blending in with the spectators. Every now and then, a spectator would unwittingly tap on a defendant's shoulder and politely ask if he could decipher the mysterious legal wrangling going on at the top of the chamber.

On one hand, these were minor details in a major court case that set out to examine for the first time the full extent of the systematic mass murder at Auschwitz. The defendants' seating arrangement and the fact that they queued up for a cola alongside everyone else would make no real difference to the outcome of the trial, which ran from December 1963 to August 1965 and received international coverage. Indeed, the neutral, businesslike manner in which the defendants were treated might be seen as evidence of the court's confidence in its power and authority. On the other hand, though, the confusion experienced by observers was telling; indeed, one might argue that this confusion points us to the real heart of the matter, highlighting the fact that these defendants had been plucked from the very center of German society. With his flushed face, snow-white hair, and impeccable dark blue suit, the main defendant, Robert Mulka, commuted between the trial and Hamburg, where he continued to run a successful business. As adjutant to the camp commander, Rudolf Höß, Mulka had been second from the top of the SS hierarchy at Auschwitz. And that was precisely the point of prosecuting Auschwitz crimes in Frankfurt. The trial didn't lead Germans to a faraway, unfamiliar place somewhere in the east. Instead, it probed these crimes right in their midst, in the middle of the booming 1960s.

"Eerie," was how another writer, Robert Neumann, described the courtroom after spending a morning in the gallery. "The way they're all sitting, in no specific seats, you can't tell them apart anymore. Each prosecutor is a potential defendant, ... each defendant your mailman, bank clerk, neighbor."[2] Pharmacists, engineers, businessmen, janitors, accountants, bank tellers: these were the professions of the men brought before the court. Oswald Kaduk, "one of the cruelest, most brutal, and coarsest SS men at the Auschwitz concentration camp," according to the court's verdict, now worked as a nurse in Berlin, where patients called him "Papa Kaduk" because of his devotion to them.[3]

Twenty-two defendants initially appeared before the court. Twenty of these remained in the dock by the time the mammoth trial ended twenty months later. The atrocities listed in the indictment stretched to seven hundred pages. In all, around twenty thousand spectators, many of them teenagers, attended the proceedings. The trial saw Auschwitz become a metonym for the Holocaust as a whole, but it sought first and foremost to address the present, a present in which every German nurse, janitor, and bank teller had a past.

"It wasn't just Adolf Eichmann who sat in the glass booth in the Jerusalem courtroom," Bauer wrote in a 1962 essay.[4] The defendants standing trial in Frankfurt weren't alone either, he believed: "The reason why people are so fiercely averse to these trials is not that they ... believe [the trials] are unjust or unethical, but because ... Frau Müller and her family, the captains of industry, the judiciary, etc., know that in the Auschwitz trial, twenty-two million people are sitting in the dock alongside the twenty-two defendants," he wrote in a letter to a friend.[5]

Whenever the windows were open, the sounds of Frankfurt's streetcars—of doors opening and closing, of wheels rattling—would enter the courtroom.

Sounds of "people making their way from Praunheim to Riederwald in time for lunch. Auschwitz was no doubt the last thing on these people's minds," Horst Krüger later recalled. "Women with string shopping bags and men with black briefcases. The squeaking and singing of the streetcars mixed to odd effect with the voice coming from the loudspeaker, which was now speaking about the children who, due to a shortage of gas, were burned alive."[6]

Shining a Spotlight on Suppressed Truths: Bauer's History Lessons

Why Frankfurt? Pure chance, Bauer said, skirting around the highly political and rather ugly truth.

The real story of how the Auschwitz trial came to be held in Frankfurt goes back to the end of the war, when the SS set fire to its courthouse in the Prussian city of Breslau (now the Polish city of Wrocław). As flames leapt from the windows, pieces of paper—some of them charred, others in shreds—sailed down to the street below. A passerby picked up eight of the few sheets that were still intact. The man, whose name was Emil Wulkan, had long been a victim of SS persecution. He held on to the yellowing papers for years before handing them over to a journalist he trusted named Thomas Gnielka, who worked for the *Frankfurter Rundschau*. Gnielka saw that these were orderly, neatly laid-out documents with blank fields for reference numbers and a contact person's telephone number. The letterhead was still clearly legible, and it specified the documents' origin: Auschwitz. On January 15, 1959, Gnielka sent the papers on to Bauer. Over Easter 1956, Bauer had moved from the small, provincial city of Brunswick to the thriving city of Frankfurt, having been promoted to the position of attorney general of the state of Hesse. He instantly recognized how politically explosive these papers were. He also recognized their evidentiary potential; he saw them as an opportunity to begin building a case against the people responsible for Auschwitz.[7]

The documents had been issued by the camp commandant's office in 1942, and they pertained to the killing of prisoners who had tried to flee. They were documents, Bauer recalled, "the likes of which the world has never seen." They were, he explained,

> the kind of preprinted forms that reflect the entire character of the "Thousand-Year Reich." On page one, it read 'Guard X shot prisoner (enter number) as he/she was fleeing.' Page two, also preprinted: "This document is hereby forwarded to the SS and Police Court of Breslau for the purposes of prosecuting the crime of manslaughter or murder." Page 3, again, preprinted: "Charges have been dropped." I am quoting these documents because they typify the way in which [the Nazis] maintained an illusion of legality. It was clear from

the outset that proceedings would be discontinued. These papers ended up with us, and that's how we here in Frankfurt chanced upon the names of numerous guards who had shot people "as they were fleeing." We sent the papers on to [the Federal Court of Justice in] Karlsruhe, and Karlsruhe sent them back, granting the attorney general's office in Frankfurt the authority to investigate Auschwitz.[8]

The evidence that ended up on Bauer's desk was anything but rare. At the time, evidence relating to Nazi crimes was readily available to any prosecutor who was interested. A significant number of people with direct knowledge of what went on in the concentration camp were still alive. According to today's estimates, more than seven thousand SS employees worked at Auschwitz. Then there were their families, many of whom lived very close to the camp in the town of Auschwitz itself. This was a town that postwar Germans tended to dismiss as a remote, dark speck somewhere in the east but which was in fact one of the Third Reich's major hubs. As the historian Norbert Frei points out, the town was familiar to Germans during the Nazi era as "Auschwitz, near Königshütte [now the Polish town of Chorzów, RS] in Upper Silesia."[9] A considerable number of former prisoners were also still alive in the 1950s, and not all of these survivors wanted to forget the past. Many were keen for their stories to be heard; one just had to be willing to listen.

On March 1, 1958, a state's attorney in Stuttgart received a tip-off about an Auschwitz criminal named Wilhelm Boger, who by then was working for an engine-manufacturing company in the Zuffenhausen district of Stuttgart.[10] Boger had begun his career with Stuttgart's "political police" in spring 1933, shortly after Fritz Bauer had been arrested in his office in the city's district court. After transferring to Auschwitz, Boger joined the camp's Gestapo, which was responsible for preventing escapes and crushing prisoner revolts. The Auschwitz Gestapo devised interrogation techniques that were even more monstrous than the daily horror of the extermination camp. Boger, in particular, was notorious for his sadistic ingenuity when it came to developing new torture methods. His most famous invention, known to prisoners as the "Boger swing," involved hanging manacled prisoners over an iron bar and repeatedly beating their exposed genitals. Years later in the courtroom in Frankfurt, Boger boasted about the effectiveness of this method. In 1958, Adolf Rögner, a former inmate of Auschwitz, sent a letter containing information on Boger's whereabouts to the state's attorney's office in Stuttgart. The investigators' response was less than vigorous. Rather than replying to Rögner, they wrote to another Auschwitz survivor, Hermann Langbein, who was now secretary general of the International Auschwitz Committee, asking whether he could help them track down information and witnesses. They found Langbein difficult to deal with, as he expected them to meet certain conditions before he would help. Frosty letters went back and forth between the parties for several months, and the investigators made little effort to push ahead in the meantime. They allowed half a year to elapse before contacting Rögner, the original informant, on August 19, 1958.

The reluctance of the Baden-Württemberg judiciary to prosecute Nazi crimes also became apparent in Ulm, a small city not far from Stuttgart. There, ten former members of SD (*Sicherheitsdienst*, or security service) death squads had been accused of participating in the massacre of 130,000 men, women, and children—more than half of Lithuania's Jewish population—by shooting them dead into mass graves. The ten defendants were to be held responsible for only a small part of the genocide in Lithuania. They were charged with the murder of 5,500 people, whom they had rounded up, beaten, forced to dig graves, and then shot in groups of ten, yelling, "Hurry up, so we can knock off work for the day!" The bloody scene resembled "an abattoir," according to a witness in Ulm.[11] And yet the perpetrators had almost avoided indictment. The prosecutors in Ulm had been on the verge of dropping the investigation when Erich Nellmann, the Stuttgart attorney general, heard about what was going on and intervened, taking the case out of the hands of the "insufficiently vigorous" local prosecutors.[12] Nellmann sent one of his own employees, a man named Erwin Schüle, to Ulm to take charge of prosecuting the massacre. Thus, though the trial was of great significance when it finally took place in 1958, it was a "chance product of a chance justice system," as a reporter for the *Süddeutsche Zeitung* put it.[13] It was an aberration, at the end of which seven of the defendants received lenient prison sentences of between three and five years, and the other three were sentenced to between ten and fifteen years.

One positive by-product of the trial in Ulm was that it helped prevent investigations into Auschwitz from drying up completely. Schüle, the prosecutor who had been sent to Ulm, was subsequently tasked with setting up the Central Office for the Investigation of National Socialist Crimes in Ludwigsburg, a small city to the north of Stuttgart. The purpose of this office was to assist prosecutors throughout the country. Public horror at the atrocities prosecuted in Ulm encouraged West Germany's eleven state ministers of justice to make funds available for a systematic investigation into Nazi crimes. However, the Central Office was only permitted to hire a maximum of eleven prosecutors to ensure that its work didn't "grow to unmanageable proportions."[14] Despite its limited personnel, it was expected to handle not only all Nazi crimes but also all crimes perpetrated against German prisoners of war and expelled Germans. Bauer was critical. "Heterogeneous things are being bundled together," he wrote. "The crimes perpetrated by the illegitimate Nazi state are one thing, and the repercussions of this state are another. Putting these things together might create the impression that we wish to create a balance sheet showing national and international wrongs, with the debits and the credits balancing each other out."[15] From December 1958, Auschwitz investigators based in Stuttgart drew on the assistance offered by the new Central Office. Yet months later, the combined efforts of Stuttgart and Ludwigsburg produced a list of just eighteen people who may have served alongside Wilhelm Boger at Auschwitz. It was a disappointing outcome.

Better progress was being made in Frankfurt. Once Bauer received permission from the Federal Court of Justice to prosecute crimes committed at Auschwitz, he summoned two young jurists from Frankfurt's regional court. The two men, Joachim Kügler and Georg Friedrich Vogel, both of whom were just thirty-three years old, were released from all other responsibilities and asked to focus exclusively on Auschwitz. This was Bauer's top priority, in stark contrast to his predecessors in Frankfurt, who had once recommended that a case against former Nazis be dropped. Not only had there been a lack of evidence, they had claimed, but "the courts' well-known opposition to political crimes dating to before the collapse" of the Nazi regime made securing a conviction unlikely.[16] Bauer brought to the job a new sense of ambition. He had no intention of waiting around for tip-offs or criminal complaints to simply land on his desk.

When Bauer had taken up his post in Brunswick in 1950, he had been one of three attorney generals in Lower Saxony. In his new position in Frankfurt, in contrast, he headed up the largest criminal prosecution apparatus in West Germany. Unlike many other German states, Hesse had just one higher regional court. From his office there, Bauer was in charge of prosecutors in all nine of Hesse's regional courts. In addition, he oversaw thirteen prisons (at the time, attorney generals were also responsible for the penal system; this is no longer the case in Germany today) and a total of 199 prosecutors. "If one also takes into account the support staff, it is a powerful, fully mobilized battalion," a correspondent for the *Frankfurter Allgemeine Zeitung* stated in 1963.[17] With these resources at his disposal, Bauer began planning his move. He recruited a senior police investigator and a few typists to support the work of Kügler and Vogel, who were later joined by a third young prosecutor named Gerhard Wiese. It was a small team, yet it was the most manpower the West German judiciary had ever devoted to investigating Auschwitz.

Bauer wasted no time in setting his young prosecutors to work. Their first task was to contact every public prosecutor in the country in order to ascertain whether they already had evidence relating to Auschwitz. The team received only a few responses, but these were enough to reveal that Auschwitz had come up in investigations beyond Stuttgart and Frankfurt. In addition, Bauer sent

Kügler and Vogel on a trip to Poland to inspect documents at the Auschwitz-Birkenau State Museum. Taking place in the middle of the Cold War, this was a delicate mission requiring a good deal of diplomatic skill.

Kügler and Vogel then issued a call for survivors to come forward as witnesses. Once the call had been transmitted all over the world by newspapers, radio shows, and Jewish organizations, the team was inundated with tales of horror. Over the following two years, not a day went by without them questioning at least one more witness. By the time the trial began, they had tracked down a total of 1,500 witnesses; of these, they called 250 to the witness stand. The prosecutors took a craftier approach when attempting to track down suspects. To determine the whereabouts of suspects originally from Silesia (the former German territory that was now part of Poland), they wrote unusually friendly letters to organizations for Silesian-German nostalgists. "We received some very nice replies providing the West German addresses of the men in question," Kügler noted.[18] Within six months, the Frankfurt team had compiled a list of 599 alleged Auschwitz criminals. This amounted to almost one in every ten SS employees at Auschwitz.

Bauer's plan was for all investigations relating to Auschwitz to be bundled together and taken over by his Frankfurt team. He wanted Wilhelm Boger to be added to Kügler and Vogel's list of 599 alleged Auschwitz criminals, along with eighteen other Auschwitz suspects who had hitherto been under investigation in the state of Baden-Württemberg. However, Hans Großmann, the head of the division responsible for Nazi investigations in the Frankfurt state's attorney's office, protested. He didn't want such a huge trial taking place in Frankfurt; instead, he argued, all of the country's Auschwitz investigations should be combined and handed over to Stuttgart.[19] His reluctance to be saddled with the work of others was understandable, but Bauer refused to back down, and his colleagues in Stuttgart were more than happy to pass on their investigations to Frankfurt. Their irksome public dispute with Hermann Langbein, secretary general of the International Auschwitz Committee, had been dragging on since November 1958, when Langbein had accused them of stalling. The Stuttgart prosecutors had been holding Wilhelm Boger in custody since October 1958, but they didn't make any more arrests until April 1959, when they apprehended three more Auschwitz suspects.[20] Shortly afterward, they handed the suspects over to their colleagues in Frankfurt.

Step by step, Bauer's team in Frankfurt built a case aiming to reveal the historical truth of Auschwitz as a whole and not just the fragments of truth that had hitherto emerged whenever criminal complaints happened to land on prosecutors' desks. By the early 1960s, it was likely that only a few perpetrators would ever face trial, so Bauer was determined to ensure that these few trials had a paradigmatic, illuminating quality. "The passage of fifteen or twenty years since these appalling events curtails our ability to see justice done on a wide scale," he wrote in one essay. But, he added, the passage of time would not prevent "all sides from identifying and recognizing the truth. This is what we must strive toward by all means necessary. It might stem the old familiar tide of convenient amnesia, provide legal clarification on what was right and wrong, and, without hypocrisy or self-righteousness, make the public aware of all citizens' past and future responsibility for what happens in their country on both a political and a human level."[21]

Bauer wanted to apply the same approach to Nazi crimes beyond Auschwitz, and so he also placed the Nazis' euthanasia program on his prosecutors' agenda. He assigned the job of investigating euthanasia to the thirty-three-year-old Johannes Warlo, instructing Warlo to put a small but representative selection of the program's main leaders in the dock and to present a case that would provide insights into the wider historical context.[22] Warlo planned to bring to trial four key figures behind Nazi euthanasia. A correspondent for *Der Spiegel* predicted that the trial would be "in all likelihood, the most spectacular . . . in German judicial history."[23] And indeed, if things had turned out differently, this trial might well have been a "spectacular" judicial milestone whose significance matched that of the Auschwitz trial. The central defendant was to be Professor Werner Heyde, the physician in charge of the Nazis' "mercy killing" program. Heyde had been arrested by the Allies after the war, but in 1947, he had escaped from a prisoner transport truck during a layover in Würzburg, the small city where he had worked almost all his life. A major manhunt was launched, but Heyde evaded recapture for many years, despite the fact that there were plenty of people who knew exactly where he was. Under the assumed name of Dr. Fritz Sawade, he lived for several years in the northern German city of Kiel, where he wrote thousands of expert medical reports for the regional social court. The jurists who requested these reports knew, or at least suspected, who Dr. Sawade really was. Eventually, after a conscientious professor in Kiel threatened to go public with the doctor's true identity, Heyde turned himself in to the state's attorney's office in Frankfurt on November 12, 1959. But in February 1964, he hanged himself with a belt from a radiator in his cell in Butzbach prison, putting an abrupt end to the prosecutors' investigations.[24]

The judges did little to help the investigators' work. Citing health reasons, they decided not to remand the other three leaders of the Nazi euthanasia program in custody. Consequently, one of these leaders absconded to Argentina, and another threw himself from the ninth floor of an office building. Only the third man, Dr. Hans Hefelmann, who had headed up the child euthanasia program, was brought to court, but after six months, the director of the University

Neurological Clinic in Giessen certified that due to a neurological disorder, Hefelmann was unfit for trial.[25] The medical report stated that Hefelmann had just two years left to live, but after the trial collapsed, he went on to outlive this prognosis more than tenfold, as the frustrated Warlo later noted.

Bauer was determined that the systematic murder of sick and disabled people, which had been repressed after the war, be brought out into the open now, and he urged Warlo not to give up. Under the Nazi regime, states' attorney generals and higher regional court presidents had turned a blind eye to euthanasia. Twenty of these jurists were still alive. The state's attorney's office in Stuttgart had twice attempted to halt criminal proceedings against these twenty on legal grounds: once in March 1961 and again in August 1962. Bauer had his Frankfurt team take over, instructing them to draw up a bill of indictment while Warlo prepared a completely new euthanasia trial, one involving fewer high-ranking physicians.[26] In the end, though, the Frankfurt judges acquitted the defendants.[27] "Frenetic applause" erupted in the courtroom as the verdict was announced, the *Frankfurter Allgemeine Zeitung* noted with disgust. Warlo was speechless. "The result is utterly unsatisfactory," he later wrote. "One has to wonder what is going on."[28]

Bauer remained resolved to bring to Frankfurt high-profile Nazi cases that prosecutors in other states had been delaying or ignoring. After discussions with Hesse's ministry of justice, he offered a reward of 20,000 Deutschmarks for the capture of Josef Mengele, the notorious doctor who had performed sadistic experiments on Auschwitz inmates, particularly twins. The reward was double the amount offered for the final commandant of Auschwitz, Richard Baer, an indication of the huge symbolic value Bauer saw in making Mengele face justice.[29] Mengele had fled to South America after the war; it would later emerge that he had ended up in Paraguay. He stayed in touch with his family back in his Bavarian hometown of Günzburg, but 20,000 Deutschmarks wasn't enough to loosen local residents' tongues. The Mengele family business had long been the largest employer in Günzburg, and so the whole town kept silent.

Martin Bormann was another high-ranking Nazi Bauer was keen to capture and prosecute. As head of the Nazi Party chancellery, Bormann had been the mouthpiece and chief interpreter of "the Führer's will" during the war's final stages. Bauer put Warlo in charge of the case against Bormann, who had mysteriously disappeared in 1945 and whose whereabouts remained the subject of wild conjecture. Bormann's seat had remained empty during the Nuremberg trial, where he had been convicted and sentenced *in absentia*. The connection with Nuremberg may partly explain why Bormann was so important to Bauer: if Bauer's prosecutors managed to track this prominent Nazi down and try him in Frankfurt, it would give the German judiciary an opportunity to contribute belatedly to the achievements of Nuremberg. But Bauer also believed a trial against Bormann would provide the German public with an important history lesson. In a 1964 interview, he explained: "Unfortunately, not many people in Germany know that toward the end of the war, Hitler ordered that the entire German population was to be annihilated in the event of defeat. He put Bormann in charge . . . of executing this order. [Bormann] would have needed the support of the Wehrmacht, but it refused to comply and intercepted the order."[30] Bauer clearly believed that any German who heard about this historical incident would be cured of nostalgia. He perhaps overstated Bormann's historical role, but his decision to channel considerable resources into finding Bormann again demonstrates the importance Bauer attached to revealing the hidden realities of the Nazi period.[31] The search for Bormann remained unsuccessful, and many years later, DNA analysis proved that Bormann had in fact died, possibly by suicide, in the last days of the Third Reich.[32]

The Auschwitz investigations illustrate Bauer's determination to foster a public reckoning with the past. He asked the renowned Institute for Contemporary History in Munich to prepare expert reports on Nazi persecution for presentation in court, telling the historians that their accounts should be vivid and comprehensible to a wide audience.[33] As the reports were being read out, state-of-the-art technology would be used to project them "onto a massive screen."[34] Bauer was undeterred by the substitute judge Werner Hummerich, who objected that historical reports were "generally . . . of no value" to the court, whose purpose wasn't to examine "recent history" but "to judge the specific acts performed by individuals."[35]

But these historical reports were of immense value for what Bauer regarded as the real point of the Auschwitz trial. "There is a risk that the prosecutors will be accused of staging a show trial, but the trial must nonetheless give a broad overall picture of the policies that were implemented," he told a few colleagues behind closed doors.[36] He personally asked the historians to focus on the bigger picture in their reports. When these were presented to the court, even Joachim Kügler, one of Bauer's prosecutors, listened in "open-mouthed" amazement: "A good deal of the information was new to me," he said.[37] For example, the experts debunked the myth that Auschwitz guards had been forced to commit their crimes, explaining that guards were free to leave the camp at any time and join the regular army instead.

Bauer wanted as many people as possible to observe the trial, and so he looked for the largest possible venue. After several failed attempts to rent the Festhalle, a huge exhibition hall in Frankfurt's trade fair grounds, the city council vacated city hall and gave the court permission to use its plenary chamber for three months. After that, the trial relocated to an even larger space, the theater auditorium of the newly constructed Gallus cultural and convention center.[38] The presiding judge allowed the opening minutes of the trial to be filmed and broadcast. Twelve television crews from countries across Europe trained their cameras and spotlights at the twelve defendants, while more than two hundred journalists from all over the world took notes. Over the course of the trial, thousands of Germans visited the nearby St. Paul's Church, where Bauer and other like-minded people, including the prominent Jewish lawyer Henry Ormond, had helped organize an exhibition of artifacts from Auschwitz. Further publicity was generated after Siegfried Unseld, chairman of the legendary Suhrkamp publishing house, asked for permission to base a new play on information that emerged during the trial. Bauer was eager to be of service. "The state's attorney's office recognizes its important duty to writers and thinkers," he replied.[39] The play in question—*Die Ermittlung* (The Investigation) by the dramatist Peter Weiss—premiered in 1965 on twelve German stages simultaneously.

The trial proved to be of momentous significance, but this had little to do with the legal nuances filling the judgment, which stretched to 920 pages when it was delivered in August 1965. In fact, the verdict contained several bitter disappointments for Bauer. Yet the very fact that a judgment had now been passed on Auschwitz marked a major turning point. As is the custom in German courts, the judgment included a summary of the evidence against Auschwitz. This meant that the facts of the case could never again be ignored or denied. Bauer had already laid most of the groundwork for this tremendous achievement when the curtain went up on the trial on December 20, 1963.

Why the Atheist Invoked Jesus Rather than Moses

As preparations for the Auschwitz trial got underway, public interest in Bauer grew. Journalists wanted to find out more about the man putting Auschwitz on trial. Fritz Bauer, the Jewish investigator of Nazi crimes, seen by many Germans as a merciless prosecutor, as a wrathful avenger of six million deaths, responded by granting interviews and publishing articles and essays. In 1958, he addressed the readership of *Stimme der Gemeinde* (Voice of the Community), a religious monthly. In this article, Bauer expressed his opposition (in contrast to many prominent politicians of the time) to the death penalty, thereby indicating that his work was not driven by thirst for revenge. Quoting the Protestant theologian Friedrich Schleiermacher, Bauer wrote, "Along with the Christianization of the state, the consciousness must grow that the death penalty is not only superfluous and unnecessary, but also immoral."[40]

In the same article, Bauer took the opportunity to clarify that, contrary to widespread prejudice, Judaism is not a vengeful religion. The narrative of Cain and Abel at the start of the Hebrew Bible is not a simple tale of crime and punishment, he argued. The story's real—and frequently overlooked—point, he claimed, is that God forgave Cain for killing his brother.[41] Bauer then turned to relatively recent German history for an example of the human capacity to forgive. He recounted the story of how, following the murder of Walther Rathenau, the Weimar Republic's foreign minister, Rathenau's grieving mother sent a letter of forgiveness to the murderer's mother.[42] Bauer didn't need to point out that the Rathenau family was Jewish; he knew his readers would be well aware of this. The story was clearly intended to provide an emphatic rebuttal of the cliché of the vengeful Jew.

Yet it is striking how often Bauer appealed to Christian values to support his political arguments during this period. He frequently referred to Jesus as well as to Protestant reformers such as Luther, Calvin, and Zwingli to lend his position philosophical authority.[43] Demonstrating extensive knowledge of the New Testament, he confidently quoted from the Gospels and the Letter to the Romans.[44] In his book *Das Verbrechen und die Gesellschaft* (Crime and Society, 1957), he appealed to the values of "occidental civilization," extolling forgiveness as a specifically "Christian virtue."[45]

The Frankfurt court had already begun its preliminary examination of the Auschwitz charges when Bauer delivered a speech at the state convention of the Kirchliche Bruderschaft (Ecclesiastical Brotherhood) in Hesse and Nassau in November 1961.[46] Bauer argued that the official legality of Nazi crimes at the time they were committed in no way lessened their criminality, drawing on Protestant theology to explain why. His speech, which was littered with quotes from Protestant clerics, fitted in perfectly, in terms of both tone and content, with the other speeches delivered that night by two prominent theologians: Martin Niemöller and Hans-Werner Bartsch, the latter of whom gave a talk entitled "The State Is Not God." During the questions and answers at the end of the evening, a member of the audience asked whether the fifth commandment prohibited "a Christian" from committing tyrannicide. Rather than saying something along the lines of "I don't think I'm the right person to answer that question," Bauer responded tersely, "I think I've already addressed that point in some detail."[47]

Bauer regularly commented on the Christian churches' affairs in Germany at the time. In one essay, for example, he approvingly mentioned the resolutions recently passed by the 1957 German Protestant Church Congress, which he felt validated his position that the Nazi state's tyrannical laws had clashed with humans' moral obligations.[48] In a 1963 radio interview, he praised the encyclical issued by the recently deceased pope and mentioned the significance of the pope dying "on Holy Thursday."[49] Also in 1963, he expressed his "extreme gratitude" for a statement on a political issue made by the council of the Protestant

Church of Germany.[50] When he made such comments, Bauer, the controversial left-wing jurist, sounded like a typical respectable middle-class German citizen. More strikingly, he didn't sound Jewish. He sounded more like the grandson of a pastor than the grandson of the head of Tübingen's synagogue.

Bauer's frequent allusions to religion were not underpinned by any real religious convictions. Nevertheless, he respected the religiosity of others. This was evident when he visited friends of his, Mr. and Mrs. Meyer-Velde, to see their newborn daughter, Esther, in 1965. Holding a fat cigar in his hand, he bent over the cot, clearly enchanted by the baby clutching his thumb. "I was just afraid the ashes would drop down," the young mother would later recall.[51] When the couple asked him to be the child's godfather, Bauer, feeling honored, immediately agreed. Shortly before the baptism, which took place in an empty church in the city of Kassel, the Protestant pastor asked Bauer whether he was religious. Bauer's affable answer—"I wholeheartedly support the teachings of the Sermon on the Mount"—seemed to put the pastor's mind at rest.[52] In private, though, Bauer admitted that he was "unable to enter the realm of metaphysics. I'm more interested in moral theology. . . . I'm not a believer, and to me, metaphysics is nothing more than beautiful poetry. I find metaphysics to be of psychological, sociological, and literary interest at most."[53]

It wasn't the case that Bauer had recently discovered a preference for Christian teachings over Jewish ones. "What I find really fascinating about Jewish moral theology," he wrote to a friend in Munich named Melitta Wiedemann, "is the line you can draw from the prophets through Marx to the trade unions."[54] Bauer's interpretation of the development of Jewish teachings was idiosyncratic. (As was his relationship with Wiedemann, a wealthy Berlin-born woman who had joined the Nazi Party in 1930 and left it again in 1931. By her own account, Wiedemann—who during the Nazi era was the editor of *Contracomintern*, an "academic" journal approved by the propaganda ministry—had put Hitler up in her home for three days while he was being pursued by the SA.[55]) But in drawing a line from the Torah through Marx to the trade unions, Bauer, an avowed socialist, was professing his respect for the Torah's teachings. As he made clear back in his student days, he believed that whereas Judaism wished to free its adherents, the "Christianity of Kant" sought to discipline them.[56] In his correspondence with Wiedemann, Bauer distinguished the "acquiescent obedience" enshrined in Christianity from "the Old Testament prophets' active criticism of the state," leaving no doubt about which tradition he preferred.[57]

This didn't stop Bauer from exploiting his knowledge of Christian doctrine—much of which he gained as a student in Tübingen, where he attended two semesters of lectures on Protestant theology—to win acceptance for both himself and his causes. His decidedly Christian vocabulary obscured the one thing that set him apart from most of the Germans he sought to win over: his Jewishness. Nevertheless, this Jewish heritage continued to exert a profound influence on his work and thought.

Bauer wanted to dispel once and for all the notion that "the Jews" had killed Christ, a stigma that had plagued him when he was a schoolboy. Bauer saw an opportunity to tackle this stigma when the Oberammergau Passion Play became mired in controversy. A centuries-old tradition, the play is performed every year by residents of the Bavarian village of Oberammergau. In 1960, the American Jewish Committee called for its boycott because it continued to depict Jews as the killers of Christ. Though Bauer didn't want to issue a statement on the controversy himself, he tried to persuade the rector of the University of Frankfurt, Max Horkheimer, to take a stand.[58]

Bauer returned to the "killers of Christ" myth five years later in an essay he wrote for *Tribüne—Zeitschrift zum Verständnis des Judentums* (Tribune: A Journal Promoting Understanding of Judaism), a periodical dedicated to tackling anti-Semitism through education. Here, Bauer argued that it wasn't the Jews who killed Christ but the Romans.[59] Perhaps to project an image of objectivity, this essay makes no mention of Bauer's own Jewish upbringing. Although it deals with Jewish law and the trial of Jesus, it draws exclusively on Christian sources. Not a single rabbi is quoted. Again in 1962, when writing the afterword to a book about the Ten Commandments, Bauer avoided referring to Jewish sources, not even using them to quote the quintessential Jewish leader, Moses. Instead, he opted to draw on Thomas Mann's retelling of the biblical story of Moses.[60]

Bauer's frustration over the myth of the Jews as the killers of Christ makes it all the more surprising that in a 1962 speech, he criticized people who, "like Shylock, insist on getting their 'eye for an eye, tooth for a tooth.'"[61] Bauer was surely sensitive to the anti-Semitic clichés in this Shakespearean allusion. Yet he didn't comment on these clichés or show any sign of being offended by them, perhaps in an effort to demonstrate that, like the vast majority of Germans, he had no particular ties to the Jewish tradition.

Bauer's Strategy: Presenting a Cross Section of the Camp

In December 1964, as the evidentiary phase of the Auschwitz trial was in full swing, Bauer took part in a televised discussion with university students, one of whom posed the following question: "Do you think that an element of sadism was at play in the meticulously planned and recorded crimes of the Third Reich? Or do you think that well-behaved citizens, the kind of citizens we have just discussed, were assigned jobs and then simply did what was demanded of them, whether this be working in an engineering factory counting replacement parts or standing on a train platform counting people as they made their way to the gas chamber or wherever?" Bauer's answer was evasive: "One shouldn't generalize. That would be a mistake." The student persisted: "No, I'm not asking for a generalization—but can you see an overall tendency?"[62]

Bauer muttered a little in irritation. Unfortunately, he said, German trials weren't designed to investigate the deep underlying reasons for crimes. Clues as to why Nazi criminals behaved the way they did would not be revealed until long after the Auschwitz trial was over, when the prison psychologists had completed their work. Until then, he said, the question of whether sadism played a role would have to remain unanswered.

The student refused to let the matter go: "Take Eichmann, then, who never killed anybody. What about him? Surely he wasn't a sadist."

Eichmann, who never killed anybody. These few words encapsulated everything Bauer and his prosecutors in Frankfurt were fighting against. They conveyed what was for many West Germans a reassuring image: Eichmann at his desk, poring over rows of figures; a man who wasn't a murderer because he never personally killed anyone. What this isolated focus on the individual failed to recognize was that the entire apparatus of the Holocaust had been specifically designed—by Eichmann himself, one should add—to ensure that vast numbers of people could be killed swiftly and with as little need for direct human intervention as possible.

The mass murder at Auschwitz had been discussed in a courtroom before 1963, having been addressed in depth during the Adolf Eichmann trial, which had begun in 1961 in Israel. But the Frankfurt trial differed from the Eichmann trial in one important respect: rather than centering on a single individual, the Frankfurt trial investigated Auschwitz as a social phenomenon. Bauer and his team of prosecutors wanted to highlight the division of labor that had enabled the Nazi killing machine to run so smoothly, a division of labor that historians would later identify as the key structural feature of the Holocaust. The Frankfurt prosecutors wished to drive home the point that within this machinery, very few individuals stood right at the doors to the gas chambers; after all, Eichmann himself worked at a far geographical remove from the chambers. The savage efficiency with which the mass killings were performed depended on highly specialized tasks being distributed through the Nazi workforce in a factory-like manner.

The role played by these specialized tasks in the smooth running of Auschwitz quickly became clear during the evidentiary hearing.[63] "Death trains" organized by the Judenreferat—the division of the Reichssicherheitshauptamt (Reich Central Security Office) responsible for "Jewish affairs"— had been rolling into Auschwitz since spring 1942. Under the directorship of

SS-Obersturmbannführer Adolf Eichmann, the Judenreferat sent more than six hundred trains carrying a total of more than a million people to the camp. The workflow was as follows: First, the Reichssicherheitshauptamt would inform the camp commandant by radio or telegraph that a transport was due to arrive. The commandant's office would then instruct the heads of its various divisions—including the Schutzhaftlagerführung (the office in charge of the "protective custody camp"), the political department, the chief medical officer's office, the transportation department, the Wachsturmbann (the SS battalion responsible for preventing escapes), and the labor division—to wait on the unloading ramps for the terrified new arrivals. Each division then had its own detailed schedule of responsibilities. The SS men assigned to work on the ramps, for example, were responsible for opening the doors of the train; for driving the prisoners out of the carriages; for collecting the transportation documents from the train drivers; for dividing the new arrivals into men, women, and children, before dividing these again into those "fit to work" and those "unfit to work"; for herding the arrivals into rows of five and performing headcounts; for issuing the train drivers with receipts detailing the "transport strength"; for ordering the Aufräumkommando (cleaning squad) to seize the possessions of the Jews standing on the platform; for transporting the people who had been selected to die to the gas chambers, either by loading them onto trucks or by marching them there; for instructing the victims to undress for the "showers" before pushing them into the gas chambers; for locking the airtight doors; for driving ambulances carrying Zyklon B to the death factories; for throwing cylinders of the gas into the chambers; for observing the gassing and the victims' deaths through peepholes; for establishing that the victims were dead; for ordering the chambers to be opened again; for arranging for the bodies to be burned in the crematoria; for supervising as gold teeth were pried out, women's hair was shorn, and any remaining valuables were taken; for telegraphing the total number of deported men and women, the number of prisoners sent into the camp, and the number killed to the bookkeepers in the Reichssicherheitshauptamt; for marshalling the men and women designated "fit to work"—who never accounted for more than 25 percent of a transport—into the camp; for ordering these prisoners to shower; for supervising as they were shaved, dressed, and tattooed; and for then working these people until they died, which on average happened three months after their arrival in the camp.

Bauer instructed his prosecutors to put a "cross section of the camp" in the dock; in other words, a selection of defendants that would represent the entire system, "from the commandant's office to the prisoners who served as kapos."[64] It was no coincidence that this approach to selecting defendants had also been used by the Nuremberg prosecutors. The "cross section" presented in Frankfurt ranged from low-ranking employees to senior officers. It included men who let their basest, cruelest instincts run wild, such as Oswald Kaduk, who used to beat prisoners to death during drunken rampages through the camp.[65] It also included men who completed their tasks with driving ambition, such as the medical orderly Josef Klehr, who had been stationed in the prisoners' infirmary. Klehr would always murder a few more people than required in order to "round up" the total number of deaths in a day, bringing the number up from twenty-eight to thirty, for example, or from thirty-seven to forty.[66]

Bauer even had the SS man responsible for distributing the striped prisoner uniforms in Auschwitz indicted as an accomplice to murder. This was intended to make a statement, to illustrate Bauer's central legal thesis. Of course, distributing prisoner uniforms per se is not a crime. But Bauer's thesis was that viewing an activity like this in isolation was wholly inappropriate in the context of the vast, highly organized crime perpetrated at Auschwitz. After all, it wasn't as if some of the extermination camp's personnel were responsible for murdering prisoners while others distributed protective clothing that would limit the number of murders. The SS staff at Auschwitz didn't work against each other; they worked in their assigned roles toward the same shared objective. All of the specialized tasks allocated to individuals in their various positions within the massive apparatus of Auschwitz served this one objective. "Concentration camps have been around for a long time," Joachim Kügler, one of Bauer's prosecutors, pointed out. "They have existed in many parts of the world, and people have been abused, tortured, and starved in all of them. In my opinion, what is unique about Auschwitz is Birkenau"—the extermination camp itself—"and the unprecedented factory-like manner in which people were murdered there . . . and their remains then harvested and utilized. That had never been done before."[67]

The SS henchman stationed at the gas chamber door worked toward the same ultimate objective as the SS man who shaved the slaves selected to be worked to death. This objective was also shared by the employee who dressed prisoners in the deindividualizing striped uniforms designed to dispel any qualms the camp's staff might have. Each member of the SS personnel at Auschwitz, no matter what his or her specific duties might have been, played a role in running a killing factory, Bauer argued. To examine each cog in the machine in isolation, to ignore its function within the larger apparatus, would lose sight of Auschwitz's real purpose.

Convicting an individual concentration camp guard for "the murder of X, Y, or Z," as the historian Matthias Meusch put it, would fail to acknowledge how Nazism worked.[68] According to the traditional legal view, Eichmann was a bookkeeper who was never violent to anyone, while the SS man in the uniform warehouse simply provided prisoners with clothing. But, Bauer argued, anyone who invoked this traditional view was motivated by a desire "to privatize and thereby mitigate collective events by atomizing and parceling out the appalling things" that had been done.[69]

Masses of petrified people were deported to places like Auschwitz-Birkenau for the sole purpose of being murdered and incinerated as efficiently as possible. In such places, guards were "surrounded by a never-ending supply of people who were destined to die in any event," as the political philosopher Hannah Arendt wrote in her commentary on the Auschwitz trial.[70] As far as Bauer was concerned, the only morally acceptable option for these guards was to defy orders. All those who failed to take this course of action, opting instead to keep the machine going, knowing that the machine's only purpose was to kill, were murderers, no matter what specific tasks they performed, regardless of whether they worked in the gas chambers or the uniform warehouse.[71] Bauer instructed his prosecutors to emphasize this argument.[72]

"Had they been tried in separate groups—the SS officers, the various ranks, the doctors and pharmacists, and the prisoners who assisted the murderers—the trials would have been shorter and less complicated, and they wouldn't have struggled with the limitations" the Auschwitz trial came up against, suggested Gerhard Mauz, a legal affairs correspondent for *Der Spiegel*.[73] The presiding judge, Hans Hofmeyer, initially shared this view and would have preferred for the defendants to be tried separately,[74] but Bauer managed to win him over: "The horrific subject matter would have been divided up into manageable parts, but [such trials] would not have given a [comprehensive] picture prompting a reckoning with the past," as Mauz pointed out.[75]

"An order was issued that the Jews were to be liquidated throughout Nazi-occupied Europe; the murder instruments were Auschwitz, Treblinka, and so on," Bauer explained. He continued:

> Everyone who worked within this killing machine, regardless of what they did, was guilty of complicity in murder, provided they knew what the machinery's goal was, of course. There can be no doubt that those who worked in the extermination camps and those who knew about the camps, from the guards up to the highest levels, knew. If you are in a Schiller-style band of robbers or a group of gangsters à la "Murder, Inc.," then you are guilty of murder; no criminal lawyer in the country would be in any doubt about that. It makes no difference whether you are the boss who orders the murder from your desk, whether you provide the revolver, whether you case the scene of the crime, whether you pull the trigger yourself, whether you act as a lookout, or whether you perform some other task that has been assigned to you.[76]

The trial brought to light some individual cases of extreme sadism. There were many random acts of cruelty that hadn't been officially organized, that hadn't been planned into the system at Auschwitz. For example, the court heard how Wilhelm Boger once chanced upon a small boy who had just arrived in Auschwitz with an apple in his hand. Boger walked up to the child, grabbed him by the feet, and smashed his head against a barracks wall. Boger then calmly picked up the apple and ate it.[77] Observers of the trial also heard about how Oswald Kaduk found it amusing to grab the caps off prisoners' heads and throw them toward the barbed wire, over the line that prisoners weren't allowed to cross. Any prisoners who tried to retrieve their caps were shot dead by the watchmen, just as Kaduk intended.[78]

But in focusing on the barbarism of individuals, headlines such as "Women Burned Alive" or "A Shooting over Breakfast" distracted attention from the real issue, warned the writer Martin Walser, a view shared by Bauer: "We have nothing to do with these events, with this barbarity; that we are certain of. This cruelty is not shared. This trial is not about us. . . . Words like these enable us to distance ourselves from Auschwitz. . . . One must picture the killing factory without the props and the characteristics the defendants have been accused of. . . . The Auschwitz without these 'colors' is the real Auschwitz."[79] It was the factory-like character of Auschwitz-Birkenau, and not the sadistic excesses of individual guards, that caused a teenaged boy to write the following message on a barracks wall in his own blood: "Andreas Rappaport—lived sixteen years." And it was what prompted a nine-year-old boy to say that while he knew "a lot," he wouldn't "learn any more."[80]

"The Auschwitz problem—and I'm sure we can all agree on this—didn't begin at the gates of Auschwitz and Birkenau," Bauer said in the TV discussion with students. "People had to be brought there in the first place, so there were many, many perpetrators."[81] In some cases, however, Bauer's thesis that every single person who worked at the extermination camp bore responsibility for the killing became difficult to uphold. This was particularly apparent in the complicated case of the SS physician Franz Lucas. There was no doubt that Dr. Lucas had participated in selections on the ramps. However, former prisoners testified that he had been "the only doctor who treated us humanely." The court heard about how Lucas saw to it that prisoners received life-saving medicine and about how he tried to offer some degree of protection until the SS eventually disciplined him for "favoring prisoners." "We were quite desperate after Dr. Lucas was gone," one witness testified. "When Dr. Lucas was with us, we were so gay. Really, we learned how to laugh again."[82]

By participating in selections on the ramp, Lucas had played a role in facilitating the industrialized killings. Yet, as Hannah Arendt suggested, "let us suppose he had asked the inmates what he ought to do. Wouldn't they have begged him to stay and pay the price of participation in the selections on the ramp—which were an everyday occurrence, a routine horror, as it were—

in order to save them from the feeble-minded, Satanic ingenuity of all the others?"[83]

The judges were frustrated by Bauer's legal argument. "What are you playing at?" one of them barked at the prosecutor Gerhard Wiese during a break in the proceedings. The Federal Court of Justice was sure to quash any verdict that assigned automatic guilt, the judge insisted. "You are putting the judgment at risk," he warned.[84] In the end, the judges gave Dr. Lucas the lowest prison sentence they could: three years and three months. As the judge predicted, the Federal Court of Justice subsequently overturned this sentence, and in a retrial at the regional court, Lucas was acquitted.

The Frankfurt court immediately acquitted the SS man in charge of the uniform warehouse. From the judges' point of view, distributing prisoner uniforms was not in itself a crime. They didn't accept that everyone who assisted in the day-to-day operations of the killing factory was responsible for the outcome of mass murder. The Federal Court of Justice later objected that Bauer's argument "implies that even an action that in no way facilitated the main crime has to be punished."[85] It wasn't until 2011, when a Munich court returned a guilty verdict against the low-ranking Ukrainian extermination camp guard John Demjanjuk, that German judges finally came around to Bauer's way of thinking.[86]

One reason for the leniency of the sentences passed in Frankfurt in 1965 was that the court's interpretation of the law was extremely generous toward the defendants. In several cases, the judges downgraded the charges from murder to accessory to murder. They assigned responsibility for the crime of the Holocaust to the men who had given the orders: Hitler, Heydrich, and Himmler. According to the judges, the people who served these Nazi leaders, however willingly or unwillingly, weren't personally motivated to commit crime. Many Germans may have committed murder, the argument went, but they saw themselves as simply assisting in the performance of an act that was of no great personal importance to them. This position had already been established during the Ulm *Einsatzgruppen* trial of 1958, a trial that resulted in very light sentences for those defendants who emphasized a lack of personal identification with the crimes they committed.[87] As a result of this position, the Frankfurt court convicted even Robert Mulka, the adjutant to the commandant of Auschwitz, of the less serious crime of accessory to murder, despite the fact that he had played a major role in transforming the concentration camp into an extermination camp.

The "Prejudiced" Survivor: Bauer Faces a Wave of Hostility

The melting snow formed puddles as the rain poured down on Copenhagen. Wind swept across the old historic heart of the city, which had emerged from the war largely unscathed. It was a wind Bauer knew well from his years in exile here. He was equally familiar with the soft sounds of the Danish language, and so he conversed with ease with the young Danish journalist. It was February 26, 1963, and Bauer was being interviewed by Hans Hermann Petersen, a twenty-five-year-old reporter for Denmark's biggest tabloid, *B.T.* "Mr. Bauer speaks perfectly comprehensible Danish," the reporter later observed, just as a storm of protest was breaking out in Germany.[88]

The Danish newspaper published the Bauer interview under the headline "A New Hitler Would Have an Easy Job Today: Attorney General Dr. Fritz Bauer, the German Leading the Hunt for Nazi Leaders, Says a New Hitler Wouldn't Be Stopped." The tabloid quoted Bauer's harsh criticism of the political situation in Germany. Jews were no longer called "pigs" in Germany, he said; instead, they were told "We forgot to gas you." The freedom enshrined in the West German constitution since 1949 didn't exist in reality, he added. Schools, in particular, were among "the most authoritarian institutions in Germany today." Bauer lamented the impact of this authoritarianism on young people, Germany's hope for the future.[89]

After the press agency UPI translated and disseminated the article around the world, Adenauer's government publicly expressed misgivings about Bauer. Even the SPD party leadership under Erich Ollenhauer distanced itself from Bauer. In the state parliament of Hesse, the CDU called for Bauer's suspension. Bauer was hauled before his superior—the SPD minister of justice, Lauritz Lauritzen—and asked to explain himself. Bauer's excuse was that the newspaper had misquoted him and taken his statements out of context. After the meeting, in a debate in Hesse's parliament on April 4, 1963, Lauritzen stated that he had no intention of reining Bauer in.[90] Those who believed public officials ought never to speak their mind were "unfortunately ignoring the fact that in recent German history, the reticence of an entire generation of public officials served neither themselves nor our people well."[91] Nevertheless, public pressure prompted Lauritzen to demand a written explanation from Bauer before deciding "whether the attorney general's behavior requires action to be taken."[92]

What Bauer was reported to have said in Copenhagen wasn't all that new. For some time now, he had been maintaining a strong media presence, expressing his views in a manner that was always sharply critical, often powerfully eloquent, and sometimes polemical. In a 1962 essay, for instance, Bauer named the following as two relatively recent manifestations of *Sippenhaft*, the practice of punishing people for actions performed by their relatives: firstly, Nazi terror, and secondly—a phenomenon separated from the former by a single comma—the legal discrimination suffered in 1960s' West Germany by children born out of wedlock.[93] In the same essay, he referred to the Nazi jurist Roland Freisler as an advocate of the retributive principle in criminal law.[94] Bauer then went on to mock the contemporary West German criminal law commission and ministry of justice, which, he argued, continued to adhere to this retributive principle while claiming to have adopted new, more humane values after 1945. Desire for revenge was particularly strong in Germany, Bauer wrote: "The Germans have a remarkable predilection for grand, ominous statements."[95] Few who knew Bauer would have been genuinely surprised by the critical statements published in the Danish newspaper.

But, as his political opponents were quick to highlight, Fritz Bauer was a former emigrant criticizing Germany in a foreign language in his old country of exile, behind German voters' and taxpayers' backs. At the time, many Germans believed that returned emigrants had no right to speak in Germany's name or to express an opinion on the past; after all, they had left the country. Most of those who expressed outrage over Bauer's statements in Copenhagen emphasized in ostensibly understanding, forbearing tones that Bauer had been personally affected by the Holocaust. A commentator for the *Rheinischer Merkur*, a conservative news weekly that was virulently critical of Bauer, wrote that one should "make allowances for the fact that he was persecuted on racial grounds, that he endured the concentration camp and emigration." But the commentator also turned Bauer's biography against him, pointedly mentioning that the emigrant Bauer "did not return until 1948."[96]

"Not until 1948"—in other words, too late to help clear the rubble from German streets, too late to help rebuild Germany from scratch, and too late for Bauer to claim he had no ties to other countries. (The journalist got the year wrong, however; Bauer didn't return to Germany until 1949.) In the Hessian parliament, the speaker of the CDU, Erich Großkopf, prefaced an attack on Bauer by saying, "I know that Dr. Bauer is one of those who suffered greatly under the Third Reich, and he continues to have our sympathy, our human sympathy."[97] Bauer's position was baffling, Großkopf said, but one must make allowances for the fact that he had been personally affected by the Holocaust. In other words, Bauer couldn't help his lack of objectivity, Großkopf suggested; the attorney general was emotionally involved and therefore incapable of discussing the past with the necessary intellectual rigor.

Bauer did receive support from other sources, including newspapers such as the *Frankfurter Rundschau* and the *Süddeutsche Zeitung*. Nevertheless, he was keenly aware of his image problem, as a 1964 letter he sent to *Der Spiegel* demonstrates. The magazine had recently quoted Bauer as saying, "Whenever I drive past my old concentration camp, I stop the car, get out, and refresh my memory." Bauer wrote a letter of complaint to the editors, claiming that these words had been put into his mouth: "There is no need to publish a correction.

However, I wish to clarify that there has been a misunderstanding. I have never visited 'my' concentration camps or 'my' prisons, either in this country or abroad, and I have no intention of visiting them in the future. However, I have visited Bergen-Belsen and Dachau—camps I was not imprisoned in—when I happened to be passing through those areas. [I visited them in] the same way one might visit cemeteries where dead relatives or friends are buried."[98]

Bauer's Role Behind the Scenes

The people who flocked to Frankfurt in their thousands to watch the trial didn't catch a glimpse of Bauer. Many of them had read about the fiery attorney general with the shock of white hair and hoped to see him in the flesh. Scanning the many men in robes at the front of the courtroom, observers were puzzled as to why they couldn't see Bauer in the center of the action. Bauer didn't deliver the symbolically significant opening or closing statements as might have been expected; in fact, he stayed out of the courtroom's spotlight completely. This absence is striking, given that Bauer otherwise gave careful consideration to how he might best stage and publicize the trial.

From their seats in the gallery in the Gallus center, spectators watched the trial unfold on the raised platform ahead of them as if they were in the theater. The layout of this "stage" had been meticulously planned. The presiding judge, Hans Hofmeyer, wearing a black hat with a thin strip of silver around the brim, performed his role with consummate sensitivity, as was noted with appreciation by all sides. His composure was almost unshakeable; it was only at the end of the trial, on delivering the judgment, that some observers noticed a catch in his voice and tears in his eyes. Seated across six benches to the left of Hofmeyer were nineteen defense lawyers. Many of them had gray hair, some had many years of experience behind them, and some, such as Hans Laternser, had worked for the defense in Nuremberg. To the right sat the attorney for civil plaintiffs, the Frankfurt lawyer Henry Ormond, a resolute, white-haired man. This cast of older characters must have made the three prosecutors sent by Bauer—the quiet Vogel, the charismatic Kügler, and the unassuming Gerhard Wiese—appear even younger than they were. Most of the defendants were as old as their fathers.

Bauer was keen to step back so as not to interfere with the impact of this father-son symbolism. But in a letter to a friend, he gave the following brief and rather unconvincing explanation for his apparent withdrawal from the proceedings: it was "a kind of unwritten custom," he wrote, that attorney generals "avoided intervening in trials (or indeed personally prosecuting cases)."[99] Bauer had clearly taken a different view during the Remer trial in Brunswick in 1952, when he had prosecuted the case against Remer himself, even drawing on his own biographical details to help rehabilitate the plotters of July 20. As we have seen, Bauer had repeatedly mentioned the "Fatherland" and "our venerable German law" and had sought to strengthen his case by emphasizing his personal connection to Claus Schenk Graf von Stauffenberg. The message he had wanted to convey to his undecided audience was "This is the new Germany speaking." At the same time, Bauer had done his best to keep his experiences as an emigrant and a Jew out of the public eye. Nevertheless, by the time of the Auschwitz trial, his Jewish background was no longer any secret, and, much to his vexation, opponents frequently invoked it in order to discredit his work and accuse him of pursuing a personal vendetta.

Purely by chance, Frankfurt's regional court had initially scheduled a Jewish judge, Hans Forester, to preside over the Auschwitz trial, but Forester recused himself because of bias. He was also concerned that in the early 1960s, large sections of the German public would simply refuse to accept that a ruling from him was "in the name of the people." He feared that people would suggest—or at least imply—that his judgment was clouded by a personal desire for revenge, and so, to forestall such potential accusations, he stepped aside.[100]

Also by chance, the court had scheduled Johann Heinrich Niemöller—whose father, the theologian and pastor Martin Niemöller, had been imprisoned in concentration camps from 1937 to 1945—to serve as deputy judge. Although Niemöller didn't believe himself to be partial, the court's governing board recused him for fear that the public wouldn't trust him to come to an objective judgment. The board's "concerns about the appearance" of impartiality were deemed reason enough to release Niemöller from his duties.[101]

By the time the Auschwitz trial began, few people in Germany saw Bauer as a neutral, impartial figure. He was known first and foremost as the emigrant whom the conservative CDU Party had recently dragged into the center of a political maelstrom. If he were to now sit opposite the defendants in the courtroom—the white-haired concentration camp survivor with the lined face on one side, the twenty-two German everymen on the other—whom were Germans more likely to identify with? Bauer decided that the prosecution should project a different image, that if the trial was to make a political impact on German society, it ought not to be associated with his face.

In their late teens, the three prosecutors selected by Bauer had performed military service in the Wehrmacht. Like most Germans, neither they nor their families had suffered racial persecution under the Nazis. They were therefore unlikely to be seen as avengers. "The trial will show the world that we are determined to create a new Germany, a German democracy that respects the dignity of every individual," Bauer told journalists as the trial began.[102] The three young men conveyed the sense that they were interested in the country's future and not in settling old scores.

Of the three prosecutors, the elegant, fair-haired Joachim Kügler seemed most at home in his role. His rhetorical duels with the considerably older defense counsel Hans Laternser were among the trial's highlights.[103] Kügler's eloquence and self-assurance were so impressive that Laternser took to calling him "Staatsanwalt Klügler" (Attorney Clever).[104] Kügler identified strongly with his role, so much so that in later years, he disputed the idea that Bauer had been at the prosecution's helm. "The investigations into the Auschwitz murderers were not conducted by Bauer's office but solely by the attorneys Vogel and Kügler of the state prosecutor's office in the regional court of Frankfurt," he wrote, referring to himself in the third person, in a 2009 letter to the editor of Die Zeit. "Bauer had absolutely nothing to do with the main trial."[105] Kügler—whose relationship with Bauer had soured over the years—insisted that full credit for the Auschwitz trial go to the young prosecutors. And it may well be the case that Bauer, who had so studiously avoided being spotted by journalists in the courtroom, wouldn't have felt the need to correct Kügler's contention that the personnel in the courtroom accurately reflected the situation behind the scenes.

But whatever Kügler may have claimed in later years, the fact remains that Bauer maintained a tight hold on the reins. He directed his key players; he summoned the prosecutors to weekly meetings throughout both the investigations and the trial itself; he advised them on tactics and strategy; he told them what defendants to put in the dock; he came up with the idea of opening the trial with seven dramatic expert reports from historians; and he determined the precise form of the criminal charges.[106] Most importantly, he overcame huge opposition within the judiciary to bring the case against Auschwitz to court in the first place. He saw to it that a trial on the scale of the Nuremberg trial took place in a German court, something his three inexperienced prosecutors could never have accomplished.[107]

Bauer's prosecutors certainly performed the painstaking work of presenting evidence in court, and so no one had a more thorough understanding of the details of the case than they did. They also deserve credit for the intelligent, delicate manner in which they questioned witnesses; this was their achievement, not Bauer's. Nevertheless, it was Bauer—the white-haired concentration camp survivor and emigrant with the lined face—who directed the proceedings from start to finish.

Notes

1. See Krüger, "Im Labyrinth der Schuld. Ein Tag im Frankfurter Auschwitz-Prozeß," *Der Monat* (May 1964): 25.

2. Robert Neumann, *Vielleicht das Heitere*, 269f.
3. Quoted in Gerhard Werle and Thomas Wandres, *Auschwitz vor Gericht, Völkermord und bundesdeutsche Strafjustiz* (Munich: C. H. Beck, 1995), 166.
4. Bauer, "Widerstandsrecht und Widerstandspflicht des Staatsbürgers" (1962), republished in *Die Humanität der Rechtsordnung*, ed. Joachim Perels and Irmtrud Wojak, 197.
5. Bauer, extracts from letters to Melitta Wiedemann, undated, published to mark Bauer's death in *Gewerkschaftliche Monatshefte*, issue 19 (August 1968), 490–492.
6. Horst Krüger, "Im Labyrinth der Schuld. Ein Tag im Frankfurter Auschwitz-Prozeß," *Der Monat*, May 1964, 23f.
7. See Werner Renz, "Der erste Frankfurter Auschwitz-Prozeß. Völkermord als Strafsache," *1999: Zeitschrift für Sozialgeschichte des 20. und 21. Jahrhunderts* (September 2000): 14.
8. Bauer, *Zu den Naziverbrecher-Prozessen. Das politische Gespräch.* There are a few errors in Bauer's account in this interview of the chain of events leading to his discovery of the documents, as Werner Renz reveals in his examination of the files; see Renz, "Der 1. Frankfurter Auschwitz-Prozess 1963–1965 und die deutsche Öffentlichkeit. Anmerkungen zur Entmythologisierung eines NSGain-Verfahrens," in *NS-Prozesse und deutsche Öffentlichkeit. Besatzungszeit, frühe Bundesrepublik und DDR*, ed. Jörg Osterloh and Clemens Vollnhals (Göttingen: Vandenhoeck & Ruprecht, 2011), 352. Only verified extracts of Bauer's account are quoted here.

According to Section 13a of the German Code of Criminal Procedure, the Federal Court of Justice (Germany's supreme court) is responsible for determining the competent court in cases where an alleged crime had been committed in another country: "If venue cannot be established in any court within the territorial scope of this Federal statute, or if such court cannot be ascertained, the Federal Court of Justice shall decide which court shall be competent." The Federal Court of Justice decided that Frankfurt would be the competent court on April 17, 1959 (2 Ars 60/59).

9. Norbert Frei, *1945 und wir*, 174f.
10. See Gerhard Werle and Thomas Wandres, *Auschwitz vor Gericht*, 146.
11. Quoted in ibid., 22f.
12. See Annette Weinke, *Eine Gesellschaft ermittelt gegen sich selbst*, 14f.
13. Ernst Müller-Meiningen Jr., "Gespenstische Vergangenheit vor Gericht zitiert," *Süddeutsche Zeitung*, August 30, 1958.
14. See Marc von Miquel, "'Wir müssen mit den Mördern zusammenleben!' NS-Prozesse und politische Öffentlichkeit in den sechziger Jahren," in *"Gerichtstag halten über uns selbst ..." Geschichte und Wirkung des ersten Frankfurter Auschwitz-Prozesses*, ed. Irmtrud Wojak (Frankfurt am Main: Campus, 2001), 102.
15. Bauer, "Mörder unter uns" (1958), republished in *Die Humanität der Rechtsordnung*, ed. Perels and Wojak, 98.
16. State's attorney general of Frankfurt, report, September 3, 1953; file number IV-1574/48, vol. 2, Ministry of Justice of Hesse. Quoted in Matthias Meusch, "'Gerichtstag halten über uns selbst.' Der Hessische Generalstaatsanwalt Fritz Bauer und die Verfolgung von NS-Verbrechen," in *Recht und Justiz im gesellschaftlichen Aufbruch (1960–1975). Bundesrepublik Deutschland, Italien und Frankreich im Vergleich*, ed. Jörg Requate (Baden-Baden: Nomos, 2003), 132.
17. *Frankfurter Allgemeine Zeitung*, "Frankfurter Gesichter: Fritz Bauer," July 13, 1963.
18. Kügler, interview.

19. See the files of the state's attorney's office at the regional court of Frankfurt am Main, file number 4 Ks 2/63, vol. 1, sheet 20.
20. See Werner Renz, "Der 1. Frankfurter Auschwitz-Prozeß. Zwei Vorgeschichten," *Zeitschrift für Geschichtswissenschaft* (2002): 624–630.
21. Bauer, "Mörder unter uns," 100.
22. On Bauer's strategy, see Willi Dreßen, "NS-'Euthanasie'-Prozesse in der Bundesrepublik Deutschland im Wandel der Zeit," in *NS-"Euthanasie" vor Gericht. Fritz Bauer und die Grenzen juristischer Bewältigung*, ed. Hanno Loewy and Bettina Winter (Frankfurt am Main: Campus, 1996).
23. Quoted in Claudia Fröhlich, "Wider die Tabuisierung des Ungehorsams," 288.
24. See Johannes Warlo, "NSG-Verfahren in Frankfurt am Main. Versuch einer justiziellen Aufarbeitung der Vergangenheit," in *Ein Jahrhundert Frankfurter Justiz. Gerichtsgebäude A: 1889–1989*, ed. Horst Henrichs and Karl Stephan (Frankfurt am Main: W. Kramer Verlag, 1989), 164f. On Bauer's determination to prosecute this case in Frankfurt, see Fröhlich, "Wider die Tabuisierung des Ungehorsams," 308f.
25. See Warlo, "NSG-Verfahren in Frankfurt am Main," in *Ein Jahrhundert Frankfurter Justiz*, ed. Henrichs and Stephan, 167f.
26. See Helmut Kramer, "'Gerichtstag halten über uns selbst.' Das Verfahren Fritz Bauers zur Beteiligung am Anstaltsmord," in *NS-"Euthanasie" vor Gericht*, ed. Loewy and Winter, 91.
27. See ibid., 169.
28. Ibid., 175f.
29. See Werner Renz, "Der Frankfurter Auschwitz-Prozeß. Zwei Vorgeschichten," *Zeitschrift für Geschichtswissenschaft* (2002), 633.
30. Bauer, interview with *Me'orot* (magazine of the Zionist Youth Movement of Germany), October/November 1964, 5.
31. Peter Longerich and Jochen von Lang describe the orders Bormann issued shortly before the war ended. Bormann commanded the Wehrmacht to keep fighting and to mercilessly stamp out any doubters, but contrary to Bauer's account, he did not call for the "annihilation" of the "entire German population" in the event of defeat. See Longerich, *Hitlers Stellvertreter. Führung der Partei und Kontrolle des Staatsapparates durch den Stab Heß und die Partei-Kanzlei Bormann* (Munich: K. G. Sauer Verlag, 992), 202; and Jochen von Lang, *Der Sekretär. Martin Bormann: Der Mann, der Hitler beherrschte*, 2nd edition (Frankfurt am Main: Fischer, 1980), 322, 324.
32. After they were discovered in Berlin in 1972, Bormann's skeletal remains were stored for twenty-six years in a cardboard box in the evidence room of the state's attorney's office in Frankfurt. The prosecutors closed the case in 1998, when DNA analysis of the remains confirmed that they were indeed Bormann's. Bauer's successor as attorney general in Frankfurt subsequently had the remains cremated and dumped in the Baltic Sea.
33. Bauer, "Vermerk über eine Besprechung der altpolitischen Dezernenten der Staatsanwaltschaft bei dem Oberlandesgericht und der Staatsanwaltschaft Frankfurt (M.) und Wiesbaden vom 7. November 1962 bei Herrn Generalstaatsanwalt Dr. Bauer," memorandum of November 7, 1962, dept. 631a, no. 1800, vol. 84, sheet 89, Hessisches Hauptstaatsarchiv, Wiesbaden.
34. "Protokoll der 4. Arbeitstagung der Leiter der Sonderkommissionen zur Bearbeitung von NS-Gewaltverbrechen vom 21. Oktober 1963," minutes of the fourth meeting of the directors of the Special Commissions for Investigating Violent Nazi Crimes, October 21, 1963, dept. 503, no. 1161, Hessisches Hauptstaatsarchiv, Wiesbaden, 22f.

35. Quoted in Werner Renz, "40 Jahre Auschwitz-Prozess. Ein unerwünschtes Verfahren," *Newsletter Nr. 26 des Fritz-Bauer-Instituts*, fall 2004: 16.
36. "Protokoll der 4. Arbeitstagung der Leiter der Sonderkommissionen zur Bearbeitung von NS-Gewaltverbrechen vom 21. Oktober 1963."
37. Kügler, interview.
38. See Renz, "Der erste Frankfurter Auschwitz-Prozeß. Völkermord als Strafsache," 30.
39. Bauer to Unseld, July 15, 1964, quoted in Irmtrud Wojak, *Fritz Bauer*, 354.
40. Bauer, "Gegen die Todesstrafe" (1958), republished in *Die Humanität der Rechtsordnung*, ed. Perels and Wojak, 397.
41. See ibid., 393.
42. See ibid., 394.
43. Bauer, "Die Schuld im Strafrecht" (1962), republished in *Die Humanität der Rechtsordnung*, ed. Perels and Wojak, 254 and 268.
44. Bauer, "Der Prozeß Jesu" (1965), republished in *Die Humanität der Rechtsordnung*, ed. Perels and Wojak, 415.
45. Bauer, *Das Verbrechen und die Gesellschaft*, 205 and 193.
46. The papers were collected in a small brochure and published by Stimme-Verlag in Frankfurt in 1962. Bauer's paper, "Widerstandsrecht und Widerstandspflicht des Staatsbürgers," was republished in *Die Humanität der Rechtsordnung*, ed. Perels and Wojak.
47. Ibid., 204. (A transcript of the question-and-answer session was published along with Bauer's paper.)
48. Bauer, "Straffälligenhilfe nach der Entlassung" (1957), republished in *Die Humanität der Rechtsordnung*, ed. Perels and Wojak, 322.
49. Bauer, *Zu den Naziverbrecher-Prozessen. Das politische Gespräch*, 115.
50. Ibid. 116.
51. Meyer-Velde, interview.
52. Ibid.
53. Bauer, extracts from letters to Melitta Wiedemann, undated, published to mark Bauer's death in *Gewerkschaftliche Monatshefte*, issue 19 (August 1968). This publication does not specify the recipient of these letters, but Bauer's friend and the executor of his will, Manfred Amend, later revealed that Wiedemann was the addressee. Wiedemann also mentioned her correspondence with Bauer in a letter to Walter Fabian; see Walter Fabian's papers, call number EB 87/112, Deutsches Exilarchiv, Frankfurt am Main. The original letters have not been found.
54. Ibid.
55. Wiedemann to Walter Fabian, July 9, 1964, Walter Fabian's papers, call number EB 87/112, Deutsches Exilarchiv.
56. See *Monatsberichte des Bundes Freier Wissenschaftlicher Vereinigungen*, July 1922, call number MF B78, Leo Baeck Institute Archives, New York, 5.
57. Extracts from Bauer's letters to Wiedemann; parenthesis in the original.
58. Correspondence between Bauer and Horkheimer, 1960, call number I/2 230, Max Horkheimer Archive, Stadt-und Universitätsbibliothek Frankfurt am Main.
59. Bauer, "Der Prozeß Jesu." Bauer bases his argument here on the New Testament and Roman law. He begins by pointing out that according to Jewish law of the time, Jesus Christ had committed blasphemy and that the Jewish leaders were therefore legally correct when they said to Pilate, "We have a law, and according to that law he must die" (John 19:7). This law was unjust, Bauer acknowledges—as unjust as the blasphemy laws later introduced in the

Christian and Islamic worlds—but it was valid at the time. However, Bauer argues that the Roman occupiers didn't apply this Jewish law. Instead, they applied their own law, according to which Jesus Christ had committed a crime in claiming to be a king. The Romans pressed their own charge, applied their own law, came to their own verdict, and imposed their own punishment. Jewish justice therefore played no role in the crucifixion, Bauer maintained.

60. See Bauer, "Nachwort," in Hermann Schreiber, *Die Zehn Gebote* (Düsseldorf: Econ Verlag, 1962), 384. Bauer quoted here from Mann's novella "The Tables of the Law" (1944), a retelling of how Moses attempted to bring disparate Hebrew tribes together.

61. Fritz Bauer, "Forderungen der Gesellschaft an die Strafrechtsreform," paper delivered at the German Workers' Welfare Association's convention in Bad Godesberg, May 30–June 3, 1962, 17.

62. Bauer, *Heute abend Kellerklub. Die Jugend im Gespräch mit Fritz Bauer*.

63. With thanks to Werner Renz.

64. Wiese, interview.

65. See Werle and Wandres, *Auschwitz vor Gericht*, 166–170.

66. Ibid., 192.

67. Kügler, interview by Werner Renz, May 5, 1998; and Kügler, interview in *Fritz Bauer. Tod auf Raten*, directed by Ilona Ziok (Berlin: CV Films, 2010).

68. Meusch, "Gerichtstag halten über uns selbst," in *Recht und Justiz im gesellschaftlichen Aufbruch (1960–1975)*, ed. Requate, 144.

69. Bauer, "Im Namen des Volkes. Die strafrechtliche Bewältigung der Vergangenheit" (1965), republished in *Die Humanität der Rechtsordnung*, ed. Perels and Wojak, 84.

70. Hannah Arendt, *Responsibility and Judgment*, ed. Jerome Kohn (New York: Schocken Books, 2003), 252.

71. See Bauer, "Ideal-und Realkonkurrenz bei nationalsozialistischen Verbrechen?" *JuristenZeitung* (1967).

72. Wiese interview.

73. Gerhard Mauz, "Ein Gedränge ohne Ausweg," *Der Spiegel*, February 24, 1969.

74. Meusch, "Gerichtstag halten über uns selbst," 136. The "investigating judge" Heinz Düx, who was responsible for scrutinizing the findings of the prosecutors' investigations before deciding whether to accept the Auschwitz indictment (a role that no longer exists in German criminal courts), later said that two colleagues encouraged him to intervene. In August 1961, the colleagues in question—Dr. Würffel and von Glasenapp, judges who were not involved with the case—tried to persuade Düx to curtail the Auschwitz trial by declining to take jurisdiction over some of the defendants. See Düx, "Geheimvermerk Nr. 1," August 17, 1961, Düx's personal archive.

75. Mauz, "Ein Gedränge ohne Ausweg."

76. Ibid.

77. See Werle and Wandres, *Auschwitz vor Gericht*, 66f.

78. See ibid., 169f.

79. See Martin Walser, "Unser Auschwitz," *Kursbuch* 1 (1965): 190. Quoted in Stephan Braese, "'In einer deutschen Angelegenheit'—Der Frankfurter Auschwitz-Prozess in der westdeutschen Nachkriegsliteratur," in *"Gerichtstag halten über uns selbst . . . ,"* ed. Irmtrud Wojak, 220f. Jörg Friedrich expressed similar concerns; see Claudia Fröhlich, *"Wider die Tabuisierung des Ungehorsams,"* 317.

80. Hannah Arendt, *Responsibility and Judgment*, 255.

81. Bauer, *Heute abend Kellerklub*.

82. Arendt, *Responsibility and Judgment*, 249.
83. Ibid., 128.
84. Wiese, interview by author.
85. Federal Court of Justice ruling, published in *Neue Juristische Wochenschrift* (1969), 2,056f.
86. See the following essay by Thilo Kurz, a prosecutor at the Central Office for the Investigation of Nazi Crimes in Ludwigsburg: "Paradigmenwechsel bei der Strafverfolgung des Personals in den deutschen Vernichtungslagern?" *Zeitschrift für Internationale Strafrechtsdogmatik* 3 (2013).
87. See Michael Greve, *Der justitielle und rechtspolitische Umgang mit den NS-Gewaltverbrechen in den sechziger Jahren* (Frankfurt am Main: Peter Lang, 2001), 145ff.
88. On this controversy and its peculiar recurrence two years later, see also Ronen Steinke, "Nestbeschmutzungen. Fritz Bauer in den Interview-Affären 1963 und 1965," in *Rückkehr ins Feindesland? Fritz Bauer in der deutsch-jüdischen Nachkriegsgeschichte*, ed. Katharina Rauschenberger (Frankfurt am Main: Campus, 2013).
89. See the German translation of the full interview in *Darmstädter Echo*, April 8, 1963.
90. The stated aim of the CDU party in Hesse's state parliament was to induce this minister of justice to curb Bauer's "extravagant statements" by enforcing "a directive or two." See the minutes of the Landtag of Hesse, fifth legislative period, ninth session, April 4, 1963, 273.
91. See the minutes of the Landtag of Hesse, fifth legislative period, ninth session April 4, 1963, 278.
92. *Frankfurter Allgemeine Zeitung*, "Zeitung bleibt bei Bauer-Interview," March 2, 1963.
93. Bauer, "Die Schuld im Strafrecht" (1962), republished in *Die Humanität der Rechtsordnung* ed. Perels and Wojak, 252.
94. See ibid., 274.
95. Ibid., 249.
96. Paul Weingärtner, "Dr. Bauer und die Deutschen," *Rheinischer Merkur*, March 8, 1963.
97. Minutes of the Landtag of Hesse, fifth legislative period, ninth session, April 4, 1963, 286.
98. Letter from Bauer to Mr. Thelen, Spiegel-Verlag, dated February 18, 1964, files of the ministry of justice of Hesse, ref. Dr. Werner Heyde, file number III/4–1834/59, vol. IV, sheet 321; quoted in Wojak, *Fritz Bauer*, 388.
99. Bauer to Harlan, undated. Copies of the correspondence between Bauer and Harlan from 1962 to 1968 are stored with Thomas Harlan's papers, Fritz Bauer Institute Archives, Frankfurt am Main. Parenthesis in the original.
100. See Werner Renz, "Die Frankfurter Auschwitz-Prozesse (1963–1981)," *Hefte von Auschwitz* 24 (2009), 216.
101. Ibid.
102. Quoted in Werle and Wandres, *Auschwitz vor Gericht*, 43.
103. Großmann, interview by Werner Renz, July 29, 1998.
104. Kügler, interview by Werner Renz.
105. Letter to the editor, signed by Joachim Kügler, *Die Zeit*, July 2009, in reaction to a review of Irmtrud Wojak's biography of Bauer.
106. Wiese, interview by author.
107. See also Werle and Wandres, *Auschwitz vor Gericht*, 48f.

9

THE FIGHT FOR GAY RIGHTS
Bauer's Dilemma

The Bohemian: Bauer in Private

Over the course of the Auschwitz trial, Bauer left his apartment building on several mornings to discover that its façade had been plastered in posters of swastikas.[1] The posters were swiftly removed each time, but the culprits would soon return and stick them back up again. Bauer now kept a 6.35-mm-caliber pistol in his apartment, but his chauffeur, who doubled as his bodyguard, doubted whether the gun would be of much use in the event of an attack.[2] In the evenings, Bauer sought diversion by inviting younger, more carefree friends to his apartment. "He had such a remarkable voice," recalled one of these friends, Wolfgang Kaven, who was in his early twenties at the time. "He would alternate rapidly between growling, yelling, and softly murmuring—it was like jazz."[3]

Bauer lived in a genteel part of Frankfurt, surrounded by elegant old buildings and expensive cafés. Another resident of this neighborhood was Theodor W. Adorno, who would leave his home at the same time every morning to walk to the university, passing by the lines of new cars owned by other professors. The university's rector, Max Horkheimer—with whom Bauer exchanged the odd birthday card—lived just a few streets away.[4] Bauer himself lived in a third-floor apartment at 48 Feldbergstrasse. His building—a plain, characterless block at the end of a long row of brightly colored *Jugendstil* houses—didn't quite fit in with its surroundings, but its location was superb. From his balcony, Bauer enjoyed an unobstructed view of the manicured shrubs and vibrant flowerbeds of Frankfurt's botanical garden.

Bauer's apartment building was also home to a high-ranking civil servant of the Federal Audit Office, an imposing, severe man who, like Bauer, was picked up by a chauffeur each morning. Bauer became friends with the man's son, the aforementioned Wolfgang Kaven. This was the first of many friendships with men young enough to be Bauer's sons, and it wasn't long before tongues began to wag in Frankfurt. Rumors were further fueled when, taking a stand against the conservatism of postwar West Germany, Bauer became an advocate of gay rights.

When he first met Bauer in the stairwell, Kaven mentioned that he dreamt of becoming a journalist. Bauer encouraged him, even promising to ask around among his contacts in Frankfurt's newspaper scene. From then on, the two men would meet regularly in Bauer's apartment for a chat over a glass of wine. They would keep talking until it was late and the apartment was full of smoke, with Bauer's coughing fits the only interruptions to the flow of conversation. The chain-smoking jurist appeared to be under a great deal of pressure, Kaven recalled, but such evenings always seemed to cheer him up a little. They talked about politics, as Bauer studiously avoided personal themes. "We never had anything to eat," Kaven said, and "oddly, we always sat at his desk."[5] It would have made more sense to sit out on the balcony, where they could have admired the view and allowed the smoke to disperse. But on the balcony, the neighbors would have been able to eavesdrop, so Bauer preferred to stay indoors.

It was Bauer who befriended Kaven, not the other way around. Similarly, it was Bauer who struck up a conversation with a young trainee named Manfred Amend in the halls of the courthouse in Frankfurt. Amend, an admirer of Bauer's liberal polemic *Das Verbrechen und die Gesellschaft* (Crime and Society), asked whether he could meet the attorney general again. A meeting was arranged, and when Amend showed up at Bauer's office, he was greeted with the words, "Do you smoke?" A few days later, Bauer contacted the young trainee again, asking why he hadn't been in touch since. There was no need to be shy, Bauer said; they should continue their fascinating discussion over a glass of red wine sometime soon.[6]

On one of his visits to Bauer's apartment, Kaven brought a friend with him, the portly, highly entertaining Wolfram Schütte, another heavy smoker who years later would become editor of the culture pages of the *Frankfurter Rundschau* newspaper. Bauer made a great impression on Schütte, who subsequently raved about the attorney general's "oratory prowess" and the rhythms of his argumentation.[7] On another occasion, Bauer invited along a young lawyer named Heinz Meyer-Velde.[8] Such evenings opened up an exciting new world to Kaven. Just up the street outside the US consulate, students were demonstrating against the Vietnam war. And here was Kaven discussing politics with Bauer, the animated, combative Auschwitz prosecutor, a figure noteworthy enough to have been mentioned in the writings of Theodor Adorno. "Fritz Bauer has observed that the people presenting a hundred lazy arguments for the acquittal of the murderers of Auschwitz are the very same people advocating the reintroduction of the death penalty," Adorno had written.[9] In his speeches, Adorno referred to the attorney general as "my friend Fritz Bauer."[10]

"Anyone who know me knows that I have total faith in young people," Bauer said during an interview with students around this time.[11] He loved Tchaikovsky, especially the emotional *Pathétique* symphony: forty-five minutes of love, pain, death, and crashing cymbals.[12] He once played it for Kaven on his record player. Kaven later recalled how the attorney general with the furrowed face "drifted away" and lost himself in the music. Kaven, a bespectacled Beatles fan, secretly turned his nose up at the "slushy pathos" of the symphony. Bauer's friend in Munich, Melitta Wiedemann, was convinced that "Bauer never loved anyone as much" as Kaven.[13] With Bauer's encouragement, Kaven took up theater studies and went on to become a successful stage actor, performing in controversial political plays such as Rolf Hochhuth's *Der Stellvertreter* (The Deputy) and later in the popular children's radio show *Ein Fall für TKKG* (A Case for TKKG).

Bauer clearly enjoyed the company of young people. He was interested in their views and often stayed up late talking to them, much to the annoyance of some neighbors, who suspiciously observed the comings and goings from behind their drapes.[14] A retired police officer living in Bauer's building filed an official complaint about the "frequent visits made by undesirable elements."[15]

And so the rumors continued to spread. On paper, Bauer was still married to his Danish friend Anna Maria Petersen, whom he had married in 1943, toward the end of his exile in Denmark. Once the war was over, Petersen offered to give her husband "back his freedom," according to Bauer's sister.[16] After all, it had been nothing more than a marriage of convenience, an act of solidarity aimed at protecting Bauer from the immigration authorities. But Bauer, keen to retain his married status, declined Petersen's offer to dissolve the marriage in 1945. His friendship with Petersen endured, but he took pains to ensure that he wasn't seen together with his "wife" on the few occasions she paid him a discreet visit in Frankfurt.[17] Bauer kept Petersen hidden away like a treasured possession, and whenever his friends asked after her, he drew a veil of silence around their relationship. Petersen's last visit to Frankfurt was in July 1968, when she attended Bauer's funeral.

Bauer's surviving relatives were also far away, in Sweden. Up until his mother's death from cancer in 1955, Bauer had spent every Christmas and several summer vacations there with her.[18] After she died, Bauer had few remaining family ties. His sister and her husband, Walter Tiefenthal, who had never really liked Bauer, continued to invite him to spend winter vacations with them, but Bauer was unenthused.[19] Instead, he began to toy with the idea of spending his vacations with the same young, artistic types in whose company he was increasingly seen at theater premieres and cafés such as the stylish Operncafé and Club Voltaire, a popular haunt of Frankfurt's left-wing activists.[20] Bauer eventually succeeded in persuading one of these young men to join him on vacation.

The man in question was Thomas Harlan, and no other friendship raised as many eyebrows as this one. Described by an acquaintance as an "imperious, delicate, good-looking, intense man," Harlan was a promiscuous, self-assured theater director and filmmaker with shaggy brown hair who had once visited Israel with the notorious German actor Klaus Kinski.[21] Harlan "related anecdotes in a virtually oriental manner, never once hesitating or pausing to chat," a television journalist once noted.[22] Harlan's father was Veit Harlan, a former director of Nazi propaganda films who had once taken the eight-year-old Thomas to visit Hitler. Now in his midthirties, Thomas Harlan was a self-proclaimed Nazi hunter. In 1958, he had directed a play in Berlin about the Warsaw ghetto uprising. After the performance, he had stood up in front of the audience and read out a list of Nazi criminals now passing themselves off as respectable pillars of West German society. The names included two members of the Free Democratic Party: the Bundestag representative Ernst Achenbach and the Porsche executive Franz Alfred Six. To escape the ensuing slander lawsuits, Harlan fled to Poland. It was from there that he got in touch with Bauer.

Harlan may have initiated contact, but yet again, it was Bauer who fostered the friendship, inviting Harlan to address him by his first name rather than "Dr. Bauer": "Please don't hesitate to dispense with such unnecessary formalities," Bauer wrote.[23] It wasn't long before Bauer was using the informal German "du" form, greeting Harlan with the words "My dear Thomas!" and sending his regards to whomever Harlan happened to be dating at the time: "I tried to reach you several times today. The last time I called, a woman answered (another 'heavily pregnant' one? Are you running a maternity hospital?)."[24] In one letter, Bauer mentioned that he had pocketed the paper, which was decorated with pictures of palm trees and camels, from the last hotel he had stayed in. He was finding work increasingly stressful, he explained, and such vacations provided little escapes.

Bauer felt "exhausted" and longed for sun and sleep. "Excessive work has made me incredibly tense," he confided to Harlan a few months before the Auschwitz trial opened; "personally and professionally, I feel like a robot."[25] He worked late every night, and for the foreseeable future, every weekend was likely to be busy with speaking engagements and writing projects: "A few publishers have written asking to publish my books. All the things you long for in youth are offered to you in abundance when you're old!"[26] There is an undertone of melancholy to Bauer's letters of this time, a sadness his friends Manfred Amend and Wolfgang Kaven also detected. "I'd be content just to drink Turkish coffee or Tunisian tea with you in the afternoons," he wrote to Harlan.[27] Bauer said that he planned to take a vacation in Tenerife, Rome, or Rhodes, "somewhere that might offer body and soul respite."[28]

Bauer looked overworked, Kaven noted; the late hours had left dark rings under his eyes. One evening, Bauer begged Kaven outright to come on vacation with him, but Kaven refused.[29] In the end, the erratic Harlan agreed, and he and the sixty-year-old attorney general, who was in the middle of preparing for the Auschwitz trial, decided to take a holiday by the sea. But on April 13, 1964, shortly before they were due to depart, Veit Harlan died, throwing the pair's plans into disarray. Bracing himself for disappointment, Bauer assured Thomas Harlan that he would understand if the trip had to be canceled. Bauer then added the following curious comment, which was clearly an attempt to persuade the son of Goebbels's anti-Semitic filmmaker to go on vacation in spite of his recent bereavement: "Tension marks all of our relationships with our fathers, a tension that you, in particular, have experienced and endured. The son's fury and fervent commitment to the truth have long atoned for whatever the father's shortcomings may have been. The father, who undoubtedly loved his son above all else, also understood his own actions, but these actions didn't destroy him in the end. Instead, he managed to find a home, a place in our thoughts and memories. Veit and Thomas Harlan formed an historic alliance, and your friends stand with you and thank you."[30]

Harlan decided to go ahead with the trip and later provided a colorful account of just how much this summer vacation meant to Bauer. (One should bear in mind, though, that the verbose Harlan never let the truth get in the way of a good story. He once recounted the dramatic tale of how he had been friends with Bauer for years before finding out that it was Bauer who had instigated legal proceedings against Veit Harlan for crimes against humanity.[31] In reality, Bauer had still been living in exile in Denmark when the trial began in Hamburg in 1949.[32]) According to Harlan's overblown description of the vacation, Bauer

> came to meet me in the desert sands of Djerba, a bouquet of verdant clover in his hand, and he invited me to go swimming in the sea with him. Three kilometers from the coast, we began to drown. It was pure luck that we didn't die; the floundering Bauer pulled me down with him to the seabed when I tried to save him, but thanks to a sandbank, the water was only 1.5 meters deep. We stood there motionless for seven hours, waiting in the blazing sun for a fisherman to come and take mercy on us. The next morning was torture for Bauer, who had been struck dumb. His back was ravaged by sunburn. Luckily, I knew a traditional African remedy and ordered fresh tomatoes, which I then massaged into his back. Fritz Bauer told me this was only the third time in his

life that he had experienced human touch. The first touch was when he was five years old and his nanny kissed him goodbye, having been fired for being too affectionate toward him. The second touch was a hand on his shoulder in a prison cell in Copenhagen when a guard—a giant of a man—promised to help him flee the Germans by escaping to Sweden. The third touch was mine.³³

Contrary to gossip back in Frankfurt, it is unlikely that the relationship between Harlan and Bauer was ever anything other than platonic. Years after Bauer's death, the open-minded Harlan continued to insist that he had had a "father-son" relationship with the attorney general.³⁴ And it is true that their main topic of conversation was politics. As the voice of moderation in such discussions, Bauer would do his best to keep his hot-headed friend grounded in reality.

Harlan planned to produce films about the Nazi past. Believing that they would trigger "catharsis in the audience," Bauer assured Harlan that such films would have just as much political significance as the prosecutors' legal work: "The young people in the audience must identify with the young anti-Nazi activists in the film, and if at all possible, the 'old people' must not only be unmasked, but also induced to recognize and . . . atone" for their wrongdoings, he told the filmmaker.³⁵ Impressed by Harlan's enthusiasm for his projects, Bauer contacted television executives in the hope of securing their support. He was less impressed by Harlan's attempts to single-handedly bring fugitive Nazi leaders to justice, however. The equally unimpressed novelist Robert Neumann, another acquaintance of Harlan's, described how "the handsome, serious [Harlan] used to sit in my room talking about his dramatic unmaskings of Nazi criminals and his publishing contracts all over the world. He expected to receive copies of 10,000 documents from Warsaw the day after tomorrow, he would say. It was always 'the day after tomorrow' until eventually the publishers and the prosecutors and I stopped believing him."³⁶

Whenever he tried to talk about legal matters with Bauer, Harlan's tendency to overestimate his understanding of jurisprudence would quickly become apparent. Bauer would sometimes deliberately trip his young friend up before gently reproaching him: "One can't expect a journalist and writer to know about the law. If I were you, I would avoid polemicizing against the law in general. It would be more appropriate and sensible to polemicize against a specific unfair court ruling."³⁷ Harlan's real work was artistic, not juristic, Bauer reminded his friend on another occasion: "You are a writer, not a fact-gatherer." It would be foolish for Harlan to get lost in forensic details he didn't fully understand, Bauer warned: "If one of my German prosecutors attempted that sort of thing, I'd let him go."³⁸ Bauer dismissed some of Harlan's interpretations of recent political events as conspiracy theories: "I still don't understand what's going on with you and your Kafkaesque men (your 'men in leather coats')."[39] After Rudolf Augstein, the publisher of *Der Spiegel*, was arrested on suspicion of treason in 1962—a political scandal that eventually led to the resignation of the federal minister of defense, Franz Josef Strauss—Harlan became convinced that the same dark forces would soon come for him. "Comparing yourself with Augstein is just silly," Bauer responded. "My dear Thomas, are you suffering from megalomania? We don't know what was really behind [the Augstein arrest]. Do you honestly believe that Mr. Strauss is after you?"[40]

Tackling West Germany's Reactionary Morality Laws

There were several fashionable gay bars in Frankfurt with names like Casino am Turm (Casino by the Tower), Karussell (Carousel), and Na und? (So What?). Others had mysterious, evocative names like Barbarina, Alligator, and Le Caprice. Their clientele would sit in semidarkness behind gathered drapes, chandeliers suspended over the tables, as one observer noted: "You come to see and be seen; the many mirrors hanging in these bars are useful for people-watching."[41] The patrons were united by fear, as the state repression of homosexuality in West Germany in the 1950s and 1960s was particularly severe in Frankfurt. Just five years before Bauer moved to Frankfurt in 1956, a massive wave of arrests and prosecutions of gay men in the city had made national headlines. After being picked up by the vice squad, a seventeen-year-old male prostitute named Otto Blankenstein had agreed to inform on his clients, leading to dozens of men being charged with sodomy under Paragraph 175 of the German Criminal Code. The men were arrested at their workplaces in the middle of the day. Many lost their jobs as a result, and six committed suicide. In gay magazines of the time, men would share tips on how to "keep calm during interrogations and other police interventions." "If a certain police unit is known to treat suspects extremely harshly or to use illegal methods . . . you have a right to judicial protection as you make your statement," an anonymous correspondent advised in an edition of the magazine *Der Weg* (The Way) in the 1950s.[42]

The vice squad, which kept suspects under surveillance and spoke openly of "maintaining index-card files on homosexuals," paid regular visits to Frankfurt's gay bars to ensure that patrons' activities never went beyond a little flirting.[43] As a result, gay sex was forced out into the city's dark streets and public toilets, and the desperation that police brutality was unleashing became increasingly evident, even in the more genteel parts of the city. Right beside the immaculate botanical garden, which stretched out in front of Bauer's balcony in the Westend district, was the derelict Grüneburgpark. Every now and then, police searchlights would shatter the protection offered by the park's darkness. The police didn't raid Grüneburgpark often, but when they did, they were merciless, safe in the knowledge that no arrestees would dare to complain about their treatment publicly. Gays familiar with the Frankfurt scene immediately surrendered to the police, putting their hands in the air of their own accord in the hope that this might spare them a beating.⁴⁴

As the state's attorney general, Bauer was responsible not just for all court prosecutions in Hesse but also for the work performed by police investigators, who prepared the groundwork for state prosecutors. This presented Bauer—as a public figure who had long insisted on the importance of civil courage—with a thorny dilemma. Many of the criminal laws he was officially required to enforce were rooted in a fusty value system that continued to condemn adulterers, women who had abortions, and, most fiercely of all, homosexuals. By the 1960s, most European countries had ceased encroaching so drastically into citizens' private lives. In fact, as long ago as 1810, the Napoleonic Code had drawn a distinction between moral transgressions and legal ones. Same-sex relationships had long been decriminalized in Latin countries such as France and Italy, and homosexuality was no longer prosecuted in the Netherlands, Switzerland, Sweden, or Denmark. A debate on whether Germany should follow these countries' lead had been raging since the Weimar period. But if Bauer were to instruct police officers and prosecutors in Hesse to simply stop enforcing the German law prohibiting homosexuality, it might cost him his job. After all, such a move would amount to interfering with the course of justice.

Bauer revealed his pragmatic side in responding to this dilemma. During his tenure as the state's attorney general, there was little change in the number of convictions made under the notorious Paragraph 175. In the year before he took up his position, Hessian prosecutors had had 141 men convicted of consensual homosexual acts.⁴⁵ Ten years later, just as the Auschwitz trial was coming to a close before the eyes of the international press, 123 men were subjected to the same humiliation. Bauer wasn't prepared to risk interfering with the wheels of justice by instructing his employees to stop pursuing homosexuals. As far as Bauer was concerned, Germany's separation of powers meant that it was the legislative branch's job to lead the way. He therefore entered the political arena as a vociferous campaigner for the liberalization of Germany's criminal laws.

A Defender of Gay Rights: Bauer and the Debate on Paragraph 175

"As parallels in the animal kingdom . . . indicate, all forms of homosexuality are manifestations of the high variability in sexual behavior," Bauer wrote in his 1957 book *Das Verbrechen und die Gesellschaft* (Crime and Society), which called for the modernization of German criminal laws.⁴⁶ The *Kinsey Reports*, which had been published just a few years previously, suggested that homosexual experiences were far more common than was openly acknowledged, Bauer noted. Abolishing Paragraph 175, the German sodomy law, was a top priority for liberals seeking to dismantle the reactionary values embedded in the German Criminal Code. They saw Paragraph 175 as emblematic of German law's moralistic tendency to interfere with the autonomous, harmless actions of consenting adults.

Paragraph 175 had plenty of supporters at the time. "Socially and ethically reprehensible behavior that cannot be tolerated"—in particular bestiality and sodomy—must be punished, conservative legal experts argued.[47] Their position became even more hardline during the Adenauer years, when the debate turned into a legal culture war, the outcome of which would have a defining influence on the next few decades.

An amended version of Paragraph 175 had been introduced by the Nazis alongside the Nuremberg Race Laws in 1935, and it was this amended version that remained in effect in West Germany until 1969. Homosexual acts had been a punishable offense before the Third Reich, but the Nazis had raised the maximum sentence from six months to five years. "A male who commits lewd and lascivious acts with another male or permits himself to be so abused for lewd and lascivious acts, shall be punished by imprisonment," the amended Paragraph 175 stated, thereby giving the courts far greater scope for interpretation.[48] The Nazi supreme court provided only a vague definition of the term "lewd and lascivious acts," according to which men could be prosecuted "objectively when a general sense of shame is harmed and subjectively when there exists the lustful intention to excite either of the two men or a third party."[49] Prosecutors were therefore under no obligation to prove that there had been the slightest physical contact between men.[50] The Nazis also passed Paragraph 175a, an addendum introducing harsher penalties for special cases such as coercion, sexual acts with men under the age of twenty-one, and male prostitution.

As soon as Germany capitulated in 1945, the Allies issued "General Instructions to Judges," forbidding them to use laws that had come into force under the Nazis. Furthermore, a new criminal code drafted by the Allied Control Council in 1946 directed the legislature to at least revert to the Weimar Republic's more liberal version of Paragraph 175. However, this instruction was never followed. "From 1945 until the assembly of the [first] Bundestag, there was almost unanimous agreement in the Western occupation zones that Paragraphs 175 and 175a were not 'laws shaped by National Socialism' to such a degree that they would have to be abolished in a free democratic state," the Federal Constitutional Court ruled in 1955, thereby rejecting a constitutional appeal that had been lodged against the paragraphs by two men.[51] The Federal Court of Justice, for its part, adopted the Nazi supreme court's definition of "lewd and lascivious acts," which meant it was still unnecessary to prove that physical contact had occurred to secure convictions for homosexual acts.[52] However, the court also ruled that "committing lewd and lascivious acts" could only be considered an offense if the acts in question were "of a certain strength and duration."[53]

In 1957, another complaint was lodged with the Federal Constitutional Court, this time arguing that, in applying only to men, Paragraph 175 violated the principle of equal rights for men and women enshrined in Article 3, Paragraph 2 of the West German constitution. The court presented biologistic arguments in response: "The principle of equality" could "provide no criteria for the legislative treatment of male and female homosexuality," the court ruled, because "homosexuality is an area where biological differences justify treating the sexes differently.... Even the physical forms of the sex organs reflect men's more forceful, domineering function and women's more acquiescent, receptive function." The court went on to explain that in contrast to men, "women are involuntarily reminded by their bodies that sexual activity is associated with encumbrances" and that as a result, "physical desire (the sex drive) and tender sensitivity (eroticism) are virtually inseparable for women, whereas for men—in particular homosexual men—these two components are often completely unrelated." As for lesbians, "a woman's organs, being designed for motherhood, lead her to behave in an instinctively feminine, maternal manner—at least in a metaphorical, social sense—even if she herself is not a biological mother."[54] The judges also refused to recognize that the right to free development of the personality (enshrined in Article 2, Paragraph 1 of the constitution) applied to homosexual men, pointing out that this right is curtailed by "the moral law." The court held that this unwritten "moral law" prescribed a "healthy and natural order of life among the people"; in other words, the purpose of the moral law was to uphold the teachings of the two main Christian churches.

Conservative values continued to be enshrined in several other Adenauer-era laws. Divorce laws were strict, the state tightly controlled the distribution of contraceptives, and abortion was illegal. In a government statement of October 20, 1953, Adenauer said that his family policies aimed to achieve "a continual increase in the birth rate." "Millions of psychologically healthy families with well-brought-up children are just as important a defense against the large families of the people in the East as all our military defenses," added West Germany's first family minister, the CDU's Franz-Josef Wuermeling. "Demographers have calculated that to completely replace the parent generation, every fertile married couple will need to produce three children," he warned.[55]

In 1962, Adenauer's government drafted extensive revisions to the German Criminal Code.[56] The proposed revisions, which would constitute the most far-reaching set of penal reforms since 1871, were a declaration of war against modernizers. One of the proposals made by the ministry of justice's reform commission was to reinstate the Weimar Republic's relatively mild version of Paragraph 175. However, the explanatory notes accompanying the draft reforms swiftly dispelled any hopes that this was a sign of the state's willingness to adopt a more tolerant attitude. If homosexuality were decriminalized, homosexuals' "next mission" would be "to campaign for social acceptance of same-sex acts. They would undoubtedly exploit every opportunity the new law offered them. It is likely they would interpret the amendment to serve their own interests, claiming that the law legitimized same-sex intercourse between adult men." Rejecting any potential endeavor to gain social acceptance (an endeavor the government had a surprisingly clear understanding of), the draft emphasized "the law's power to shape morality": "In recent decades, interested parties have repeatedly claimed that same-sex intercourse is a natural and therefore unobjectionable drive. This claim can only be rejected as a strategic one.... Wherever same-sex lewdness has become rampant... it has led to degeneracy and the decay of people's moral strength."[57]

In 1962, the government planned to subsume all criminal offenses related to religion, marriage, and morality under the new title "Offenses against the Moral Order." Furthermore, by splitting up individual offenses, it intended to expand the existing twenty-eight morality clauses into forty-seven new ones. These included clauses on blasphemy, adultery, and the accessibility of contraceptives as well as seventeen offenses with the word "lewdness" in the title, five clauses on procuring, and one clause on bestiality. In addition, the government wanted to make West Germany the only country in Europe where artificial insemination using sperm from a donor (rather than from a woman's own husband) was a criminal offense.

The following year, Bauer contributed to the first major critical response to these planned morality laws. Together with the sexologists Hans Bürger-Prinz and Hans Giese, he published a collection of essays by famous authors from a range of disciplines, including Adorno, in a paperback entitled *Sexualität und Verbrechen* (Sexuality and Crime).[58] Herbert Jäger, a young research assistant, did the editorial work, and in return, Bauer assisted Jäger with his research on violent crimes committed by the Nazis. *Sexualität und Verbrechen*, which set out the case for liberalizing the laws governing sexual offenses, was a spectacular success, with fifty thousand copies sold in the first year alone.[59] (In contrast, Bauer's *Das Verbrechen und die Gesellschaft*, published six years previously, had had a print run of just three thousand copies.[60]) Bauer was neither the loudest nor the most famous liberal voice in this collection, but he was the only contributor who held an influential position within the justice system.

In his introductory essay to *Sexualität und Verbrechen*, Bauer pointed out that only four other countries in "non-communist Europe" continued to punish homosexual men, whereas the remaining fifteen countries left these men alone. Quoting the Danish criminal lawyer Stephan Hurwitz, Bauer noted that men who would be "respected citizens under Danish law" were treated as a "criminal problem" in West Germany.[61] Meanwhile, Adorno argued in his essay that "one of the most evident results of the authoritarian personality is that people with character structures predisposing them to submissiveness to totalitarianism are plagued to an exceptional degree by paranoid delusions centering on what they consider to be sexually deviant. Such people are plagued by the wild sexual fantasies they cast out from themselves and project onto outgroups."[62]

At the time *Sexualität und Verbrechen* was published, a few liberal professors of criminal law were beginning to draft an alternative bill to the one proposed by Adenauer's government. This alternative bill was published in instalments from 1966 onward. The section concerning sexual offenses, published in 1968, afforded legal protection in just two areas: personal freedom and children. "In the sexual sphere, especially, criminal law cannot offer protection to general moral states of affairs for their own sake. To do so would involve misinterpreting the law's function, using it as social policy's last resort and infantilizing citizens in an alarming manner," explained the authors, sixteen scholars from German universities, all of them tenured professors.[63] Bauer, the practitioner, was not among them.

Bauer died on June 30, 1968, and so he didn't contribute to the debate on reforming sexual offense laws that unfolded at the Association of German Jurists' annual convention in Nuremberg in September 1968. There, Karl Lackner, a representative of the ministry of justice, was forced onto the defensive after he commented that the "heterosexual structure of society" was the "invention of a simplistic social morality." When pressed to elaborate, Lackner responded that he wasn't necessarily of the opinion that it was important to preserve this "heterosexual structure." Indeed, he agreed that the "excoriation" of homosexuality was deplorable. But the very existence of such excoriation, he said, meant that "it is in society's interest to spare young people the fate of becoming homosexuals."[64]

This debate took place during the final throes of West Germany's antihomosexuality laws. A grand coalition of the CDU and the SPD had been in power since 1966, and the SPD minister of justice, Gustav Heinemann, had been working on getting the two parties to agree on a compromise package. He eventually succeeded in 1969, and as a result, homosexual acts between adults were decriminalized.

Of course, the word "adult" can be defined in different ways. Legislators initially set the age of consent for homosexual acts at twenty-one, significantly higher than the age of consent for heterosexuals. In 1973, the homosexual age of consent was reduced to eighteen, while heterosexual teenagers had the right to exercise sexual self-determination from the age of sixteen. It wasn't until 1994, as part of the process of standardizing laws in the reunified Germany, that this final remnant of Paragraph 175 was removed from the Criminal Code.

Bauer, the outspoken attorney general, deserves some credit for the progress achieved, particularly as it wasn't just the letter of the law that changed in 1969. A palpable shift in public attitudes saw support for the old reactionary morality laws dwindle. Bauer was still alive when the chief of Frankfurt's vice squad recalled his officers from the city's parks and gay bars, from Casino am Turm, Le Caprice, and Grüneburgpark. The chief admitted in a 1968 interview that consensual homosexual acts between adults were rarely punished in neighboring countries, adding that decriminalization was most likely imminent in West Germany too.[65]

Notes

1. See Irmtrud Wojak, *Fritz Bauer*, 441.
2. Kriminalhauptmeister Schmitt, "Bericht betr. Leichensache z. N. des Generalstaatsanwalts," Frankfurt am Main, July 1, 1968, Fritz Bauer Institute Archives, Frankfurt am Main, 2; and Wehrheim, interview by author, October 11, 2012.
3. Kaven, interview by author.
4. See Bauer to Horkheimer ("belated but no less warm wishes") on February 15, 1965, and Bauer to Horkheimer on July 17, 1963 (thanking Horkheimer for his good wishes), call number I/2 230, Max Horkheimer Archive, Stadt-und Universitätsbibliothek Frankfurt am Main.
5. Kaven, interview by author.
6. Amend, interview by author.
7. Wolfram Schütte, "Schopenhauers präventive Kriminalpolitik. Generalstaatsanwalt Dr. Fritz Bauer in der Schopenhauer-Gesellschaft," *Frankfurter Rundschau*, December 16, 1966.
8. Meyer-Velde, interview by author.
9. Theodor W. Adorno, *Negative Dialektik*, 282.
10. Claussen, interview by author, October 22, 2012.
11. Bauer, *Heute abend Kellerklub. Die Jugend im Gespräch mit Fritz Bauer*.
12. Kaven, interview by author. After Bauer died, Kaven requested permission to inherit Bauer's radio-gramophone.
13. Wiedemann to Walter Fabian, July 23, 1973, Fabian's papers, call number EB 87/112, German Exile Archive, Frankfurt am Main.
14. Kaven, interview by author.
15. File memo by Oberstaatsanwalt Krüger, state's attorney general's office in Frankfurt am Main, July 26, 1968, Fritz Bauer Institute Archives, Frankfurt am Main.

16. Tiefenthal, interview by Walter Fabian.
17. Ibid.
18. Ibid.
19. Bauer to Thomas Harlan, undated (probably 1963). Copies of the correspondence between Bauer and Harlan from 1962 to 1968 are stored in the Fritz Bauer Institute Archives, Frankfurt am Main.
20. Kaven and Amend, interviews by author.
21. Robert Neumann, *Vielleicht das Heitere*, 15.
22. Jean-Pierre Stephan, *Thomas Harlan. Das Gesicht deines Feindes. Ein deutsches Leben* (Frankfurt am Main: Eichborn, 2007), 7.
23. Bauer to Harlan, May 10, 1965.
24. Bauer to Harlan, April 5, 1965.
25. Bauer to Harlan, July 7, 1963.
26. Bauer to Harlan, December 31, 1964.
27. Bauer to Harlan, dated "Easter Saturday."
28. Bauer to Harlan, undated.
29. Kaven, interview by author.
30. Bauer to Harlan, most likely April 1964.
31. See Stephan, *Thomas Harlan. Das Gesicht deines Feindes*, 94f.
32. See Wojak, *Fritz Bauer*, 439.
33. Quoted in Stephan, *Thomas Harlan. Das Gesicht deines Feindes*, 140f.
34. Ibid., 103.
35. Bauer to Harlan, March 18, 1965.
36. Neumann, *Vielleicht das Heitere*, 15.
37. Bauer to Harlan, dated July 13.
38. Bauer to Harlan, dated "Saturday."
39. Bauer to Harlan, undated.
40. Bauer to Harlan, dated 1964.
41. Gerd Jürgen Grein, "Der Homosexuelle in Frankfurt am Main" (master's dissertation, Universität Frankfurt, 1968), 82.
42. Pery, "Die Rechte des Beschuldigten und Angeklagten," *Der Weg zu Freundschaft und Toleranz* 3 (July 1953): 23f.
43. Kriminalinspektor Herbert Kosyra, "Die Homosexualität–ein immer aktuelles Problem," *Kriminalistik* (1962), 113.
44. Christian Setzepfandt, interview by author, October 11, 2012. (Setzepfandt, a former city councillor in Frankfurt, is currently working on a history of the city's gay scene.)
45. "Wegen Verbrechen und Vergehen wider die Sittlichkeit verurteilte Personen in Hessen 1955 bis 1965," file reference 4,044, vol. 2, file name "Unzucht," files of Hesse's ministry of justice (department 505, no. 2,530), Hessisches Statistisches Landesamt, Wiesbaden.
46. Bauer, *Das Verbrechen und die Gesellschaft*, S. 58.
47. Quoted in Jürgen Baumann, *Paragraph 175. Über die Möglichkeit, die einfache, nichtjugendgefährdende und nichtöffentliche Homosexualität unter Erwachsenen straffrei zu lassen (zugleich ein Beitrag zur Säkularisierung des Strafrechts)* (Berlin and Neuwied: Luchterhand, 1968).
48. English translation by Warren Johannson and William Perry, "Homosexuals in Nazi Germany," *Simon Wiesenthal Center Annual* 7 (1990).
49. English translation by Clayton J. Whisnant, *Queer Identities and Politics in Germany: A History, 1880–1945* (New York: Harrington Park Press, 2016), 215.

50. See *Entscheidungen des Reichsgerichts in Strafsachen*, vol. 73 (Berlin: de Gruyter), 78, 80f.

51. *Entscheidungen des Bundesverfassungsgerichts*, vol. 6 (Tübingen: Mohr Siebeck), 389ff.

52. *Entscheidungen des Bundesgerichtshofs in Strafsachen*, vol. 4 (Cologne: Carl Heymanns Verlag), 323f, republished in *Neue Juristische Wochenschrift* (1954), 519.

53. *Entscheidungen des Bundesgerichtshofs in Strafsachen*, vol. 1, 293.

54. *Entscheidungen des Bundesverfassungsgerichts*, vol. 6, 389ff.

55. Quoted in Hans-Georg Stümke, *Homosexuelle in Deutschland. Eine politische Geschichte* (Munich: C. H. Beck, 1989), 140.

56. *Entwurf eines StGB 1962 mit Begründung*, Deutscher Bundestag, fourth legislative period, *Drucksache* IV/650.

57. Ibid.

58. Fritz Bauer et al., ed., *Sexualität und Verbrechen* (Frankfurt am Main: Fischer, 1963).

59. Herbert Jäger provided this figure; see Thomas Horstmann and Heike Litzinger, *An den Grenzen des Rechts*, 51.

60. See the production records of Ernst Reinhardt Verlag Munich, Reinhardt Verlag Archives. With thanks to Bettina Hölzl.

61. Bauer, "Sexualstrafrecht heute" in *Sexualität und Verbrechen*, ed. Bauer et al., republished in *Die Humanität der Rechtsordnung*, ed. Perels and Wojak, 303.

62. Theodor W. Adorno, "Sexualtabus und Recht heute," *Sexualität und Verbrechen*, ed. Bauer et al., 301.

63. Ernst-Joachim Lampe et al., *Alternativentwurf eines StGB, Besonderer Teil, Sexualdelikte* (Tübingen: Mohr), 9.

64. *Sitzungsbericht K des 47. Deutschen Juristentages* (Munich: C. H. Beck), 102.

65. Grein, "Der Homosexuelle in Frankfurt am Main," 107.

10

BAUER'S PATH TO ISOLATION

A Fear of Intimacy: The Jurist's Relationship with Other Jews

It was while reading the newspaper one day in August 1964 that a seventeen-year-old girl in Frankfurt learned that her father, Hersz Kugelmann, had just given testimony at the Auschwitz trial. In an unwavering voice and the soft accent of Będzin, the southern Polish city in which he had grown up, Kugelmann had described at the trial his arrival at Auschwitz-Birkenau. Standing on the ramp in front of bellowing SS men making their selections with precise hand gestures, he had watched as his parents and his older daughters, aged just nine and six, were led away to the gas chambers.[1] Years later, Kugelmann was unable to talk about this trauma with his daughter Cilly, who had been born after the war.[2]

"Our parents told us nothing," Cilly Kugelmann said. "We didn't know the facts, but we sensed deep unease, the shadow of a horrific history. I find it difficult to put our feelings into words. I'd describe the atmosphere as oppressive, tragic. There was little laughter; it was as if fun and light-heartedness were barred from entering our home. These years were symbolized for me by the pills my parents swallowed to manage their physical and psychological pain."[3]

Cilly Kugelmann sought solace in the company of Jewish teenagers who found their German surroundings equally oppressive, their schools equally grim, and their families equally damaged. Members of the Zionist Youth Movement of Germany, which had been founded in 1958, eschewed alcohol, cigarettes, rock 'n' roll, and all the other forms of escapism available in 1960s Germany, recalled another member of the movement's Frankfurt branch, Micha Brumlik: "At night, we would sit in front of a roaring fire and swear a sacred oath that as soon as we finished school, we would leave Germany and emigrate to Israel."[4] The teenagers, who produced a kind of student magazine entitled *Me'orot* (Star), looked up to Fritz Bauer, the Jewish jurist confronting the former Nazis. When Kugelmann and Brumlik learned that Bauer had agreed to an interview with the magazine, they were "awestruck."[5]

The attorney general seemed to pay attention to the two young Zionists sitting in front of his desk. Unlike other adults, he listened to them patiently. He answered "even the dumbest questions" about the Nazi trials, Kugelmann noted.[6] And yet he was oddly uncommunicative throughout the meeting.

Decades later, non-Jewish people who had met Bauer when they were young gushed about his warmth and love of debate. Always animated, always challenging, he traveled from podium to podium in the 1960s, encouraging young people to tell him about their political hopes and dreams, engaging them in debate until they found themselves tied up in their own contradictions. The son of the Frankfurt writer Hans Frick once asked, "Mr. Bauer, are you a communist?" Bauer took a deep breath, cleared his throat, and gave a long explanation to the ten-year-old seated beside him on the sofa. Afterward, the child told his father, "I'd like to talk to Mr. Bauer when I'm older and I know a bit more about politics. He took me really seriously. He's not like other people."[7]

But according to Cilly Kugelmann, there was nothing paternal, nothing warm about Bauer's behavior during their interview.[8] He mentioned nothing about Judaism or Israel, subjects close to the interviewers' hearts—not even in the small talk at the end of the interview. He could have said a great deal about these subjects if he had wanted to. By this time, his work had brought him to Israel many times, and he had been grappling with the idea of Zionism since he was a young man himself. As a student in Heidelberg, he had taken part in heated debates on Zionism, and after the outbreak of the Six-Day War in 1967, he was one of the first to ask Frankfurt's Jewish community how he could make a donation to Israel.[9] Yet in the interview, Bauer remained silent on such topics.

Ever since his return from exile, Bauer had been playing down the one thing that distinguished him from most of the Germans he sought to win over. He didn't want people to identify him with his Jewishness. He had no Jewish friends. He maintained a professional distance from the few other returned Jewish emigrants he encountered at work, and he had nothing to do with them outside working hours. As illustrated by the threatening letters flooding his office, many Germans were already convinced that a "Jewish clique" in Frankfurt's judiciary was leading a witch-hunt. Bauer was no doubt keen to avoid fueling this paranoia any further.

At the time, Frankfurt—and more precisely, the Westend district where Bauer lived and the synagogue was located—was the center of Jewish life in Germany.[10] One of the leaders of the city's Jewish community was a jurist named Paul Arnsberg. Like Bauer, who was four years younger, the intellectual Arnsberg had been dismissed from the civil service in 1933 and had worked as a journalist after going into exile. The secretary general of the Central Council of Jews in Germany, Hendrik George van Dam, was also a jurist. After the war, while Bauer was working in Brunswick, van Dam had helped establish the justice system in Oldenburg, another city in Lower Saxony. Bauer generally kept his distance from such figures, though he did give a speech to Vienna's Jewish community in the 1960s, having been invited by someone he was interested in for professional reasons: the famous "Nazi hunter" Simon Wiesenthal.[11] It is likely that Bauer accepted the invitation in the hope of having an opportunity to glean some information from Wiesenthal in private. Bauer's focus was their common work, not their shared identity.

On another occasion in the 1960s, Bauer was invited to a dinner organized by the Hamburg-based publisher of *Die Zeit*, Gerd Bucerius. Bauer was taken aback to find himself seated next to the newspaper's literary editor, Marcel Reich-Ranicki.[12] Bauer and Reich-Ranicki didn't hit it off, partly, perhaps, because Bauer was annoyed at being placed next to *Die Zeit*'s only Jewish editor (and not, for example, next to the Protestant resistance member Marion Gräfin Dönhoff). Yet the host's seating plan wasn't completely wrong-headed; after all, Reich-Ranicki had expressed support for Bauer's work. In the edition of *Die Zeit* published on May 22, 1964, the literary editor had called on German writers to attend the Auschwitz trial in order to demonstrate that they counted among the people who wished to "uncover" the past, not cover it up.[13] The relationship between Bauer and Reich-Ranicki may have been put under strain that evening because so many people were observing them, wondering if the two Jews would get on with each other. In any case, Bauer was later quick to point out that he had found Reich-Ranicki insufferable.

More than two hundred concentration camp survivors came to Frankfurt to give testimony at the Auschwitz trial. Some had written Bauer warm letters when the investigations into Auschwitz were launched back in 1959, having heard that he himself was a survivor and returned emigrant.[14] They presented him with a stone from the camp, which he kept in his office.[15] But on a personal level, Bauer kept his distance from the witnesses. In several press interviews of the time, he referred to the tattoos marking Auschwitz survivors' "right hands." In fact, numbers had been tattooed onto prisoners' left hands. Bauer had first noticed the tattoo—which reminded him of the branding "on an animal being led to slaughter"—on a young woman sitting next to him in a café in Frankfurt, he said in an August 1963 radio interview: "As she was drinking her coffee, [the sleeve of] her sweater rode up and I saw the Auschwitz number on her right hand . . . blue, visible."[16] Later, when the trial was underway and the first witnesses were about to testify, Bauer made the same mistake: the public would soon be able to see the tattoos, he told a journalist, when hundreds of survivors took the stand and raised their right hands to swear their oaths.[17] A year later, as the trial was coming to a close, Bauer made the error a third time.[18] It may seem like a small detail, but had Bauer spent time getting to know survivors personally, he wouldn't have got it wrong.

Bauer met a couple of times with the secretary general of the International Auschwitz Committee, Hermann Langbein, to discuss how they might work together on gathering evidence. But Bauer had one important request: that Langbein never refer publicly to their collaboration. The reason for such caution was obvious to Henry Ormond, the attorney representing civil plaintiffs at the Auschwitz trial, who warned the committee against holding a press conference on the status of Bauer's investigation: "You would only provide the defense with arguments to support their claim that Eastern propaganda is driving the entire trial."[19]

On August 1, 1959, Langbein wrote Bauer a furious letter criticizing the latter for accepting the release of the suspect Klaus Dylewski from custody.[20] Bauer took umbrage at Langbein's presumptuous tone. "I respect Mr. Langbein and greatly appreciate his assistance," Joachim Kügler, one of the young prosecutors, later remarked. "But we (Vogel and I) both resisted any attempt by Mr. Langbein to call the shots. . . . It was like a journalist from some newspaper coming and saying, 'Listen to me, I'm going to tell you prosecutors how to do your job.'"[21] Despite his annoyance, Bauer urged his team to exercise tactical restraint so as to avoid attracting public attention to their collaboration with the International Auschwitz Committee.[22]

By this stage, Bauer had almost entirely pulled back from his relationship with Langbein. To keep the secretary general at a safe distance, Bauer's communication now took the form of short, polite, formulaic letters, and he no longer met with Langbein in person, sending subordinates to meetings instead. Bauer avoided personal relationships with Holocaust victims, though these only wanted to offer him their support, because he was determined to protect the prosecution's credibility and maintain an image of political objectivity and impartiality. He would pay a high price for this detachment.

In 1965, Langbein published a book about the recently concluded Auschwitz trial, in which he praised the judges, the civil attorney, and even the defense lawyers. The prosecutors, in contrast, were fiercely criticized, but it was Bauer—the trial's instigator, to whom Langbein had once written hopeful letters about "our" Auschwitz proceedings—who received the most severe punishment: He wasn't mentioned once in the two-volume work, a glaring omission that reveals the degree of Langbein's anger and disappointment.[23] Bauer "is a gaping absence throughout [Langbein's] account" of the trial, notes Katharina Stengel, Langbein's biographer.[24] The survivors' organization had once seen Bauer as a natural ally, but it now treated him like a traitor. Bauer's Jewish background made his putative betrayal even worse.

In their interview with Bauer in September 1964, Cilly Kugelmann and Micha Brumlik eventually managed to squeeze in one question about Jewish life in contemporary Germany. Some had argued that the trials of Nazi criminals might actually be harmful to Jews today, they said. Was this true? Bauer changed the topic and evaded the question, and the young Zionists were too shy to press him for an answer.[25]

The tragedy is that Bauer pushed away the one group that would have truly accepted him, thereby maneuvering himself into a position even more isolated than that of his parents and grandparents during the Weimar period. They had always insisted that they were German *and* Jewish. Thus, when others tried to negate their German identity, they could at least find a sense of belonging in their Jewish group identity. Bauer, in contrast, had decided in 1945 to distance himself from everything Jewish in the hope that this would allow him to be fully recognized as German. He made a habit of quoting canonical German writers such as Fichte, Goethe, and Schiller; he emphasized the fact that he had gone to school with Hitler's would-be assassin, Stauffenberg; and he celebrated as "Germanic" Stauffenberg's right to resist the dictator. In his will, which he wrote six months before his death on New Year's Eve 1967, Bauer stipulated that his body was to be cremated, adding that "the ashes must not be inurned."[26] Given that the Jewish tradition forbids cremation, this was a deeply un-Jewish request. Toward the end of his life, though, Bauer realized that all these attempts to distance himself from his Jewish heritage had ultimately been of little benefit. When the East German state publishing house presented at the 1967 Frankfurt Book Fair a "Brown Book" containing the names of Nazi jurists, numerous West German politicians expressed indignation at Bauer's refusal to confiscate the publication. Referring to the controversy, Bauer wrote in a letter to a friend, "It is appalling to see how such incidents unite this country's brown elements and incite witch-hunts. And it is the Jew who is burned to death."[27]

"At the age when most people retire, Fritz Bauer was startlingly active, unfinished, going through crises," recalled the Frankfurt-based writer Horst Krüger, who became friends with Bauer shortly after attending the Auschwitz trial. "There was always something simmering inside him. He smoked an inordinate amount and had a worrying cough. He railed against society, but he battled with himself above all. He began to talk a lot about his childhood, about the torment of his difficult upbringing. Right before he died, he was thinking about undergoing psychoanalysis. At sixty-four years of age, he was ferociously questioning himself. What other German jurist would do that? They're 'done'—and they all look that way too."[28]

A few years after Bauer's death, during an interview conducted in the tranquil surroundings of an upmarket hotel in Switzerland, Bauer's sister, Margot, remarked that her brother "was like a sabra: He didn't want people to see how tender he was inside."²⁹ "Sabra" is a quintessentially Jewish term. The Yiddish word for the prickly pear—a soft, sweet cactus fruit covered in spines—it refers to people born in Israel, who are said to be equally prickly on the outside and soft on the inside. In invoking this familiar Israeli metaphor, Margot Bauer—who by then was almost seventy and had never returned from Scandinavia—revealed a great deal about her relaxed, affectionate attitude toward her Jewish heritage. It's impossible to imagine her brother, who had returned to Germany after the war to bring about political change, drawing attention to his Jewishness with such ease.

"He Was Impossible to Talk To": Bauer and His Young Team of Prosecutors

The young man whispering to the two gray-haired Nazi criminals was by now a well-known figure in the city. His blond hair was styled into a fashionable pompadour; his slightly stocky frame was dressed in a perfectly tailored suit; and with his soft, warm Hessian accent and strong, clear delivery, his voice effortlessly filled the courtroom. He still wore the trademark black horn-rimmed spectacles he had worn while delivering the closing statement at the Auschwitz trial three years ago. Back then, he had been a state prosecutor. He had since changed sides.

The young man in question, Joachim Kügler, was now working as a defense attorney in the very same courthouse. Bauer was also involved in the trial that was currently in progress, though he himself was not present in the courtroom. In November 1967, on the very first day of the trial, one of the two defendants, a man named Adolf Heinz Beckerle, had railed against the state's attorney general, claiming that he, the defendant, had lost his livelihood as a result of the "brutal persecution" he had suffered. Bauer, safely enthroned up in his office, was the driving force behind this persecution, according to Beckerle; the lowly prosecutor leading the case in the courtroom was just Bauer's minion.

Kügler was on Beckerle's defense counsel. The trial, which became known as the "Frankfurt diplomat trial," was an historic one. In his closing statement in August 1968, Kügler raised some fundamental questions about the West German judiciary's engagement with the Nazi past. In doing so, he implicitly cast doubts on the Auschwitz trial. He spoke about the uneasiness that ought to accompany any attempt now, a quarter of a century after the war had ended, to determine the truth. It was obvious, Kügler claimed, that people living under the Nazi regime had had no degree of independence. They had been mere "human material," he said, and as such, they hadn't had the option of choosing between right and wrong. Kügler therefore questioned whether it was in

Figure 10.1. Prosecutor Joachim Kügler started out as Bauer's protégé in the Auschwitz trial—and turned into his opponent. Credit/Source: *Fritz Bauer Institute*.

the "common good" to keep prosecuting Nazi crimes. There was no doubt, he said, that such trials caused damage. With its slogan of "You can vote again," the far-right National Democratic Party of Germany (Nationaldemokratische Partei Deutschlands, or NPD) had won seats in the state parliaments of Hesse and Bavaria in 1966 and of Bremen, Rhineland-Palatinate, Lower Saxony, and Schleswig-Holstein in 1967. Right-wing extremists wouldn't have enjoyed such success were it not for the recent trials of former Nazis, Kügler argued.[30]

Bauer didn't live to hear his former protégé utter these rancorous words. But the very public rift between the state's attorney general and Kügler had been growing for years. Bauer was still alive when Kügler began defending Nazi criminals, and he watched from the sidelines as Hans Laternser, the most aggressive defense lawyer in the Auschwitz trial, welcomed Kügler into his lawyers' guild. Bauer heard Laternser describe Kügler as "the prosecutor with the most extensive expertise" when it came to Nazi crimes.[31] Back in 1961, Bauer had still believed that the general public recognized "the necessity of such trials" and that virtually "the entire younger generation and a large proportion of the older one" supported them.[32] The public reaction to the Auschwitz trial punctured this optimism. One survey found that only 60 percent of Germans had even heard of the trial.[33] In an interview conducted after the verdict had been delivered, Bauer told an Israeli journalist that "the educational effect of these trials has been minimal, if indeed they have had any effect at all."[34] Sixty-three percent of men and 76 percent of women believed that the state should stop prosecuting Nazi crimes—and Kügler, the talented young lawyer whom Bauer had once had great hopes for, was their key witness.[35]

Bauer had always depended on the loyalty of his hand-picked young prosecutors, but the demands he placed on them over the years sorely tested this loyalty. He was so worried about other colleagues sabotaging the Auschwitz investigations that from 1963 to 1965, he insisted his Auschwitz prosecutors work in a separate building he had rented for them next to the building where the other prosecutors were based.[36] They felt "abandoned and alone" in this spartan, uncomfortable outpost far from Bauer's huge office, Kügler recalled.[37] To make matters worse, they faced hostility from other members of Frankfurt's judiciary, including judges who privately threatened them with "armed neutrality."[38] Such animosity was par for the course for anyone working on Bauer's Nazi cases.

Many older jurists who had painstakingly worked their way up through the judiciary looked on with suspicion as Bauer filled important positions with inexperienced prosecutors. The only asset these new hires shared was that they had begun their studies after the fall of the Third Reich. They may have studied under professors who had been implicated in the Nazi regime, but at least they hadn't gained their qualifications within the system that had barracked trainees in Nazi training camps. Bauer therefore fast-tracked the careers of Kügler and other new recruits.

One of these other recruits was the thirty-three-year-old Johannes Warlo. Warlo looks even younger in photos taken at the time; his wavy blond hair combed smooth, he appears earnest and a little wary, as if he is trying hard to be taken seriously.[39] Apart from a stint working as a prosecutor of white-collar crime, Warlo had very little experience when he was hired. He was ordered to report directly to Bauer, who immediately entrusted him with the euthanasia investigations and the proceedings against Martin Bormann, two highly sensitive and important cases. Warlo was given an office with two long-serving prosecutors whose mistrust immediately became apparent. When he returned from the restroom, he would catch them scurrying away from the top-secret Nazi files on his desk. On hearing of this, Bauer quickly provided Warlo with his own office. It was small and dark, but at least it was safe from prying eyes. Whenever Warlo passed by his more established colleagues in the courthouse, their conversations would fall silent.[40]

Bauer, who liked Warlo's down-to-earth manner, once asked for the latter's opinion on the modern checkered wallpaper hanging in his office. Warlo replied that it reminded him of a funeral parlor, prompting Bauer to burst out laughing. On another occasion, Bauer upbraided Warlo for drafting a pleading that met the exact requirements set by judges in earlier cases. "Are you the kind of person who's only interested in pleasing the judges?" he asked. Bauer couldn't stand servility; he wanted his prosecutors to stand up for themselves, not kowtow to their superiors. "He expected us to disagree with others—and with him, too," Warlo explained.[41] During a job interview with a junior lawyer in 1956, Bauer demanded to know the applicant's view on the debate raging in Berlin about the fate of the Kaiser-Wilhelm Gedächtniskirche (Memorial Church). The debate centered on the question of whether the church, which had been badly damaged during the war, should be rebuilt or torn down entirely. Bauer believed it ought to be torn down, but the applicant, Gerhard Wiese—a fourth-generation Berliner—vehemently disagreed. Neither of the men budged from their positions, but Bauer subsequently selected this opinionated applicant to join the Auschwitz prosecution team.[42]

Bauer's "young guard," as they were known around the courthouse, were in the direct line of fire when he decided to tackle the older generation of jurists. He initiated proceedings against sixty-eight Hessian judges for Nazi crimes and perverting the course of justice after an East German report entitled *Gestern Hitlers Blutrichter, heute Bonner Justiz-Elite* (Yesterday, Hitler's Blood Judges; Today, Bonn's Judicial Elite) revealed these judges' pasts.[43] This was to be the largest prosecution of Nazi jurists in the country's history; never before had a West German prosecutor stirred up so much trouble with his own colleagues. Bauer urged the team responsible for Nazi crimes to act as swiftly as possible, as it was imperative to have the investigation up and running before the statute of limitations for manslaughter elapsed in 1960.[44] The prosecutors' investigations achieved little in legal terms, as all the defendants were acquitted in the end. Unwilling to convict their colleagues, the judges who heard the cases ruled that the defendants had been unaware of the unlawfulness of their actions during the Nazi period.[45] But in shining a spotlight on the Nazi pasts of several jurists, the trials had an important political impact. One of the major figures affected was the federal attorney general, Wolfgang Fränkel, who was forced to retire after revelations about his involvement with the Nazi regime became public in 1962. Such developments only isolated Bauer further, however. During this period, he was often heard to say, "Whenever I leave my office, I find myself in enemy territory."[46]

Nevertheless, Bauer was ensconced in a secure position and could afford to shrug off the hostility he faced in the judiciary. In contrast, the young prosecutors directly conducting investigations into their superiors had their entire careers ahead of them. Once, during a conference for criminal lawyers in the

1960s, Bauer sat alone at breakfast while the other participants sat around chatting at their tables. Nobody wanted to sit with him, until eventually, to his relief, a young legal scholar named Ernst-Walter Hanack joined him. "The state's attorney general cut a lonely figure," Hanack recalled.[47] Meanwhile, back in Frankfurt, few people took any interest in the welfare of the prosecutors working on Bauer's contentious cases. These young men, who were harboring grave worries about their careers, were disheartened to find that even Bauer was largely uninterested in the difficulties they faced.

Their situation was exacerbated by a change in personnel. In October 1963, the ministry of justice sent Bauer a deputy, a man who could scarcely have been more different from Bauer himself. The fifty-six-year-old Ulrich Krüger was tall, wiry, and athletic, with a pronounced Adam's apple and a sharp hooked nose.[48] Known for his extreme fastidiousness, Krüger would order his subordinates to rewrite documents containing even the tiniest error. He never touched cigarettes. Prior to 1945, Krüger had worked as a prosecutor at a Nazi "special court" in Frankfurt, where he had been responsible for political trials.[49] After the war, nobody accused Krüger of being overly zealous during his tenure at the "special court." It was true that he had joined an SA cavalry unit in 1933, but a denazification commission decided he had only done this because the president of Frankfurt's higher regional court had demanded that every trainee be a member of a Nazi organization. Krüger's membership in the Nazi Party, which he joined in 1937, was excused for the same reason. Now, in fall 1963, the ministry of justice was sending him to the state's attorney general's office in Frankfurt in the hope that he would act as a counterbalance to the headstrong Bauer. Rather than attempting to resist the move, Bauer responded pragmatically, delegating all the bureaucratic tasks he hated to his punctilious new deputy. These tasks included handling personnel matters such as leave requests, evaluations, and—crucially—promotions. Bauer probably assumed that such tasks were of little political import. This was a mistake that would have serious repercussions for his young prosecutors.

In putting Krüger in charge of personnel, Bauer placed the professional advancement of his few loyal followers in the hands of someone far less favorably disposed toward them. From the moment they were hired, the young jurists personally selected by Bauer had had to put up with antagonistic colleagues who resented their rapid career progression. Bauer's protégés were widely viewed within the Frankfurt judiciary as upstarts who could only afford to be impertinent toward older colleagues because they were being protected by the attorney general. But it seemed that Bauer could no longer be counted on to protect them. The "young guard" now had to submit their applications for promotion and their requests for additional resources to Krüger, who invariably turned them down. Krüger thereby allowed the Nazi investigations—of which he was no fan—to founder, both in the state's attorney general's office, where Johannes Warlo worked, and in the prosecutor's office in Frankfurt's regional court, where the Auschwitz prosecutors Joachim Kügler, Georg Friedrich Vogel, and Gerhard Wiese were based. Meanwhile, jurists working in politically innocuous areas overtook Warlo, Kügler, Vogel, and Wiese on the career ladder, progressing to higher, better paid grades. The young guard was left behind.

Kügler, who "always steered well clear" of Bauer's deputy, eventually sought advice from Warlo.[50] During their discussion, Kügler reminded Warlo that Bauer had once promised them their dedication wouldn't be forgotten, that he would always look out for them. Over the previous two years, Kügler had delivered the performance of a top lawyer while earning an entry-level salary. For the duration of the Auschwitz trial, he had gone home with a net salary of 1,300 Deutschmarks per month (the equivalent of around $325 at the time).[51] Kügler wasn't the only one unhappy with his pay. Hesse's other state prosecutors and judges were also protesting their low salaries—for good reason, according to a 1965 article in *Die Zeit*: "Judges are looking on helplessly as [remuneration for] roughly comparable government legal positions keeps sailing upward."[52] Kügler had hoped that now that the Auschwitz trial had been successfully concluded, he would be promoted to a higher pay grade. After making his closing statement at the trial, he had asked Bauer to be transferred to a less stressful position. He wanted to be moved away from Nazi crimes, away from the firing line of the ill-humored Krüger, and back onto the career ladder. But Bauer refused. "We've lived a fulfilled life when we've moved things forward by the breadth of a matchstick," Bauer told Kügler.[53]

The sixty-year-old concentration camp survivor's earnestness did not satisfy Kügler, who was concerned about his career development. The two men seemed to inhabit different worlds. Bauer's personal experiences may have taught him that nothing is more important than politics and that one must be prepared to make sacrifices, but Kügler wanted to be able to enjoy life. "You're an expert now," Bauer said, and advised Kügler to keep working on Nazi trials.[54] This is ultimately what Kügler decided to do, but not in the way Bauer had in mind.

The young guard's disappointment in Bauer may have been exacerbated by the fact that he was clearly capable of being considerate toward other people. Indeed, he could be extremely generous toward low-ranking staff. Bauer had a chauffeur, Heinz Eichwald, whom he had brought with him from Brunswick to Frankfurt. Some of Bauer's colleagues at the courthouse found Eichwald rather rough, with his brawny appearance and gruff manner. It was so smoky inside Bauer's car—a black and silver Opel Kapitän with wraparound windshields

front and back and more chrome accessories than an American limousine—
that the young prosecutors became nauseous whenever they traveled in it, but
the smoke never bothered Eichwald.[55] Bauer made no secret of his fondness for
his chauffeur—whom according to Bauer's sister, he loved "like a son"—and
once even paid for Eichwald and Eichwald's wife to visit Israel.[56]

In December 1962, as Bauer and his chauffeur were on their way to Göttingen University, where Bauer was supposed to give a talk, their car skidded on
an icy street, overturned, and crashed into some trees. The following Saturday,
Eichwald died in hospital as a result of his injuries.[57] Bauer, who had survived
unscathed, placed a death notice in the *Frankfurter Neue Presse*. In the notice,
the usually undemonstrative Bauer quoted from "Ich hatt' einen Kameraden"
(I Had a Comrade), a rousing soldiers' anthem known to be popular among the
lower classes. The song's second verse appeared in the middle of the notice:

> A bullet came a-flying
> Is it my turn or yours?
> He was swept away,
> He lies at my feet,
> Like he was a part of me.[58]

When they saw the death notice, Bauer's young guard, accustomed to being
treated coldly by Bauer, were aghast at the manner in which their boss presented
himself as a caring friend to his employees.[59]

Did Bauer really do nothing to help the prosecutors being snubbed because
of their work on Nazi trials? In 1967, Warlo had to get the union involved to make
sure he wasn't passed over yet again in the next round of promotions.[60] By this
stage, some members of management were voicing complaints about Krüger's
political machinations, but Bauer remained silent. If he took his deputy to task
behind closed doors, it never became apparent, and so the young guard became
even more convinced that their loyalty to Bauer was unreciprocated.

Out of courtesy, Kügler waited for a few weeks after the trial concluded
before resigning. "In the civil service, nonconformists are seen as outsiders," he
told a journalist shortly afterward.[61] In an interview with another journalist, he
said, "How do we live today? Certainly not in harmony. The judiciary demonstrates that we live in conflict with each other."[62] Decades later, Kügler was still
bitter: "Don't expect any thanks from the state," he warned.[63]

Kügler rented a small office diagonally opposite the regional court and
began offering his services as a defense lawyer. His expertise put him in high
demand, particularly among those accused of Nazi crimes, and he was able to
charge substantial fees. He never contacted Bauer again. "He was impossible to
talk to anyway," Kügler said. Whenever the two men ran into each other in the

courthouse, the expressions on their faces spoke volumes. "He just kept walking. 'Hello'. That's all he said." [64]

"The Left Keeps Offering Its Utopias": Disillusionment at the End

Bauer could always count on his popularity among students and young artists. Back in 1961, the student newspaper *Diskus* had published a front-page article by "The State's Attorney General Dr. Fritz Bauer."[65] A representative of the Sozialistischer Deutscher Studentenbund (Socialist German Students' Union, or SDS), Joachim Perels, was present at an April 1968 meeting between Bauer and the president of the higher labor court, Hans G. Joachim, which resulted in the launch of a new legal journal. Entitled *Kritische Justiz* (Critical Justice), the journal aimed to provide a forum for voices outside the conservative mainstream. Perels and another young participant in the meeting, a trainee lawyer named Jan Gehlsen, came up with the journal's name. Bauer was pleased with their allusion to the 1920s' journal of the Republican Association of Judges, *Die Justiz* (Justice).[66]

Bauer had a good relationship with the members of the SDS. As a result, when stones and Molotov cocktails began flying around the streets of Frankfurt, newspapers published by the conservative Axel Springer company were quick to accuse the left-wing, antiauthoritarian Hessian attorney general of not cracking down hard enough on the "career revolutionaries of the SDS."[67] In fact, several student protesters were brought to trial in Frankfurt, and their treatment was not particularly lenient. Yet of all the members of the German judiciary criticized for not being punitive enough, Bauer was the only one mentioned by name: "Mr. Fritz Bauer has just suspended the rule of law," the *Welt am Sonntag* lamented in April 1968.[68]

In 1967, two communards named Fritz Teufel and Rainer Langhans found themselves facing criminal charges in Berlin. In response to a recent fire in a department store in Brussels that had killed more than three hundred people, Teufel and Langhans had distributed pamphlets. "A burning department store with burning people, that sizzling Vietnam feeling—of being there, of burning too—is a feeling we've been sorely lacking in Berlin up to now," the pamphlets read. "Burn, warehouse, burn."[69] Did this constitute incitement to violence? No, it was just satire, believed the jurist Manfred Amend, who was a friend of Bauer's. According to Amend, the communards' irony was comparable to that of the Irish writer Jonathan Swift in "A Modest Proposal," a 1729 satire suggesting that impoverished Irish peasants sell off their numerous children as delicacies to rich English ladies and gentlemen. Bauer mentioned the Swift comparison in a conversation with the attorney general of Berlin a short while later.⁷⁰ The judges also adopted this liberal perspective and ultimately acquitted the communards.

The verdict had scarcely been delivered when a department store really did go up in flames, but in Frankfurt, not Berlin. On the night of April 2, 1968, Andreas Baader, Gudrun Ensslin, and Thorwald Proll planted incendiary devices in two department stores on the Zeil, a shopping promenade not far from Bauer's office. As the devices had been set to go off after closing time, no one was killed in the fires. Nevertheless, the attacks triggered fear throughout the country and brought shame to Bauer, the liberal. The violence must have come as a bitter blow to someone with so much faith in Germany's young protesters. Bauer had eagerly awaited the arrival of a generation who would hold their parents to account for Nazi crimes. But now this confrontation seemed to have taken an ominous turn. In resorting to violence, in attempting to instill fear into society, Bauer believed the young rebels had made a grave strategic mistake.⁷¹

Bauer accused the protesters of having their heads in the clouds. He told his friend Amend that growing uneasiness about their precarious employment prospects was the likely reason why students were becoming increasingly radical. There weren't enough jobs for all the sociologists and political scientists graduating from West German universities, he said.⁷² But he also admitted that his own generation had been dangerously divorced from reality at times: "We emigrants cherished our own delusions. Willy Brandt and I used to publish an emigrants' newspaper. We thought there was a positive side to the fact that Germany lay in ruins. Once the rubble was cleared away, we would build the cities of the future. Big, bright, and humane. Bauhaus. Gropius. Mies van der Rohe. That's what we believed back then. Everything would be reinvented on a grand scale. But then along came other people who said, 'But the sewers are still intact beneath the rubble!' So German cities were rebuilt around the sewers."⁷³ Bauer criticized the left for being similarly naïve and out of touch with reality in the late 1960s: "The left keeps offering its utopias," he grumbled in a meeting with the young writer Gerhard Zwerenz. "But what good is a utopia when the cities have been built around the sewers?"⁷⁴

Bauer felt a deep sense of anxiety and pessimism as he observed the state's repressive crackdown on the 1968 protest movement: "Look at the early years of the Bonn Republic! No Wehrmacht. No strongman politics. Now look at today's politics and the emergency laws that have been introduced. Line up a ruler. What direction is it pointing? Toward the right! Where's it all going to lead in the long term? To a dystopia at best! Thankfully we're old. We won't live to see it."⁷⁵

There was a rupture in Bauer's private life around this time, too. He had always enjoyed the company of young artists, and the theater director and filmmaker Thomas Harlan had long been a close friend. Once, when going through a particularly difficult time, Bauer had written wistfully to Harlan, "Sometimes I think the sun over Ascona combined with Thomas Harlan would be the best medicine and psychotherapy for me."[76] A few years later, in 1967, Harlan tried to convince Bauer to buy a property in Switzerland. The two of them could live there, Harlan said, and form a little artists' colony, plus it could double as a retirement home for Bauer, whom Harlan expected to foot the entire bill.

Bauer had demonstrated generosity on several occasions in the past, but the idea of purchasing property was a step too far for him. It was "too damn expensive," he told Harlan, pointing out that in any case, he planned to keep working until 1971.[77] (As a victim of the Nazis, Bauer was entitled to retire three years later than the statutory retirement age.) He felt "no shortage" of longing for southern Europe, "but what would be the point in me having a villa there at the moment, seeing as I would only be able to visit it for a couple of weeks, and seeing as its future might be endangered by a virus or viruses (I mean that symbolically!)?" Bauer wrote, alluding darkly to his deteriorating health.[78]

Harlan wasn't prepared to give up so easily, and Bauer had to fob him off repeatedly. At one point, Bauer, who obviously found it difficult to admit to himself that he was being taken advantage of, even apologized for not being as wealthy as Harlan seemed to think. The letters went back and forth until Bauer eventually plucked up the courage to end the friendship. But even in his last lines to Harlan, Bauer was apologetic. He was sorry if he seemed "callous," he wrote.[79]

Notes

1. Fritz Bauer Institute, ed., *Der Auschwitz-Prozess. Tonbandmitschnitte, Protokolle und Dokumente*, 3rd edition (Berlin: Directmedia Publishing, 2007), DVD-ROM, 15,481.
2. Cilly Kugelmann, interview by author, October 17, 2012.
3. Quoted in Olivier Guez, *Heimkehr der Unerwünschten*, 133.
4. Quoted in Elke Wittich, "Mit 17 hat man noch Träume. Die Zionistische Jugend Deutschlands wird 50–viele Aktivisten blicken wehmütig zurück," *Jüdische Allgemeine*, July 23, 2009.
5. Prof. Micha Brumlik, interview by author, October 17, 2012.
6. Kugelmann, interview by author.
7. See Hans Frick, *Henri* (Reinbek: Rowohlt, 1970), 42ff.
8. Kugelmann, interview by author.
9. See P. A. (Paul Arnsberg), "Nachrufe: Generalstaatsanwalt Dr. Fritz Bauer," *Frankfurter Jüdisches Gemeindeblatt*, July/August 1968, 15.
10. See Dan Diner, "Im Zeichen des Banns," in *Geschichte der Juden in Deutschland von 1945 bis zur Gegenwart*, ed. Michael Brenner, 55–58.

11. See Tom Segev, *Simon Wiesenthal. Die Biographie* (Munich: Siedler Verlag, 2010), 222.
12. Amend, interview by author.
13. See Stephan Braese, "'In einer deutschen Angelegenheit'—Der Frankfurter Auschwitz-Prozess in der westdeutschen Nachkriegsliteratur," in *"Gerichtstag halten über uns selbst . . . ,"* ed. Irmtrud Wojak, 217–219.
14. See Werner Renz, "(Un-) Begründete Selbstkritik. Überlegungen zu einer skeptischen Bilanz Fritz Bauers. In memoriam Fritz Bauer (1903–1968)," *Tribüne. Zeitschrift zum Verständnis des Judentums* 190/2 (2009): 129, footnote 19.
15. Tiefenthal, interview by Walter Fabian.
16. Bauer, *Zu den Naziverbrecher-Prozessen. Das politische Gespräch*, 116.
17. Bauer, "Nach den Wurzeln des Bösen fragen," *Die Tat*, March 7, 1964, 12.
18. See Bauer, "Antinazistische Prozesse und politisches Bewußtsein. Dienen NS-Prozesse der politischen Aufklärung?" in *Antisemitismus. Zur Pathologie der bürgerlichen Gesellschaft*, ed. Hermann Huss and Andreas Schröder (Frankfurt am Main: Europäische Verlagsanstalt, 1965), 172.
19. Henry Ormond to Hermann Langbein, April 11, 1960, quoted in Katharina Stengel, *Hermann Langbein. Ein Auschwitz-Überlebender in den erinnerungspolitischen Konflikten der Nachkriegszeit* (Frankfurt am Main: Campus, 2012), 435.
20. See Katharina Stengel, *Hermann Langbein. Ein Auschwitz-Überlebender in den erinnerungspolitischen Konflikten der Nachkriegszeit*, 419.
21. Kügler, interview by Werner Renz.
22. See meeting minutes by Vogel, August 4, 1959, file number 4 Js 444/59, sheet 54, Hessisches Hauptstaatsarchiv, Wiesbaden.
23. Langbein to Bauer, March 31, 1961, call number N1 HL E/1797: 96, Österreichisches Staatsarchiv, Vienna; quoted in Stengel, *Hermann Langbein*, 438.
24. Stengel, *Hermann Langbein*, 438.
25. See Bauer, "Interview mit der Zeitschrift der Zionistischen Jugend Deutschlands," *Me'orot*, October/November 1964; and Brumlik, interview by author.
26. Bauer's handwritten will, December 31, 1967, Manfred Amend's personal archive.
27. Bauer to Harlan, late 1967.
28. Horst Krüger, "Fremdling in der Stadt. Gedenkblatt für Fritz Bauer," *Die Zeit*, July 12, 1968.
29. Tiefenthal, interview by Fabian.
30. See "Verteidiger bezweifelt den Sinn der NS-Verfahren," *Frankfurter Allgemeine Zeitung*, August 8, 1968.
31. Hans Laternser, *Die andere Seite im Auschwitz-Prozess 1963/1965* (Stuttgart-Degerloch: Seewald, 1966).
32. Bauer, "Der SS-Staat in Person," *Weltbild*, January 13, 1961, 4.
33. See Bauer, "Im Namen des Volkes. Die strafrechtliche Bewältigung der Vergangenheit" (1965), republished in *Die Humanität der Rechtsordnung*, ed. Perels and Wojak, 78.
34. Amos Elon, *In einem heimgesuchten Land. Reise eines israelischen Journalisten in beide deutsche Staaten* (Munich: Kindler, 1966), 376.
35. See Bauer, "Im Namen des Volkes. Die strafrechtliche Bewältigung der Vergangenheit," 78.
36. Wiese, interview by author.
37. Kügler, interview by Renz.
38. Warlo, interview by author.
39. Warlo's personal archive.

40. Warlo, interview by author.
41. Ibid.
42. Wiese, interview by author.
43. See Matthias Meusch, *Von der Diktatur zur Demokratie. Fritz Bauer und die Aufarbeitung der NS-Verbrechen in Hessen (1956–68)* (Wiesbaden: Historische Kommission für Nassau, 2001), 246ff., 251.
44. See Claudia Fröhlich, "Wider die Tabuisierung des Ungehorsams," 287.
45. See Meusch, *Von der Diktatur zur Demokratie*, 245, 250f.
46. Quoted in Helga Einsele, "Worte der Erinnerung," in *Fritz Bauer. Eine Denkschrift*, ed. Hessisches Ministerium der Justiz (Wiesbaden: Hessisches Ministerium der Justiz, 1993), 21.
47. Quoted in Thomas Horstmann and Heike Litzinger, *An den Grenzen des Rechts*, 80.
48. Warlo, interview by author, and photos from Warlo's personal archive.
49. See Ulrich Krüger's *Spruchkammer* (denazification court) files, call number Abt. 520 F-Z Nr. 6441, Hessisches Hauptstaatsarchiv, Wiesbaden.
50. Kügler, interview by Renz; and Warlo, interview by author.
51. Kügler, interview by Renz.
52. Gerhard Ziegler, "Das karge Brot des Richters. Für 1300 Mark Gehalt Ankläger im Auschwitz-Prozeß," *Die Zeit*, December 24, 1965.
53. Quoted in Jürgen Serke, "Der Moralist," *Stern*, April 18, 1974.
54. Kügler, interview by Renz.
55. Günter Wehrheim, interview by author, October 17, 2012.
56. Tiefenthal, interview by Fabian.
57. See *Frankfurter Rundschau*, "Den Unfallfolgen erlegen," December 12, 1962.
58. *Frankfurter Neue Presse*, death notice, December 12, 1962.
59. Warlo and Wiese, interviews by author; Kügler, interview by Renz.
60. Warlo, interview by author.
61. Quoted in Ziegler, "Das karge Brot des Richters."
62. Quoted in Jürgen Serke, "Der Moralist," *Stern*, April 18, 1974.
63. Kügler, interview by Renz.
64. Ibid.
65. *Diskus. Frankfurter Studentenzeitung*, "Generalstaatsanwalt Dr. Fritz Bauer, Im Gleichschritt marsch? Widerstandspflicht aus Nächstenliebe," vol. 11 (December 1961).
66. Dr. Joachim Perels, interview by author, February 20, 2013. Bauer had originally been in favor of a different title for the journal: "Kampf ums Recht" (Fight for the Law).
67. William S. Schlamm, "Suspendierte Justiz," *Welt am Sonntag*, April 21, 1968.
68. Ibid.
69. Kommune I, "Warum brennst du, Konsument?," pamphlet no. 7, May 24, 1967, accessed December 28, 2017, https://www.historicum.net/persistent/old-purl/5138!.
70. Amend, interview by author.
71. Perels, interview by author.
72. Amend, interview by author.
73. Quoted in Gerhard Zwerenz, "Gespräche mit Fritz Bauer," 92f.
74. Ibid.
75. Ibid.
76. Bauer to Harlan, dated 1964.
77. Bauer to Harlan, dated June 30, probably 1967.
78. Ibid.
79. Bauer to Harlan, dated October 20, probably 1967.

11

1968

The Body in the Bathtub

THE MOURNERS EXCHANGED QUESTIONING GLANCES AS THEY STOOD around the coffin in the small cemetery chapel. Their skepticism was understandable. The sudden death of a man who had been the target of hatred, death threats, and political attacks for much of his life was bound to seem suspicious.

The state of Hesse paid for the musicians and allowed Theodor W. Adorno to select the music, three string quartets by Beethoven.[1] Only Bauer's closest friends and family members were gathered around the coffin, which was decorated with large-leaved oil plants.[2] As Thomas Harlan noted, earlier that day a much bigger crowd had attended the funeral ceremony in Frankfurt, a grand affair funded by the state government: "Admirers from the police force; plainclothes railway police officers; Danes, more Danes, Danes everywhere; numerous Swedish social democrats; old workers who used to be in the Reichsbanner; a bunch of Spanish Republican volunteers; owners of porn movie theaters; liberals; free spirits; hustlers; Alexander Kluge; Herbert Schneider; the executor Amend; ballet masters and mistresses; Pina."[3] The Beethoven quartet faded to silence and the congregation said their final goodbyes to Bauer. On July 20, 1968, his ashes were taken to Gothenburg in Sweden and buried in his parents' grave.[4]

Bauer's deputy, Ulrich Krüger, knew right away that questions would be asked about Bauer's sudden death. He therefore ordered a forensic autopsy soon after Bauer's body was discovered in his bathroom, even though there was no evidence to suggest that Bauer had died as the result of an assault or suicide.

Bauer's heart had stopped beating while he was taking a bath. At least twenty-four hours elapsed before his body was found on Monday, July 1, 1968. That morning, Bauer had failed to respond when his chauffeur came to pick him up, and eventually concerned colleagues sent someone to break down his apartment door.

On the evening of Saturday, June 29, Bauer had been in a good mood, "bright and cheerful," a neighbor said in a statement. Bauer spent much of that warm summer evening sitting out on the balcony with her. He even asked her to provide him with more cookies that week, as he had none left; there had been no sign of despondency or suicidal thoughts.[5] It is likely that he drew his bath in the early hours of Sunday, June 30.

Bauer's death was the subject of much speculation among his acquaintances. His estranged artist friend Thomas Harlan began to murmur dramatically that Bauer had committed suicide because he was so disillusioned by the continued existence of the Nazi old boy network.[6] In a literary text republished in its original form in the year 2000, the writer and filmmaker Alexander Kluge, a distant acquaintance of Bauer's, described the bathwater Bauer's body was found in as blood red.[7] A 2010 documentary by an admirer of Bauer's rehashed these dark rumors of suicide while hinting at the possibility that Bauer had been the target of a murder plot.[8] There was no evidence to support any of these theories in the autopsy conducted by the Frankfurt coroner Joachim Gerchow, however.

On January 24, 1969, Gerchow summarized his findings on nine typewritten pages. His report is now filed along with the toxicology and medical reports at the Hessian ministry of justice. The Fritz Bauer Institute in Frankfurt, which was founded in 1995, also keeps a copy. Professor Gerchow established that Bauer had taken the sedative Revonal before getting into the bath.[9] He had taken a total of five tablets, a dose that was not medically advisable but had not led to any signs of poisoning in this case, Gerchow wrote. Bauer had admitted to his neighbor on the balcony that he was generally unable to sleep without "chemicals."[10] His blood alcohol content was found to be moderate.[11] Gerchow therefore came to the same conclusion as that reached by the police detectives who had first inspected Bauer's apartment on July 1, 1968: there was "no evidence of suicide" nor of any criminal activity.[12]

Bauer's final moments weren't a thrilling denouement. Instead, their quiet drama revealed the price he paid for a life so intense that it "ultimately sapped his physical vitality," as the former Federal Criminal Police Office criminologist Dieter Schenk put it in his 2012 reexamination of the circumstances of Bauer's death.[13]

Bauer's state of mind had darkened considerably toward the end of the 1960s. In a letter to two artist friends, he wrote, "There has been a barrage of criminal charges; the world is conspiring against me, as you can see from the newspapers. I work sixteen hours a day. My wife is here, but I have no time for her. I don't know what's going to become of me."[14] On one hand, the hostility Bauer faced spurred him on: "Sometimes I feel like throwing in the towel," he admitted, "but what stops me is the pleasure this would give my opponents.

I'm a prisoner of my own history."[15] On the other hand, the constant antagonism was wearing him down: "'How dare you ask us to sacrifice ourselves?' Colleagues who served as judges in Nazi special courts during the war say this right to my face. I can't even respond anymore!"[16] Bauer joked about the abusive late-night phone calls to his apartment: "My Nazis still haven't grasped that I'm not in bed before midnight!"[17] But in truth, they were exhausting him. He was a fitful sleeper at the best of times, always had been, but to make matters worse, the phone calls were no longer sporadic; on some nights the phone rang at carefully timed intervals throughout the night. Bauer was being "well and truly hounded," recalled Wolfgang Kaven, the young friend in whom he confided.[18] Things were obviously getting to the attorney general.

"The strong aversion in this country to confronting the past is growing even stronger and taking an ominous turn," Bauer wrote to Harlan on January 31, 1967. Bauer had recently met in a hotel with Adolf von Thadden (or "Adolf II," as Bauer called him), one of the founding members and the soon-to-be chairman of the far-right Nationaldemokratische Partei Deutschlands (National Democratic Party of Germany, or NPD). "We spoke for three hours," Bauer wrote. "Grotesque and bizarre! What makes things worse is that he is an exceptionally intelligent, skilled politician. He 'hopes to keep the party in line,' he said, though he may have been lying to me. I don't believe that he himself is worried about opening Pandora's box. But unless an economic miracle takes place, the party is going to become a formidable force, winning 20 to 25 percent of the vote. And then what little we've achieved will be destroyed."[19] In April 1968, not long before Bauer's death, the NPD topped off a series of election successes by winning a record 9.8 percent of the vote in Bauer's home state, Baden-Württemberg. Many journalists believed this success would be repeated in the upcoming Bundestag election.

In the late 1960s, word went around the staff at the Hessian attorney general's office that Bauer's doctor had warned him to take better care of his heart. But Bauer continued to smoke as much as ever, and his meals "mainly consisted of black coffee and cigarettes," his employee Johannes Warlo recalled.[20] Thick cigar smoke would billow through Bauer's office from early in the morning. Back in 1963, a reporter had asked him how many cigarettes he smoked in a day. Bauer responded with another question: "How long does it take me to smoke a cigarette?" "Around five minutes, I guess," the reported replied. "Then divide eighteen hours by five minutes and you'll arrive at my daily consumption," Bauer said.[21]

Those opposed to the prosecution of Nazi crimes were becoming increasingly well organized in the latter years of Bauer's life. At the annual convention of the Association of German Jurists in late September 1966, "which focused on

Nazi trials, the deep mistrust of the trials (and me) was evident," Bauer wrote.²² Meanwhile Bauer—by now both the oldest and longest-serving state's attorney general in the country—threw himself into a frenzy of activity.²³ He was constantly either traveling or writing. In 1967, the conference of German ministers of justice gave him yet another responsibility, one that was sure to trigger a new wave of protests: as director of a new commission, he was to analyze all the material on Nazi crimes stored in East Berlin archives.²⁴ Bauer may have seemed as combative as ever, but "he was aging," a close colleague in Frankfurt noticed.²⁵ His "volcanic temper, which his disciplined intellect had always attempted to keep in check, erupted less frequently," a friend commented as he reflected on the signs of Bauer's deteriorating health.²⁶ The furious, empathetic, restless Bauer had spent his entire life operating at full steam, expecting his body to simply keep up, but now the enormous physical toll was becoming apparent.

Fritz Bauer died "like a burnt-out crater," his estranged protégé, Joachim Kügler, said.²⁷ One of the most eloquent of Bauer's many obituaries was published in the *Frankfurter Allgemeine Zeitung*. "Everyone who knew him could see there was a fire burning inside him," it read, "a fire that ultimately consumed him."²⁸ Bauer would have been sixty-five years old on July 16, 1968.

Bauer's successor as attorney general of Hesse was Horst Gauf, a jovial man with big, thick spectacles who liked to tinker around with electronics in his spare time, building things like transistor circuits and alarm systems. "For a long time I wasn't sure whether to study law or physics," he told a reporter in early 1969.²⁹ A member of the SPD, the forty-four-year-old Gauf paid tribute to his predecessor, calling him "a great role model, a titan a hundred years ahead of his time."³⁰ But the new attorney general quickly made it clear he had no intention of following in Bauer's footsteps: "I don't want to give myself a heart attack."

In 1968, the year Bauer died, the West German judiciary began to abandon most of its efforts to prosecute Nazi criminals, largely because of a minor legal amendment that came into force just a few weeks after Bauer's death. Had Bauer known about the amendment, he would no doubt have protested vociferously.³¹ But it was adopted without much fuss. Hidden in the details of an apparently unnoteworthy new introductory law to an act on regulatory offenses, it quietly passed through the Bundestag in spring 1968 and only began to make headlines in September 1968.³² The amendment allowed thousands of Germans implicated in Nazi crimes to breathe a deep sigh of relief and left legal experts scratching their heads and wondering what exactly had just happened.

The amendment functioned like a ball rebounding off the cushion in a game of pool. At first glance, it appeared to affect just the general provisions concerning the punishment of accomplices set out in Section 50, Paragraph 2 of the German Criminal Code. Where previously this paragraph had stated that judges *could* punish an accessory to a crime more leniently than the main offender, it now stated that an accessory who lacked the "special personal characteristics" of the main offender, such as his or her base motives, *must* be given a lighter sentence.[33]

The many Nazi criminals categorized as accessories to the Holocaust had hitherto received light sentences because judges had been *permitted* to exercise leniency in such cases. Now judges were *obliged* to treat accessories to murder more leniently than the murderers themselves. This may seem like a small technicality. However—and this is where the pool ball ricochets off the cushion and starts rolling toward its real target—as well as reducing the range of sentences judges were permitted to impose on accessories to crimes, the amendment reduced the statute of limitations for investigating accessories. As a result, this supposedly minor change had profound consequences.

The new statute of limitations for accessories to crimes was fifteen years, which suddenly meant that the statute of limitations for accessories to Nazi crimes had elapsed back in 1960. From now on, it would only be possible to prosecute the few Nazi criminals who had themselves carried out horrific murders and who therefore couldn't claim to lack the "special personal characteristics" of murderers. The amendment, which came into force on October 1, 1968, rendered all other Nazi criminals legally untouchable. There was no hope of ever prosecuting them now, as Adalbert Rückerl, the disheartened director of the Central Office for the Investigation of Nazi Crimes, told a reporter in early 1969: "It's too late. Once the statute of limitations has run out, there's no reviving a case."[34]

It's impossible to tell whether the change to the statute of limitations was the result of a cunning legal ploy or simply an oversight. What we do know is that the amendment can be traced back to a high-ranking ministry official in Bonn named Eduard Dreher, who had once worked as an attorney at a Nazi "special court" in Innsbruck. Dreher was in contact with the Bundestag representative Ernst Achenbach, a member of the Freie Demokratische Partei (Free Democratic Party, or FDP) who had been involved in deporting Jews from France and now also worked as a defense lawyer for people accused of Nazi crimes. Achenbach's adviser, Werner Best—who had been Hitler's plenipotentiary in occupied Denmark at the time Bauer was arrested there by the Gestapo—was looking for legal strategies to secure amnesties for his old friends.

The minister of justice had originally announced that the reform of Section 50, Paragraph 2 would not result in a reduction of the statute of limitations for serious crimes. He entrusted his official, Dreher, with the task of inserting a clause ensuring that long statutes of limitations remained in place. Yet there is no sign of any such clause in the draft amendments; ministry records give no indication as to why.[35] The documents that might contain information on what led to this omission are missing; they have been "expunged," suspects the historian Michael Greve.[36]

Twenty Nazi criminals were convicted and sentenced in 1968. Charges against far more suspects were dropped that year. A total of 282 defendants were notified that the cases against them had been dropped due to the new statute of limitations.[37] In 1969, an eight-line ruling forced prosecutors in Berlin to abandon years of investigations into numerous former employees of the Reich Central Security Office. In 1970, Bauer's successor, Gauf, quietly instructed his prosecutors to stop investigating high-ranking jurists who had failed to speak out against the Nazis' euthanasia program. As a result, the euthanasia trial that Bauer had fought long and hard for never took place.[38]

The halls of the attorney general's office in Frankfurt seemed subdued now that Bauer was gone. The same quiet atmosphere that prevailed in most other West German prosecutors' offices descended here too. A couple of minor, sporadic trials of individual Nazi criminals, including some from Auschwitz, took place after 1968. But the prosecutors now avoided the glare of publicity; their new boss, Gauf, had nothing to say to the public anyway.

"Bauer was a powder keg," said one of his prosecutors, Johannes Warlo. "Gauf was a pile of sand."[39] Warlo's criticism is perhaps a little unfair, given that Gauf's reluctance to take on Nazi crimes was by no means unusual for the time. In Frankfurt, however, Gauf's passivity was striking, because up to 1968, the world had seen just how much could be achieved by a German prosecutor with the necessary determination.

Notes

1. Alexander Kluge, *Chronik der Gefühle. Band II Lebensläufe* (Frankfurt am Main: Suhrkamp, 2000), 239.
2. Ibid.
3. Thomas Harlan, *Heldenfriedhof. Roman* (Berlin: Eichborn Berlin Verlag, 2006), 405f.
4. Cremation records of 196, quoted in Dieter Schenk, "Die Todesumstände von Generalstaatsanwalt Fritz Bauer (1903–1968)," *Einsicht 08. Bulletin des Fritz-Bauer-Instituts*, fall 2012, 40.
5. Ulrich Krüger, file note, July 26, 1968, files of the attorney general's office, Frankfurt am Main, Fritz Bauer Institute Archives.
6. See Jean-Pierre Stephan, *Thomas Harlan. Das Gesicht deines Feindes*, 141.
7. See Kluge, Chronik der Gefühle, 240.
8. *Fritz Bauer. Tod auf Raten.*

9. Gerchow's report specifies that Bauer had taken Revonal. Some secondary sources erroneously state that he had taken Veronal, another sedative.

10. Ulrich Krüger, file note, July 26, 1968, files of the attorney general's office, Frankfurt am Main, Fritz Bauer Institute Archives, 1–2.

11. Prof. Joachim Gerchow, "Abschließendes Gutachten über das Ergebnis der Obduktion und die weiteren Untersuchungen, 24. Januar 1969," Fritz Bauer Institute Archives.

12. Kriminalhauptmeister Schmitt, "Bericht betr. Leichensache z. N. des Generalstaatsanwalts," Frankfurt am Main, 1. Juli 1968, Fritz Bauer InstituteArchives, 2.

13. Schenk, "Die Todesumstände von Generalstaatsanwalt Fritz Bauer (1903–1968)," *Einsicht 08. Bulletin des Fritz-Bauer-Instituts*, fall 2012, 43. Schenk reexamined the findings of the forensic and criminal investigations in the light of current scientific knowledge. He also found that there is no evidence of suicide or the involvement of a third party in Bauer's death.

14. Bauer to Harlan, undated, probably 1967.

15. Bauer to Harlan, spring 1965.

16. Quoted in Gerhard Zwerenz, "Gespräche mit Fritz Bauer," 89.

17. Bauer to Harlan, undated letter written on stationery from the Europäischer Hof Hotel in Baden-Baden, probably fall 1967.

18. Kaven, interview by author.

19. Bauer to Harlan, January 31, 1967.

20. Warlo, interview by author.

21. Bauer, quoted in *Der Spiegel*, "Personalien," November 13, 1963.

22. Bauer to Harlan, October 1966.

23. See Bauer's personnel file, eulogy by Attorney General Mützelburg in Haus Dornbusch, July 1968, Hessisches Hauptstaatsarchiv, Wiesbaden.

24. See *Frankfurter Rundschau*, "Bauer soll NS-Material sichten," October 20, 1967.

25. Warlo, interview by author.

26. Eckard Wiemers, "Heilen statt Strafen," *Vorwärts*, July 18, 1968.

27. Quoted in Jürgen Serke, "Der Moralist," *Stern*, April 18, 1974.

28. *Frankfurter Allgemeine Zeitung*, "Nachruf auf Fritz Bauer," July 2, 1968.

29. Quoted in *Der Spiegel*, "Register," January 13, 1969.

30. Quoted in Gerhard Ziegler, "Name ohne Glanz. Der neue Generalstaatsanwalt in Hessen," *Die Zeit*, February 7, 1969.

31. See ibid.

32. See Michael Greve, "Amnestie von NS-Gehilfen. Die Novellierung des § 50 Abs. 2 StGB und dessen Auswirkungen auf die NS-Strafverfolgung," *Einsicht 04. Bulletin des Fritz-Bauer-Instituts* fall 2010, 57.

33. Section 50, paragraph 2 (now Section 28) of the German Criminal Code read: "If special personal traits, conditions, or circumstances (special personal characteristics) that establish the perpetrator's liability are absent in the participant, their sentence shall be mitigated pursuant to the legal provisions."

34. Quoted in Annette Weinke, *Eine Gesellschaft ermittelt gegen sich selbst*, 136.

35. See ibid., 137.

36. Greve, "Amnestie von NS-Gehilfen," 56, footnote 12.

37. See Michael Greve, *Der justitielle und rechtspolitische Umgang mit den NS-Gewaltverbrechen in den sechziger Jahren*, 387–393.

38. *NS-»Euthanasie« vor Gericht*, ed. Hanno Loewy and Bettina Winter.

39. Warlo, interview.

BIBLIOGRAPHY

Adler, Leo. *Wandlungen bei dem Oberrat der Israelitischen Religionsgemeinschaft Württembergs, Feiertagsschrift der Israelitischen Kultusvereinigung Württemberg und Hohenzollern*, September 1962, Archiv Stadtbibliothek Stuttgart.
Adorno, Theodor W. *Negative Dialektik. Jargon der Eigentlichkeit. Dritter Teil: Modelle. Gesammelte Schriften*, vol. 6, edited by Rolf Tiedemann. Frankfurt am Main: Suhrkamp, 1986.
———. "Sexualtabus und Recht heute." In *Sexualität und Verbrechen. Beiträge zur Strafrechtsreform*, edited by Fritz Bauer, Hans Bürger-Prinz, Hans Giese, and Herbert Jäger, 299–317. Frankfurt am Main: Fischer, 1963.
Albrecht, Peter-Alexis. *Der Weg in die Sicherheitsgesellschaft. Auf der Suche nach staatskritischen Absolutheitsregeln*. Berlin: Berliner Wissenschafts-Verlag, 2010.
Albrecht, Willy. "Jeanette Wolff, Jakob Altmaier und Peter Blachstein. Die drei jüdischen Abgeordneten des Bundestags bis zum Beginn der sechziger Jahre." In *Leben im Land der Täter. Juden im Nachkriegsdeutschland (1945–1952)*, edited by Julius H. Schoeps, 236–253. Berlin: Jüdische Verlagsanstalt Berlin, 2001.
Angermund, Ralph. *Deutsche Richterschaft 1919–1945*. Frankfurt am Main: Fischer, 1990.
Arendt, Hannah. *Responsibility and Judgment*, edited by Jerome Kohn. New York: Schocken Books, 2003.
Bar-Zohar, Michael. *Ben-Gurion*, vol. 3. Tel Aviv: Am Oved, 1978.
Bass, Gary J. *Stay the Hand of Vengeance: The Politics of War Crimes Tribunals*. Princeton, NJ: Princeton University Press, 2000.
Bauer, Fritz. "Antinazistische Prozesse und politisches Bewußtsein. Dienen NS-Prozeße der politischen Aufklärung?" In *Antisemitismus. Zur Pathologie der bürgerlichen Gesellschaft*, edited by Hermann Huss and Andreas Schröder, 168–188. Frankfurt am Main: Europäische Verlagsanstalt, 1965.
———. "Das Ende waren die Gaskammern" (1960). Republished in *Die Humanität der Rechtsordnung. Ausgewählte Schriften Fritz Bauers*, edited by Joachim Perels and Irmtrud Wojak, 91–96. Frankfurt am Main: Campus, 1998.
———. "Das Land der Kartelle." *Geist und Tat. Monatsschrift für Recht, Freiheit und Kultur* (June 1952): 167–171.
———. "Das Nansen-Amt." *C.V.-Zeitung*, June 23, 1938.
———. *Das Verbrechen und die Gesellschaft*. Munich and Basel: Ernst Reinhardt Verlag, 1957.
———. "Der Prozeß Jesu" (1965). Republished in *Die Humanität der Rechtsordnung. Ausgewählte Schriften Fritz Bauers*, edited by Joachim Perels and Irmtrud Wojak, 411–426. Frankfurt am Main: Campus, 1998.
———. "Der SS-Staat in Person." *Weltbild*, January 13, 1961.
———. "Die glückliche Insel Dänemark." *C.V.-Zeitung*, December 24, 1936.
———. *Die Kriegsverbrecher vor Gericht*. Zürich and New York: Europa Verlag, 1945.
———. *Die rechtliche Struktur der Truste. Ein Beitrag zur Organisation der wirtschaftlichen Zusammenschlüsse in Deutschland unter vergleichender Heranziehung der Trustformen in den Vereinigten Staaten von Amerika und Rußland*. Mannheim: Bensheimer, 1927.

———. "Die Wirtschaftsgesetzgebung in der Ostzone." *Deutsche Nachrichten*, April 14, 1947.
———. "Ein bisschen Arsenik. Blick hinter die Kulissen der Wirtschaft." *Deutsche Nachrichten*, April 28, 1947.
———. "Eine Grenze hat Tyrannenmacht. Plädoyer im Remer Prozeß" (1952). Republished in *Die Humanität der Rechtsordnung. Ausgewählte Schriften Fritz Bauers*, edited by Joachim Perels and Irmtrud Wojak, 169–180. Frankfurt am Main: Campus, 1998.
———. "Einwanderer in Skandinavien, Offiziöse Zahlen und Daten." *C.V.-Zeitung*, April 29, 1937.
———. "Forderungen der Gesellschaft an die Strafrechtsreform," paper delivered at the German Workers' Welfare Association's convention in Bad Godesberg, May 30–June 3, 1962. *Schriften der Arbeiterwohlfahrt* 14 (1962): 5–20.
———. "Gegen die Todesstrafe" (1958). Republished in *Die Humanität der Rechtsordnung. Ausgewählte Schriften Fritz Bauers*, edited by Joachim Perels and Irmtrud Wojak, 393–397. Frankfurt am Main: Campus, 1998.
———. "Glückliche Insel Dänemark." *C.V.-Zeitung*, December 24, 1936.
———. "Hochschule und Politik." *Monatsberichte des Bundes Freier Wissenschaftlicher Vereinigungen*, September 1921.
———. "Ideal- und Realkonkurrenz bei nationalsozialistischen Verbrechen?" *JuristenZeitung* 22 (1967): 625–628.
———. "Im Kampf um des Menschen Rechte" (1955). Republished in *Die Humanität der Rechtsordnung. Ausgewählte Schriften Fritz Bauers*, edited by Joachim Perels and Irmtrud Wojak, 37–49. Frankfurt am Main: Campus, 1998.
———. "Im Namen des Volkes. Die strafrechtliche Bewältigung der Vergangenheit" (1965). Republished in *Die Humanität der Rechtsordnung. Ausgewählte Schriften Fritz Bauers*, edited by Joachim Perels and Irmtrud Wojak, 77–90. Frankfurt am Main: Campus, 1998.
———. "Juden in Europas Norden." *C.V.-Zeitung*, September 22, 1938.
———. "Justiz als Symptom" (1962). Republished in *Die Humanität der Rechtsordnung. Ausgewählte Schriften Fritz Bauers*, edited by Joachim Perels and Irmtrud Wojak, 365–376. Frankfurt am Main: Campus, 1998.
———. *Krigsförbrytarna inför domstol*. Stockholm: Natur och kultur, 1944.
———. *Monopolernes Diktatur*. Copenhagen: Forlaget Fremad, 1948.
———. "Mörder unter uns" (1958). Republished in *Die Humanität der Rechtsordnung. Ausgewählte Schriften Fritz Bauers*, edited by Joachim Perels and Irmtrud Wojak, 97–100. Frankfurt am Main: Campus, 1998.
———. "Nach den Wurzeln des Bösen fragen." *Die Tat*, March 7, 1964.
———. "Nachwort." In Hermann Schreiber, *Die Zehn Gebote*, 383–384. Düsseldorf: Econ Verlag, 1962
———. "Nationale Front?" *Politische Information*, February 1, 1945.
———. "Nürnberg." *Deutsche Nachrichten*, October 14, 1946.
———. *Ökonomisk Nyorientering*. Copenhagen: Martins Forlag, 1945.
———. "Panorama in Helsingör." *C.V.-Zeitung*, July 29, 1937.
———. *Pengar i går, i dag och i morgon*. Stockholm: Bokförlaget Natur och Kultur, 1944.
———. *Penge*. Copenhagen: Martins Forlag, 1941.
———. "Recht oder Unrecht ... mein Vaterland." *Deutsche Nachrichten*, June 24, 1946.
———. "Scham bei der Lektüre. Richter zerstörten die Demokratie." *Die Zeit*, September 29, 1967.

———. "Sexualstrafrecht heute" (1963). Republished in *Die Humanität der Rechtsordnung. Ausgewählte Schriften Fritz Bauers*, edited by Joachim Perels and Irmtrud Wojak, 297–313. Frankfurt am Main: Campus, 1998.

———. "Sinn und Wert der studentischen Korporation." *Monatsberichte des Bundes Freier Wissenschaftlicher Vereinigungen*, September 1921.

———. "Sozialismus und Sozialisierung." *Deutsche Nachrichten*, May 12, 1947.

———. "Straffälligenhilfe nach der Entlassung" (1957). Republished in *Die Humanität der Rechtsordnung. Ausgewählte Schriften Fritz Bauers*, edited by Joachim Perels and Irmtrud Wojak, 315–339. Frankfurt am Main: Campus, 1998.

———. "Widerstandsrecht und Widerstandspflicht des Staatsbürgers" (1962). Republished in *Die Humanität der Rechtsordnung. Ausgewählte Schriften Fritz Bauers*, edited by Joachim Perels and Irmtrud Wojak, 181–205. Frankfurt am Main: Campus, 1998.

———. "Wiedergutmachung und Neuaufbau." *Deutsche Nachrichten*, September 4, 1945.

Bauer, Fritz, Hans Bürger-Prinz, Hans Giese, and Herbert Jäger, ed. *Sexualität und Verbrechen*. Frankfurt am Main: Fischer, 1963.

Baumbach, Dr. "Der Bankrott der Strafjustiz." *Deutsche Juristen-Zeitung* 1 (1928): 38–43.

Borth, Helmut. "Das Amtsgericht Stuttgart." In *Das Oberlandesgericht Stuttgart – 125 Jahre von 1879 bis 2004*, edited by Eberhard Stilz, 233–237. Villingen-Schwenningen: Neckar-Verlag, 2004.

Brenner, Michael. *Jüdische Kultur in der Weimarer Republik*. Munich: C. H. Beck, 2000.

Buchholz, Michael. "Zur Geschichte der Freien Wissenschaftlichen Vereinigung." In *Freie Wissenschaftliche Vereinigung. Eine Berliner anti-antisemitische Studentenorganisation stellt sich vor – 1908 und 1931*, edited by Manfred Voigts, 210–225. Potsdam: Universitätsverlag Potsdam, 2008.

Buchloh, Ingrid. *Veit Harlan. Goebbels' Starregisseur*. Paderborn: Schöningh, 2010.

Diner, Dan. "Im Zeichen des Banns." In *Geschichte der Juden in Deutschland von 1945 bis zur Gegenwart*, edited by Michael Brenner, 15–66. Munich: C. H. Beck, 2012.

Dreßen, Willi. "NS-'Euthanasie'-Prozesse in der Bundesrepublik Deutschland im Wandel der Zeit." In *NS-"Euthanasie" vor Gericht. Fritz Bauer und die Grenzen juristischer Bewältigung*, edited by Hanno Loewy and B. Winter, 35–58. Frankfurt am Main: Campus, 1996.

Drumbl, Mark A. *Atrocity, Punishment, and International Law*. Cambridge: Cambridge University Press, 2007.

Eichler, Anja, ed. *Spott und Respekt – die Justiz in der Kritik*. Petersberg: Michael Imhof Verlag, 2010.

Eichmüller, Andreas. *Keine Generalamnestie. Die Strafverfolgung von NS-Verbrechen in der frühen Bundesrepublik*. Munich: Oldenbourg Verlag, 2012.

Einsele, Helga. "Worte der Erinnerung." In *Fritz Bauer. Eine Denkschrift*, ed. Hessisches Ministerium der Justiz, 19–22. Wiesbaden: Hessisches Ministerium der Justiz, 1993.

Elon, Amos. *In einem heimgesuchten Land. Reise eines israelischen Journalisten in beide deutsche Staaten*. Munich: Kindler, 1966.

———. *The Pity of It All: A Portrait of Jews in Germany, 1743–1933*. London: Picador, 2004.

Faust, Anselm. *Der Nationalsozialistische Deutsche Studentenbund. Studenten und Nationalsozialismus in der Weimarer Republik*, vol. 1. Düsseldorf: Schwann, 1973.

Frei, Norbert. *1945 und wir. Das Dritte Reich im Bewußtsein der Deutschen*. Munich: C. H. Beck, 2005.

Fröhlich, Claudia. *"Wider die Tabuisierung des Widerstands." Fritz Bauers Widerstandsbegriff und die Aufarbeitung von NS-Verbrechen*. Frankfurt am Main: Campus, 2006.

Geschichtswerkstatt Tübingen, ed. *Zerstörte Hoffnungen. Wege der Tübinger Juden*. Tübingen: Theiss, 1995.

Giordano, Ralph. *Die Bertinis*. Frankfurt am Main: Fischer, 1982.

Göppinger, Horst. *Juristen jüdischer Abstammung im "Dritten Reich." Entrechtung und Verfolgung*, 2nd edition. Munich: C. H. Beck, 1990.

Greve, Michael. "Amnestie von NS-Gehilfen. Die Novellierung des § 50 Abs. 2 StGB und dessen Auswirkungen auf die NS-Strafverfolgung." *Einsicht 04. Bulletin des Fritz-Bauer-Instituts*, fall 2010.

———. *Der justitielle und rechtspolitische Umgang mit den NS-Gewaltverbrechen in den sechziger Jahren*. Frankfurt am Main: Peter Lang, 2001.

Guez, Olivier. *Heimkehr der Unerwünschten. Eine Geschichte der Juden in Deutschland nach 1945*. Munich: Piper, 2011.

Guggenheimer, E. "Aus der Geschichte des Synagogenbaus." In *Festschrift zur Einweihung der Synagoge in Stuttgart*, edited by Israelitische Kultusvereinigung Württemberg und Hohenzollern, 25–31. Stuttgart: Israelitische Kultusvereinigung Württemberg und Hohenzollern, 1952.

Hachenburg, Max. *Lebenserinnerungen eines Rechtsanwalts und Briefe aus der Emigration*. Stuttgart: Verlag W. Kohlhammer, 1978.

Haffner, Sebastian. *Geschichte eines Deutschen. Die Erinnerungen 1914–1933*, 6th edition. Stuttgart and Munich: dtv, 2001.

Hambrock, Matthias. *Die Etablierung der Außenseiter. Der Verband nationaldeutscher Juden 1921–1925*. Cologne: Böhlau, 2003.

Harel, Isser. *Das Haus in der Garibaldistraße*. Frankfurt am Main: Ullstein, 1976.

Hiller, Kurt. *Leben gegen die Zeit, Band 1: Logos*. Reinbek: Rowohlt, 1969.

Horstmann, Thomas, and Heike Litzinger. *An den Grenzen des Rechts. Gespräche mit Juristen über die Verfolgung von NS-Verbrechen*. Frankfurt am Main: Campus, 2006.

Jäger, Herbert. "Strafrecht und nationalsozialistische Gewaltverbrechen." In *Der Unrechts-Staat. Recht und Justiz im Nationalsozialismus*, edited by Redaktion Kritische Justiz, 143–157. Frankfurt am Main: Nomos, 1979.

Jünger, Ernst. *Jahre der Okkupation*. Stuttgart: Klett, 1958.

Grein, Gerd Jürgen. *Der Homosexuelle in Frankfurt am Main*. Master's dissertation, Universität Frankfurt, 1968.

Kant, Immanuel. *Die Metaphysik der Sitten. Werkausgabe Band VIII*, edited by Wilhelm Weischedel. Frankfurt am Main: Suhrkamp, 1977.

Kempner, Robert M. W. "Generalstaatsanwalt Dr. Fritz Bauer gestorben. Ein Streiter ohne Furcht und Tadel/Ein Leben für das Recht." *Das Reichsbanner*, July/August 1968.

Kienle, Markus. *Das Konzentrationslager Heuberg bei Stetten am Kalten Markt*. Ulm: Klemm & Oelschläger, 1998.

Kluge, Alexander. *Chronik der Gefühle. Band II Lebensläufe*. Frankfurt am Main: Suhrkamp, 2000.

Koch, Arnd. "Binding vs. v. Liszt. Klassische und moderne Strafrechtsschule." In *Der Strafgedanke in seiner historischen Entwicklung*, edited by Eric Hilgendorf and Jürgen Weitzel, 127–145. Berlin: Duncker & Humblot, 2007.

Köhler, Lotte, and Hans Saner, ed. *Hannah Arendt/Karl Jaspers Briefwechsel 1926–1969*, 2nd edition. Munich: Piper, 1987.

Kosyra, Kriminalinspektor Herbert. "Die Homosexualität - ein immer aktuelles Problem." *Kriminalistik* (1962): 113.

Krüger, Horst. "Im Labyrinth der Schuld. Ein Tag im Frankfurter Auschwitz-Prozeß." *Der Monat* (May 1964): 19–29.
Lang, Jochen von. *Der Sekretär. Martin Bormann: Der Mann, der Hitler beherrschte*, 2nd edition. Frankfurt am Main: Fischer, 1980.
Lankenau, Arne. *"Dunkel die Zukunft – Hell der Mut!" Die Heidelberger Studentenverbindungen in der Weimarer Republik 1918–1929.* Heidelberg: Universitätsverlag Winter, 2008.
Laternser, Hans. *Die andere Seite im Auschwitz-Prozess 1963/1965.* Stuttgart-Degerloch: Seewald, 1966.
Laubenthal, Klaus, and Helmut Baier. *Jugendstrafrecht.* Berlin: Springer, 2006.
Lechner, Silvester. *Das KZ Oberer Kuhberg und die NS-Zeit in der Region Ulm/Neu-Ulm.* Stuttgart: Silberburg-Verlag, 1988.
Lehrmann, Dr. Ch. "Ansprache." In *Festschrift zur Einweihung der Synagoge in Stuttgart*, edited by Israelitische Kultusvereinigung Württemberg und Hohenzollern, 15–19. Stuttgart: Israelitische Kultusvereinigung Württemberg und Hohenzollern, 1952.
Liszt, Franz von. "Organisation und Organisationsformen im studentischen Leben" (1908). Republished in *Freie Wissenschaftliche Vereinigung. Eine Berliner anti-antisemitische Studentenorganisation stellt sich vor – 1908 und 1931*, edited by Manfred Voigts, 29–30. Potsdam: Universitätsverlag Potsdam, 2008.
———. *Zeitschrift für die gesamte Strafrechtswissenschaft* 9 (1889).
Loewy, Hanno, and Bettina Winter, ed. *NS-"Euthanasie" vor Gericht. Fritz Bauer und die Grenzen juristischer Bewältigung.* Frankfurt am Main: Campus, 1996.
Longerich, Peter. *Hitlers Stellvertreter. Führung der Partei und Kontrolle des Staatsapparates durch den Stab Heß und die Partei-Kanzlei Bormann.* Munich: K. G. Sauer Verlag, 1992.
Marx, Alfred. *Das Schicksal der jüdischen Juristen in Württemberg und Hohenzollern 1933–1945.* N.p.: Neckar Verlag, 1965.
Meier, Bernd-Dieter, Dieter Rössner, and Heinz Schöch. *Jugendstrafrecht.* Munich: C. H. Beck, 2007.
Merrit, Anna, and Richard Merrit, ed. in *Public Opinion in Semisovereign Germany: The HICOG Surveys, 1949–1955.* Champaign: University of Illinois, 1980.
Merseburger, Peter. *Der schwierige Deutsche. Kurt Schumacher.* Stuttgart: Deutsche Verlags-Anstalt, 1995.
———. *Willy Brandt (1913–1992). Visionär und Realist.* Frankfurt am Main: Deutsche Verlags-Anstalt, 2002.
Meusch, Matthias. "'Gerichtstag halten über uns selbst' – Der Hessische Generalstaatsanwalt Fritz Bauer und die Verfolgung von NS-Verbrechen." In *Recht und Justiz im gesellschaftlichen Aufbruch (1960–1975). Bundesrepublik Deutschland, Italien und Frankreich im Vergleich*, edited by Jörg Requate, 131–148. Baden-Baden: Nomos, 2003.
———. *Von der Diktatur zur Demokratie. Fritz Bauer und die Aufarbeitung der NS-Verbrechen in Hessen (1956–1968).* Wiesbaden: Historische Kommission für Nassau, 2001.
Michalski, Gabrielle. *Der Antisemitismus im deutschen akademischen Leben in der Zeit nach dem 1. Weltkrieg.* Frankfurt am Main: Peter Lang, 1980.
Müller, Ingo. "Nürnberg und die deutschen Juristen." In *Gegen Barbarei. Essays Robert M. W. Kempner zu Ehren*, edited by Rainer Eisfeld and Ingo Müller, 257–280. Frankfurt am Main: Athenäum Verlag, 1989.
Müller, Roland. *Stuttgart in der Zeit des Nationalsozialismus.* Stuttgart: Konrad Theiss Verlag, 1995.

Neumann, Robert. *Vielleicht das Heitere. Tagebuch aus einem andern Jahr.* Munich: Heyne, 1968.
Pätzold, Kurt, and Manfred Weißbecker. *Rudolf Heß. Der Mann an Hitlers Seite.* Leipzig: Militzke, 2003.
Perels, Joachim. "Zur rechtlichen Bedeutung des Auschwitz-Prozesses. Eine kritische Intervention." In *Gesellschaft und Gerechtigkeit. Festschrift für Hubert Rottleuthner*, edited by Matthias Mahlmann, 492–298. Baden-Baden: Nomos, 2011.
Pery, "Die Rechte des Beschuldigten und Angeklagten." *Der Weg zu Freundschaft und Toleranz* 3 (July 1953): 23–27.
Radbruch, Gustav. *Einführung in die Rechtswissenschaft*, 7th/8th editions (1929), republished in *Gustav Radbruch. Gesamtausgabe Band 1*, edited by Arthur Kaufmann, 211–406. Heidelberg: C.F. Müller Verlag, 1987.
Renz, Werner. "(Un-) Begründete Selbstkritik. Überlegungen zu einer skeptischen Bilanz Fritz Bauers. In memoriam Fritz Bauer (1903–1968)." *Tribüne. Zeitschrift zum Verständnis des Judentums* 190/2 (2009): 124–132.
———. "40 Jahre Auschwitz-Prozess. Ein unerwünschtes Verfahren." *Newsletter Nr. 26 des Fritz-Bauer-Instituts* (fall 2004): 13–16.
———. "Der 1. Frankfurter Auschwitz-Prozess 1963–1965 und die deutsche Öffentlichkeit. Anmerkungen zur Entmythologisierung eines NSG-Verfahrens." In *NS-Prozesse und deutsche Öffentlichkeit. Besatzungszeit, frühe Bundesrepublik und DDR*, edited by Jörg Osterloh and Clemens Vollnhals, 349–362. Göttingen: Vandenhoeck & Ruprecht, 2011.
———. "Der 1. Frankfurter Auschwitz-Prozeß. Zwei Vorgeschichten." *Zeitschrift für Geschichtswissenschaft* (2002): 622–641.
———. "Der erste Frankfurter Auschwitz-Prozeß. Völkermord als Strafsache." *Zeitschrift für Sozialgeschichte des 20. und 21. Jahrhunderts* (September 2000): 11–48.
———. "Fritz Bauer zum Zweck der NS-Prozesse. Eine Rekonstruktion." *Einsicht 07. Bulletin des Fritz-Bauer-Instituts* (spring 2012): 40–46.
Rosenberger, Arthur. "Was wir tun" (1908). Republished in *Freie Wissenschaftliche Vereinigung. Eine Berliner anti-antisemitische Studentenorganisation stellt sich vor – 1908 und 1931*, edited by Manfred Voigts, 70–73. Potsdam: Universitätsverlag Potsdam, 2008.
Rüping, Hinrich, and Günter Jerouschek. *Grundrisse der Strafrechtsgeschichte*, 5th edition. Munich: C. H. Beck, 2007.
Sauer, Paul, and Sonja Hosseinzadeh, *Jüdisches Leben im Wandel der Zeit. 170 Jahre Israelitische Religionsgemeinschaft, 50 Jahre neue Synagoge in Stuttgart.* Gerlingen: Bleicher Verlag, 2002.
Schaffstein, Friedrich, and Olaf Miehe. *Weg und Aufgabe des Jugendstrafrechts.* Darmstadt: Wissenschaftlliche Buchgesellschaft, 1968.
Schenk, Dieter. *Auf dem rechten Auge blind. Die braunen Wurzeln des BKA.* Cologne: Kiepenheuer & Witsch, 2001.
———. "Die Todesumstände von Generalstaatsanwalt Fritz Bauer (1903–1968)." In *Einsicht 08. Bulletin des Fritz-Bauer-Instituts* (fall 2012): 38–43.
Schmid, Richard. "Fritz Bauer 1903–1968." *Kritische Justiz* 1 (1968): 60–61.
Schmoeckel, Matthias. *Rechtsgeschichte der Wirtschaft. Seit dem 19. Jahrhundert.* Tübingen: Mohr Siebeck, 2008.
Schonfeld, Walter T. *Nazi Madness.* London: Minerva, 2000.
Schöningh, Claudia. *"Kontrolliert die Justiz." Die Vertrauenskrise der Weimarer Justiz im Spiegel der Gerichtsreportagen von* Weltbühne, Tagebuch *und* Vossische Zeitung. Munich: Fink, 2000.

Schulz, Birge. *Der Republikanische Richterbund (1921–1933)*. Frankfurt am Main: Peter Lang, 1982.
Schwarz, Jürgen. *Studenten in der Weimarer Republik. Die deutsche Studentenschaft in der Zeit von 1918 bis 1923 und ihre Stellung zur Politik*. Berlin: Duncker & Humblot, 1971.
Segev, Tom. *Simon Wiesenthal. Die Biographie*. Munich: Siedler Verlag, 2010.
Sender Freies Berlin, ed. *Um uns die Fremde. Die Vertreibung des Geistes 1933–45*. Berlin: Haude & Spener, 1968.
Singelnstein, Tobias, and Peer Stolle. *Die Sicherheitsgesellschaft. Soziale Kontrolle im 21. Jahrhundert*, 3rd edition. Wiesbaden: Verlag für Sozialwissenschaften, 2011.
Smith, Bradley F. *The American Road to Nuremberg*. Stanford: Hoover Institution Press, 1982.
Stadtarchiv Ulm, ed. *Zeugnisse zur Geschichte der Juden in Ulm. Erinnerungen und Dokumente*. Ulm: Stadtarchiv Ulm, 1991.
Stangneth, Bettina. *Eichmann vor Jerusalem. Das unbehelligte Leben eines Massenmörders*. Zürich and Hamburg: Rowohlt, 2011.
Steffensen, Steffen. "Fritz Bauer (1903–1968). Jurist und Volkswirt." In *Exil in Dänemark. Deutschsprachige Wissenschaftler, Künstler und Schriftsteller im dänischen Exil*, edited by Willy Dähnhardt und Birgit S. Nielsen, 171–177. Heide: Westholsteinische Verlagsanstalt Boyens & Co., 1993.
Steinbach, Peter. "Einführung." In Eberhard Zeller, *Oberst Claus Graf Stauffenberg. Ein Lebensbild*, 2nd edition, VII–XXVII. Paderborn: F. Schöningh, 2008.
Steinke, Ronen. *The Politics of International Criminal Justice: German Perspectives from Nuremberg to The Hague*. Oxford: Hart Publishing, 2012.
Stengel, Katharina. *Hermann Langbein. Ein Auschwitz-Überlebender in den erinnerungspolitischen Konflikten der Nachkriegszeit*. Frankfurt am Main: Campus, 2012.
Stephan, Jean-Pierre. *Thomas Harlan. Das Gesicht deines Feindes. Ein deutsches Leben*. Frankfurt am Main: Eichborn, 2007.
Stickler, Matthias. "Zwischen Reich und Republik. Zur Geschichte der studentischen Verbindungen in der Weimarer Republik," in *"Der Burschen Herrlichkeit." Geschichte und Gegenwart des studentischen Korporationswesens*, edited by Harm-Hinrich Brandt and Matthias Stickler, 85–107. Würzburg: Veröffentlichungen des Stadtarchivs Würzburg, 1998.
Stümke, Hans-Georg. *Homosexuelle in Deutschland: Eine politische Geschichte*. Munich: C. H. Beck, 1989.
Taus, Gerhard. "Studentische Vereinigungen, Begriffe und Abkürzungen." In *Freie Wissenschaftliche Vereinigung. Eine Berliner anti-antisemitische Studentenorganisation stellt sich vor – 1908 und 1931*, edited by Manfred Voigts, 12–16. Potsdam: Universitätsverlag Potsdam 2008.
Taylor, Telford. *The Anatomy of the Nuremberg Trials*. Boston: Back Bay Books, 1992.
Uhlman, Fred. *Der wiedergefundene Freund*. Zürich: Diogenes, 1998.
———. *The Making of an Englishman. Erinnerungen eines deutschen Juden*. Zürich: Diogenes, 1998.
Utz, Friedemann. *Preuße, Protestant, Pragmatiker. Der Staatssekretär Walter Strauß und sein Staat*. Tübingen: Mohr Siebeck, 2003.
Venohr, Wolfgang. *Stauffenberg. Symbol des Widerstands. Eine politische Biographie*, 3rd edition. Munich: Herbig, 2000.
Voigts, Manfred, ed. *Freie Wissenschaftliche Vereinigung. Eine Berliner anti-antisemitische Studentenorganisation stellt sich vor – 1908 und 1931*. Potsdam: Universitätsverlag Potsdam, 2008.

Walser, Martin. "Unser Auschwitz." *Kursbuch* 1 (1965): 189–200.
Warlo, Johannes. "NSG-Verfahren in Frankfurt am Main. Versuch einer justiziellen Aufarbeitung der Vergangenheit." In *Ein Jahrhundert Frankfurter Justiz. Gerichtsgebäude A: 1889–1989*, edited by Horst Henrichs and Karl Stephan, 155–183. Frankfurt am Main: W. Kramer Verlag.
Wehler, Hans-Ulrich. *Deutsche Gesellschaftsgeschichte. Vierter Band: Von Beginn des Ersten Weltkriegs bis zur Gründung der beiden deutschen Staaten 1914– 1949*. Munich: C. H. Beck, 2003.
Weinke, Annette. "Von Nürnberg nach Den Haag?" In *Leipzig – Nürnberg – Den Haag. Neue Fragestellungen und Forschungen zum Verhältnis von Menschenrechtsverbrechen, justizieller Säuberung und Völkerstrafrecht*, edited by Helia-Verena Daubach, 20–33. Düsseldorf: Justizministerium des Landes NRW, 2007.
———. *Eine Gesellschaft ermittelt gegen sich selbst. Die Geschichte der Zentralen Stelle Ludwigsburg 1958–2008*, 2nd edition. Darmstadt: Wissenschaftliche Buchgesellschaft, 2009.
Weinmann, Günther. "Das Oberlandesgericht Stuttgart von 1933 bis 1945." In *Das Oberlandesgericht Stuttgart – 125 Jahre von 1879 bis 2004*, edited by Eberhard Stilz, 37–62. Villingen-Schwenningen: Neckar Verlag, 2004.
Weis, Stefanie. *Leben und Werk des Juristen Karl Hermann Friedrich Julius Geiler (1878–1953). Ein Rechtswissenschaftler in Zeiten des Umbruchs*. Hamburg: Verlag Dr. Kovač, 2013.
Weiss, Michael. *Bücher, Buden, Burschenschaften. Tausend Semester Tübinger Studentenleben*. Tübingen: Attempto-Verlag, 1991.
Wojak, Irmtrud. *Fritz Bauer (1903–1968). Eine Biographie*. Munich: C. H. Beck, 2009.
Zapf, Lilli. *Die Tübinger Juden. Eine Dokumentation*. Tübingen: Katzmann-Verlag, 1981.
Zeller, Eberhard. *Oberst Claus Graf Stauffenberg. Ein Lebensbild*, 2nd edition. Paderborn: F. Schöningh, 2008.
Zelzer, Maria. *Weg und Schicksal der Stuttgarter Juden*. Stuttgart: Klett, 1964.
Ziemann, Benjamin. *Die Zukunft der Republik? Das Reichsbanner Schwarz-Rot-Gold 1924–1933*. Bonn: Friedrich Ebert Stiftung, 2011.
Zorn, Wolfgang. "Die politische Entwicklung des deutschen Studentums 1918–1931." In *Darstellungen und Quellen zur Geschichte der deutschen Einheitsbewegung im neunzehnten und zwanzigsten Jahrhundert*, edited by Kurt Stephensen, Alexander Scharf, and Wolfgang Klötzer, 223–307. Heidelberg: Universitätsverlag Winter, 1965.
Zwerenz, Gerhard. "Gespräche mit Fritz Bauer." *Streit-Zeit-Schrift* 2 (September 1968): 89–93.
Zwerenz, Ingrid, ed. *Anonym. Schmäh- und Drohbriefe an Prominente*. Munich: Rütten & Loening, 1968.

INDEX OF NAMES

Achenbach, Ernst, 159, 192
Adenauer, Konrad, 7, 9, 77, 87, 88, 93, 146, 164–167
Adorno, Theodor W., 108, 156–158, 166–167, 188
Altmaier, Jakob, 80
Amend, Manfred, 110, 123, 157, 159, 183–184
Angermair, Rupert, 99
Apfel, Alfred, 40, 53
Arendt, Hannah, 8, 19, 143–144
Arnsberg, Paul, 172
Augstein, Rudolf, 162

Baader, Andreas, 184
Baer, Richard, 134
Bartsch, Hans-Werner, 137
Bauer, Ella, 20, 22–25, 72
Bauer, Julius, 20
Bauer, Ludwig, 19–25, 72
Bauer, Margot. *See* Tiefenthal, Margot
Baumann, Jürgen, 14, 57
Beckerle, Adolf Heinz, 176
Ben-Gurion, David, 6–8
Bernays, Murray, 118
Best, Werner, 192
Beyerle, Josef, 55, 60
Blachstein, Peter, 80
Blankenstein, Otto, 162
Bloch, Robert, 51, 67, 90
Boger, Wilhelm, 129, 131–132, 144
Böll, Heinrich, 9
Bormann, Martin, 134–135, 178
Brandt, Willy, 12, 73–74, 78, 184
Brecht, Bertolt, 34, 37
Brenner, Michael, 24
Brumlik, Micha, 171, 175
Bucerius, Gerd, 173
Buck, Karl, 65
Bürger-Prinz, Hans, 166
Butler, Samuel, 112

Chesterton, Gilbert K., 110
Cohn, Haim, 7

Dam, Hendrik George van, 172
Demjanjuk, John, 145
Dickopf, Paul, 3, 5
Dill, Gottlob, 67
Dönhoff, Marion Gräfin, 173
Dorls, Fritz, 86
Dreher, Eduard, 192
Drumbl, Mark, 116
Dylewski, Klaus, 174

Ehrenburg, Ilja, 51
Eichmann, Adolf, 1–8, 126–127, 140–142
Eichwald, Heinz, 181–182
Einstein, Walter, 38–39
Ensslin, Gudrun, 184

Ferencz, Benjamin, 116
Fichte, Johann Gottlieb, 175
Forester, Hans, 149
Foucault, Michel, 115
Frank, Hans, 119
Fränkel, Wolfgang, 179
Frei, Norbert, 129
Freisler, Roland, 98–99, 146
Frick, Hans, 172

Gauf, Horst, 191, 193
Gehlen, Reinhard, 4
Gehlsen, Jan, 183
Geiler, Karl, 43, 45, 78, 109
Gerchow, Joachim, 189
Gerlach, Adolf, 55–56
Giese, Hans, 166
Giordano, Ralph, 79
Gnielka, Thomas, 128
Goebbels, Joseph, 87, 160
Goerdeler, Carl Friedrich, 101

203

Index of Names

Goethe, Johann Wolfgang von, 34, 38, 74, 120, 175
Göring, Hermann, 33
Grass, Günter, 9, 12
Greve, Michael, 193
Gropius, Walter, 51, 184
Großkopf, Erich, 147
Großmann, Hanns, 132
Gumbel, Emil Julius, 33

Hachenburg, Max, 45
Haffner, Sebastian, 32
Hanack, Ernst-Walter, 180
Harel, Isser, 6
Harlan, Thomas, 159–161, 185, 188–190
Harlan, Veit, 159–160
Harpprecht, Renate, 13–14
Hart, Leo. *See* Herz, Leo
Hedler, Wolfgang, 95
Hefelmann, Hans, 133–134
Hegel, Georg Wilhelm Friedrich, 23, 110–112
Heinemann, Gustav, 167
Heinig, Kurt, 81
Hermann, Lothar, 2, 5
Herz, Leo, 90
Herzl, Theodor, 23
Heß, Rudolf, 33
Heuss, Theodor, 94–95
Heyde, Werner, 133
Hiller, Kurt, 90
Hirsch, Erich, 73
Hirsch, Gustav, 18–19
Hirsch, Leopold, 21, 71
Hirsch, Minna, 24
Hirsch, Otto, 24
Hirsch, Paula, 73
Hirsch, Robert, 24, 26
Hochhuth, Rolf, 158
Hofmeyer, Hans, 143, 148
Horkheimer, Max, 70–71, 74, 89, 139, 156
Höß, Rudolf, 127
Hummerich, Werner, 135
Hurwitz, Stephan, 70, 167

Iwand, Hans Joachim, 99

Jackson, Robert, 118
Jacob, Alaric, 117

Jacoby, Erich H., 80
Jäger, Herbert, 108, 166
Jagow, Dietrich von, 50–51
Jaspers, Karl, 7
Joachim, Hans G., 183
Jünger, Ernst, 33
Junker, Werner, 4

Kaduk, Oswald, 127, 142, 144
Kant, Immanuel, 38–39, 92, 110–112, 138
Katz, Rudolf, 25, 80
Kaven, Wolfgang, 66, 156–158, 160, 190
Kinski, Klaus, 159
Klagges, Dietrich, 91–92
Klehr, Josef, 142
Kluge, Alexander, 188–189
Krapp, Otto, 89
Kreisky, Bruno, 73
Krüger, Horst, 125–126, 128, 175
Krüger, Ulrich, 180–182, 188
Krupp, Gustav, 116
Kugelmann, Cilly, 171–172, 175
Kugelmann, Hersz, 171–172
Kügler, Joachim, 3, 131–132, 135, 142, 148, 150, 174, 176–178, 181–182, 191

Lackner, Karl, 167
Landauer, Julius, 26
Langbein, Hermann, 129, 132, 174
Langhans, Rainer, 183
Laternser, Hans, 148, 150, 177
Lauritzen, Laurits, 146
Lehr, Robert, 88
Liszt, Franz von, 70, 109–111
Lucas, Franz, 144–145

Mann, Thomas, 139
Maor, Michael, 1–2, 6
Marx, Karl, 138
Mauz, Gerhard, 143
Mengele, Josef, 134
Mergenthaler, Christian, 60
Merkatz, Hans-Joachim von, 92
Merseburger, Peter, 64
Meyer-Velde, Esther, 138
Meyer-Velde, Gisela, 66, 138
Meyer-Velde, Heinz, 36, 66, 138, 157
Mielke, Helmut, 26, 58

Index of Names

Mies van der Rohe, Ludwig, 51, 184
Mühsam, Erich, 53
Mulka, Robert, 127, 145

Nathansen, Henri, 25–26
Nellmann, Erich, 130
Neumann, Richard, 91
Neumann, Robert, 127, 161
Neurath, Konstantin von, 19
Niemöller, Johann Heinrich, 149
Niemöller, Martin, 137, 149
Nietzsche, Friedrich, 25, 112

Ollenhauer, Erich, 146
Ormond, Henry, 136, 148, 174
Ossietzky, Carl von, 53
Oven, Wilfred von, 87

Perels, Joachim, 107, 183
Petersen, Anna Maria, 73, 158
Petersen, Hans Hermann, 73, 146
Philipp, Karl-Wolfgang, 90
Plank, Ernst, 65
Pollock, Friedrich, 71
Proll, Thorwald, 184

Radbruch, Gustav, 53–54, 70, 109–115, 120
Rathenau, Emil, 32
Rathenau, Walther, 32–33, 44, 80, 137
Reich an der Stolpe, Siegfried, 12
Reich-Ranicki, Marcel, 173
Reinowksi, Hans, 81
Remer, Otto Ernst, 86–88, 93, 95–96, 98, 102, 148
Reuter, Ernst, 94
Rieger, Martin, 67
Roeder, Manfred, 96
Rögner, Adolf, 129–130
Rosenthal, Ernst, 90–91
Rothfels, Hans, 95–96
Rückerl, Adalbert, 192
Ruggaber, Karl, 65, 67

Schenk, Dieter, 89
Schiller, Friedrich, 23, 37, 79, 101–102, 175
Schinnar, Felix, 4
Schirach, Baldur von, 119
Schleiermacher, Friedrich, 136

Schmid, Carlo, 68, 78
Schmid, Richard, 71, 78
Schopenhauer, Arthur, 37
Schramm, Percy, 100
Schüle, Erwin, 4–5, 130
Schumacher, Kurt, 57–59, 64–68, 74, 78–80, 90
Schütte, Wolfram, 157
Simon, Erich, 90–91
Six, Franz Alfred, 159
Staff, Curt, 92
Stangneth, Bettina, 5
Stauffenberg, Claus Schenk Graf von, 19, 87, 93–95, 98–99, 102, 149, 175
Stengel, Katharina, 174
Swift, Jonathan, 112, 183

Taylor, Telford, 118
Teufel, Fritz, 183
Thadden, Adolf von, 190
Tiefenthal, Margot, 17–19, 23, 27, 68, 72, 175–176
Tiefenthal, Walter, 68, 70, 158
Topf, Erich Günther, 88, 96
Tucholsky, Kurt, 53

Uhlman, Fred, 22, 42, 57, 59–60, 67
Uhlmann, Manfred. *See* Uhlman, Fred
Unseld, Siegfried, 136

Vogel, Georg Friedrich, 131–132, 148, 150, 174, 181
Vorberg, Reinhold, 3

Walser, Martin, 9, 144
Warlo, Johannes, 133–134, 178–179, 181–182, 190, 193
Weiss, Peter, 136
Wergeland, Henrik, 26
Wiedemann, Melitta, 138, 158
Wiese, Gerhard, 131, 145, 148, 179, 181
Wiesenthal, Simon, 7, 173
Wojak, Irmtrud, 8
Wolf, Ernst, 99
Wuermeling, Franz-Josef, 165
Wulkan, Emil, 128

Zelzer, Maria, 26
Zinn, Georg August, 4, 9
Zwerenz, Gerhard, 184
Zwerenz, Ingrid, 9

RONEN STEINKE is a political journalist for *Süddeutsche Zeitung*. He holds a doctorate in law and has published numerous articles, academic and otherwise, on law and history.

SINÉAD CROWE teaches English at the University of Hamburg and is a translator. She co-translated Pierre Jarawan's *The Storyteller* with Rachel McNicholl.

www.ingramcontent.com/pod-product-compliance
Lightning Source LLC
Chambersburg PA
CBHW020332240426
43665CB00043B/440